W9-BYU-668

POLITICAL TRACTS OF WORDSWORTH, COLERIDGE AND SHELLEY

POLITICAL TRACTS OF WORDSWORTH, COLERIDGE AND SHELLEY

EDITED
WITH AN INTRODUCTION,
BY

R. J. WHITE
*Fellow of Downing College,
Cambridge*

CAMBRIDGE
AT THE UNIVERSITY PRESS
1953

PUBLISHED BY
THE SYNDICS OF THE CAMBRIDGE UNIVERSITY PRESS

London Office: Bentley House, N.W.1
American Branch: New York
Agents for Canada, India, and Pakistan: Macmillan

Printed in Great Britain by The Carlyle Press, Birmingham 6

CONTENTS

INTRODUCTION

1. The Poets and their Age

The texts reprinted in this volume were originally intended by their authors as 'Tracts for the Times'—the distressed and dangerous times of the Napoleonic wars and the immediately post-war years. The first in time, Wordsworth's *Convention of Cintra*, was published in 1809. The last, Shelley's *Philosophical View of Reform*, was composed in 1820. Coleridge's two lay sermons belong to the years 1816 and 1817 respectively, the darkest of the post-war years. In each case, the author was passionately convinced that what he had to say was of vital and immediate importance to his countrymen. Time, indeed, was of the essence. Wordsworth, writing far into the night in his Lakeland cottage, felt himself to be at the very heart of the storm. Coleridge, composing lay sermons in his attic-room over Dr Gillman's house on Highgate Hill, may have been what Carlyle called him—'a sage escaped from the inanity of life's battle'—but he was well aware that he was still 'attracting towards him the thoughts of innumerable brave souls still engaged there'. Shelley, self-exiled at the Villa Valsovano near Leghorn, was awakened by the distant fratricidal tumult of Peterloo as by a trumpet:

> As I lay asleep in Italy
> There came a voice from over the sea . . .

Not that any of them can be said to have had the slightest effect upon the immediate course of events. *The Convention of Cintra* was published too late, and most of the copies went as paper-linings for the trunk-makers. As for the *Lay Sermons*, they were preached to the converted, and when they were sampled by the liberal intelligence of a Sarah Wedgwood they appeared to be 'an affectation of the most sublime and important meaning and so much no-meaning in reality . . .'[1] As for

[1] Emma Darwin, *A Century of Family Letters*, vol. 1, pp. 109-10.

Shelley's *Philosophical View of Reform*, it remained unpublished until 1920. These works cannot be said to belong to the great tradition of political pamphleteering which is represented by Lilburne and Swift, Defoe, Paine and Cobbett. Their authors were rather 'recluse men of genius' than working politicians or men of the market-place. Their very detachment from the necessary disciplines of parliamentary life and from the detailed exigencies of administration enabled them to see more clearly and to feel more deeply the great movements which ebb and flow in the minds and emotions of ordinary men and women. They were aware of this advantage, and cherished it. 'The slave of custom is roused by the rare and the accidental alone,' Coleridge observed; 'but the axioms of the unthinking are to the philosopher the deepest problems . . . '.[1] Wordsworth attributed no small part of the deficiency of the statesmen who sanctioned the Convention of Cintra to the fact that 'a ruling minister of a long-established government', accustomed to managing the 'formal machine' of state, knows far too little of 'the instincts of natural and social man; the deeper emotions; the simpler feelings; the spacious range of the disinterested imagination'.[2] The strength and value of the work here presented may indeed be said to spring chiefly from the philosophic detachment of the poets, and from the consequent freshness and profundity of their vision. What they lack in the immediate effectiveness, the aplomb, and the pertness of the typical pamphleteer, is more than compensated by their relevance to the permanent problems of the human predicament.

In their immediate purposes, these men were attempting the impossible. Oppressed to the point of outrage by the evils of the day and the hour, they wished to summon their countrymen to an immediate re-examination of the principles on which personal and public action alike should be based. All else, it seemed to them, were futile tinkering. At the very least, the tinkerers should be told, frequently and firmly, that even in their most cherished acts of expediency their minds and habits are conditioned by the presence of principles, albeit principles

[1] *Statesman's Manual*, p. 29. [2] *Convention of Cintra*, p. 170.

of which they are unaware in explicit formulation. The most that could be asked or expected was that the working governors of the political machine should know, fitfully perhaps, what they were doing; that, in the midst of their concern for the particular, they should have some notion that particulars are related to universals. Coleridge's bitterest complaint of the ministers of 1817—'the Castlereagh gang'—was that they were literally, 'unprincipled'.[1] Nor could Wordsworth find any deeper cause for the dishonesty of the Convention of Cintra than the hand-to-mouth insensibility of the routine statesman. To Shelley, the sole hope for his country in the year of Peterloo lay in the cultivation of that great organ of moral truth—the imagination. Not that the ministers of that day were more indifferent to philosophic principles than the ministers of any other day. 'From Mr Coleridge', Lord Liverpool endorsed a long letter from the poet, in 1817,

> stating that the great object of his writings has been to rescue speculative philosophy from false principles of reasoning and to place it on that basis, or give it that tendency, which would make it best suited to the interests of religion as well as of the State; at least, I believe this is Mr Coleridge's meaning, but I cannot well understand him.[2]

For an 'unprincipled' statesman, it was a good guess.

There was the impossibility: that the ministers of the Crown, or men of affairs in general, should have had the time, aptitude, or inclination to enquire into the distinction between the Reason and the Understanding, or to read history—particularly that of the Old Testament—in the light of Ideas, or to endue themselves with the spirit of Poetry and Platonic philosophy. And, of course, in their less impassioned moods, the poets knew this. While it is important to emphasize their conviction of the immediate relevance of their work, we should still attend even more seriously to the tone of prophecy, the concern for the longer and larger day of futurity. They were, as Shelley put it in immortal phrase, 'the mirrors of the gigantic shadows which

[1] *Unpublished Letters of S. T. Coleridge*, ed. E. Leslie Griggs, vol. II, p. 224.
[2] C. D. Yonge, *Life and Administration of Lord Liverpool*, vol. II, pp. 300-7.

futurity casts upon the present. . . . Eternity warning Time'.[1] It is for this reason that we should still read them. No other work written in English in the nineteenth century bears so clearly the stamp of a timeless relevance.

2. The Philosophy of History

The texts have been arranged according to an order of ideas rather than according to the order in which they were composed. *The Statesman's Manual* is, in every sense, the basic text. With its concern for the primary importance of principles, it sets both the tone and the tenor of all that follows. Its priority is inevitable but unfortunate, for it would be difficult to conceive of a work more likely to repel the reader at first sight, with its twenty-six pages of text, its thirty pages of notes and appendices, and its rash of Biblical texts and scholastic quotations. Its sub-title—'The Bible the best guide to Political Skill and Foresight'—might have been deliberately designed to offend the modern intelligence, with its suggestion of religious fundamentalism. Its declared form—'A Lay Sermon addressed to the Higher Classes of Society'—might well frighten away the uninitiated with its premonitory snuffle of snobbery. Historically, one might imagine, few documents were ever calculated to offend more susceptibilities. England in 1816 was noisy with machine-breaking and bread-rioting—on the verge of revolution, it seemed to many. And the contribution of the Philosopher of Highgate was to hand out tracts to the higher classes recommending the study of the Old Testament as a manual for statesmen. Nor was he content to stop at that. A second, and much longer *Sermon*—this time addressed primarily to the middle classes—was to follow within twelve months, and there is reason to believe that a third, addressed to the labouring classes ('to unvizard our Incendiaries'), was on the way.[2] Likewise, a long letter went off to the Prime Minister, exposing the meretricious philosophy of Locke and Hume, tracing its

[1] *Defence of Poetry*, p. 206, and *Philosophical View of Reform*, p. 259.
[2] *Unpublished Letters*, vol. II, p. 179.

infection of the arts and sciences in modern Europe, and pointing out its horrid effects upon political thinking.

> As long as the principles of our gentry and clergy are grounded in a false philosophy, which retains but the name of logic, and has succeeded in rendering metaphysics a term of opprobrium, all the Sunday and national schools in the world will not preclude schism and Jacobinism in the middle and lower classes. The predominant philosophy is the keynote. . . .[1]

Now, what his age, including Lord Liverpool, thought of all this was probably best summed up by Hazlitt who 'reviewed' the first *Lay Sermon* in *The Examiner*[2] before it appeared, on the grounds that he knew what anything by Coleridge would be as well before publication as after. That observation really means that Hazlitt, like most other people, never bothered to read Coleridge's political prose writings, but contented himself with phrases like 'German Metaphysics' or 'Transcendental Moonshine' or 'Opium-dreams'.[3] As far as the first *Lay Sermon* is concerned, that is what most people have done ever since. *The Statesman's Manual* is, like *Sordello* and *Finnegan's Wake*, one of the fabulous monsters which lie stranded on the shores of literature, splendid, terrifying, and unknown. And yet, that *The Statesman's Manual* is a masterpiece in its kind is unlikely to be disputed by anyone who passes through its repellent jaws and delivers himself to the wonders of its inward parts. Here are the very caverns of Xanadu, opening one into another, with the sacred river sounding ever onwards through eternity. Let anyone who is content to suppose, on the strength of unacquaintance, that Coleridge always wrote turgid prose, venture into the wondrous passages marked 'Appendix C',[4] on the Tri-unity of the soul, the philosophy of nature and the omnipresence of deity; let him then go on to the great celebration of 'the Idea' in Appendix E;[5] and then let him ask himself whether anyone has handled the English language with such magnificence

[1] See note 2, p. ix, above. [2] *The Examiner*, 8 September 1816.

[3] See Thomas Carlyle, *Life of John Sterling*, ch. VIII, for ingenious phraseology of this kind. [4] Appendix A, in the present text (p. 31).

[5] To be found in Appendix B, in the present text. The passage begins at the last paragraph on p. 47.

and power, on a philosophic theme, since the great Platonists of the seventeenth century. 'Too often', Coleridge observed, 'my readers may justly complain of the involution and entortillage of my style.' He would account for the fact that his sentences are 'more *piled up* and *architectural* than is endurable in so illogical an age as the present, in which all the cements of style are dismissed, and a popular book is only a sequence of epigrams and aphorisms on one subject', by his continuous reading—among other things—of 'our English writers from Edward VI to James II'.[1] It is a strange reflection on the reading habits of our time that those who profess the greatest admiration for the literature of seventeenth-century England should have left unexplored the most remarkable prose work of this greatest heir of the seventeenth-century tradition.

Less surprising, but more disastrous, from the point of view of understanding Coleridge's thought, is the failure of scholars to make use of this key-work. Apart from F. J. A. Hort[2] and Professor Basil Willey,[3] those who have taken it upon themselves to expound Coleridge as a political and social thinker seem to have left it severely alone. John Stuart Mill, for example, whose essay on Coleridge[4] has become a *locus classicus* for the subject, seems never to have read it. No one who had read Appendix C of *The Statesman's Manual* could possibly describe Coleridge's philosophy, as Mill described it, as 'the Germano-Coleridgean Philosophy', nor could anyone who had read the main text of that work have identified his philosophy of history with that of Herder and Michelet. Mill contrived to admire Coleridge's views on what he would doubtless call 'practical' questions—the function of the National Church, the true nature of landed property, and the corporate purposes of the state,—while remaining largely ignorant of the nature of the philosophical basis from which those views took their

[1] *Unpublished Letters*, vol. II, pp. 10-11.

[2] *Cambridge Essays*, 1857.

[3] *Nineteenth Century Studies*, 1949, ch. I.

[4] *Dissertations and Discussions of John Stuart Mill*, vol. I, 1859. The Coleridge essay is republished in *Mill on Bentham and Coleridge*, with an Introduction by F. R. Leavis, Chatto and Windus, 1950.

departure. More than half of his celebrated essay is thereby rendered not merely useless, but positively misleading.

Mill described 'the Germano-Coleridgian school' as 'the first who inquired with any comprehensiveness or depth, into the inductive laws of the existence and growth of human society . . . they thus produced . . . a philosophy of society, in the only form in which it is yet possible, that of a philosophy of history'. He rightly ascribed to 'that great series of great writers and thinkers from Herder to Michelet' the achievement of transforming history, from a tale told by an idiot, into a science of causes and effects. By making 'the facts and events of the past have a meaning and an intelligible place in the gradual evolution of humanity', they had made history into prophecy, affording to mankind 'the only means of predicting and guiding the future, by unfolding the agencies which have produced and still maintain the Present'. This was all perfectly true, but it had very little to do with Coleridge, nor had Coleridge very much to do with it. Coleridge's philosophy of history is to be found in *The Statesman's Manual*, and it is a very different thing from the historicism of the 'cause-and-effect' or 'prophetic' school of Herder and Michelet. It was true, again, that Coleridge possessed a philosophy of society, but it was not *derived* from his philosophy of history. It was not indeed historical at all in the sense in which Mill—and for that matter Herder or Michelet, Burke or Macaulay, Marx or Buckle,—employ the term. It was poetic. History, for Coleridge, was a poem whose author is God. And human society was an aspect of the universal and timeless poem. The first thing, and the last thing, to remember about Coleridge is that he was a poet. His philosophy of history and of society was one with his philosophy of poetry.

The purpose of the historian, to Coleridge, is the same as that of the poet: to convert a series of events, which constitute the straight-line of real or imagined history, into a whole, so that the series shall assume to our understandings 'a circular motion—the snake with its tail in its mouth'.[1] Or, to employ

[1] *Unpublished Letters*, vol. II, p. 128.

another of Coleridge's favourite images, to produce past, present and future 'as boys produce the circle of light by a piece of kindled charcoal whirled rapidly round'.[1] This purpose is imposed upon the historian by the fact that, in history, men and events are not related to each other simply in a straight-line of cause and effect, but enact, in every generation, even in every moment, the part of universals as well as the part of particulars. The superiority of Sir Walter Scott's achievement in *Old Mortality*, as compared with *Ivanhoe*, Coleridge ascribed to the fact that in *Old Mortality* the reader is made to feel, without for one moment leaving 'the past', that he is experiencing the permeating life of universal and timeless ideas: that he is living the past in the present and the present in the past. *Ivanhoe* might have been as great a novel as *Old Mortality* if Scott had realized, in this instance too, that 'the contest between the loyalists and their opponents can never be obsolete'. As it was, he had concerned himself in 'a mere contest of indifferents, of minim-surges in a boiling tea-kettle', and the result was tedious antiquarianism and moral anachronism.[2] Coleridge could never bear conducted tours over battlefields or ruined castles. Gazing at a wall in Carnarvon Castle, he 'wished the guide fifty miles off that was telling me, "In this chamber the Black Prince was born" (or whoever it was)'. He positively disliked 'things contingent and transitory' in history, as intrusions upon his contemplation of the men and events of the past as 'things of now, for ever, and which were always'.[3]

Now, the Bible, Coleridge thought, afforded this kind of history *par excellence*. It was, he always said, the book that 'found' him at his deepest level, and was literally the Book of Revelation because it enabled men to find themselves as partakers in the timeless life of ideas. It was the key to the science of life, and the best guide to political skill and foresight, because it was the archetype and pattern of history itself. In it, freedom

[1] Alice D. Snyder, *Coleridge on Logic and Learning*, pp. 111-12.

[2] *Table Talk*, etc. from Allsop's *Letters, Conversations and Recollections of S. T. Coleridge*, 1836, under the date 8 April, 1820.

[3] *Anima Poetae*, ed. E. H. Coleridge, ch. III.

and necessity were reconciled. It afforded the synthesis of the free world of ideas—of Reason, which was taught to men, under Providence, by the Greeks:—and the necessitated world of sense as represented to men's Understanding by the Romans. Coleridge regarded the Hebrews as 'the fixed mid-point of the living line towards which the Greeks, as the ideal pole, and the Romans, as the material, were ever approximating; till the coincidence and final synthesis took place in Christianity, of which the Bible is the Law and Christendom the phenomenon'.[1] The history portrayed in the Old Testament is not to be regarded as allegory, but as symbol. An allegory is merely a translation, or copy, of abstract notions into picture-language—an abstraction from the objects of the senses. A symbol, on the other hand, enables us to see the universal in the particular because it partakes of the reality which it portrays. In the Bible, every person appears as a self-subsisting individual and yet belongs to the universal life. The events and persons of the Bible, therefore, have both a particular and a universal significance; they belong to their temporal life of the past, as history, and yet belong to the present and to the future and to all time. They are at once portraits and ideals. In the Bible we see the stream of time continuous as life; but we also see in it the symbol of eternity. Past and future are virtually contained in the present.[2]

Coleridge's reflections upon the significance of the Bible contain the essence of his interpretation of history, and that essence is poetic. He looks upon its persons as, on another plane, he looks upon the persons of Shakespeare's plays. Shakespeare's characters partake equally of the individual and the universal, of time and eternity.

In every one of his various characters we still feel ourselves communing with the same human nature. Everywhere we find individuality, nowhere is mere portrait. The excellence of his productions consists in a happy union of the universal with the particular. . . . It was Shakespeare's prerogative to have the

[1] *Coleridge's Treatise on Method*, ed. Alice D. Snyder, p. 51.
[2] *Statesman's Manual*, p. 25.

universal, which is potentially in each particular, opened out to him, the *homo generalis*, not as an abstraction from observation of a variety of men, but as the substance capable of endless modifications. . . .[1]

In Shakespeare, as in the Bible, the persons are not copies but imitations, not allegoric but symbolic. They belong, perfectly literally, to all time. To achieve this is the prerogative of genius. The Bible achieves it at the highest level because it is the work of men under the direct inspiration of God. Shakespeare achieves it because he possessed genius, partaking on the human plane of the divine power of creation. Coleridge achieved it in *The Ancient Mariner*, and spent the rest of his life translating his experience of the creative mind into terms of a philosophy of life, in showing to men that the way of creative genius is the way of ordinary humanity. Even if all men do not possess ideas, all men are possessed by them.[2] If it is unlikely, and even undesirable, that every man should bring forth an *Ancient Mariner*, or a *Macbeth*, 'the dullest wight is at times a Shakespeare in his dreams',[3] and he owes it to God, and to himself, to try to make his dreams come true, to acknowledge that the potential works in him, even as the actual works upon him. As Professor Lowes has remarked, 'the Road to Xanadu . . . is the road of the human spirit'.[4]

3. Poetry and Politics

The Statesman's Manual was addressed to the higher classes, and represents its author's persuasion that the reformation of English society must begin at the top. His purpose here, as in everything that he wrote, was the re-education of the 'educated' —those who really govern society, whether as the Clerisy or the Magistracy. To attempt general illumination first, would be to 'spur-arm the toes of society . . . to attempt to *popularize*

[1] *Coleridge's Treatise on Method*, ed. Alice D. Snyder, pp. 31-6.

[2] S. T. Coleridge, *On the Constitution of Church and State according to the Idea of Each*, ch. 1.

[3] *Statesman's Manual*, p. 40.

[4] J. Livingston Lowes, *The Road to Xanadu* (1945), p. 433.

science . . . will only effect its *plebification*'.[1] The preliminary to all other reform was 'the recurrence to a more manly discipline of the intellect on the part of the learned themselves, in short, a thorough recasting of the moulds in which the minds of our gentry, the characters of our future land-owners, magistrates and senators, are to receive their shape and fashion'.[2] This necessarily meant an abjuration of Lockian philosophy and re-education in a life-giving philosophy of Ideas—'true philosophy, or the power and habit of contemplating particulars in the unity and fontal mirror of the idea. . . .'[3] Men so educated would at once grasp the fact that 'the Bible alone contains a science of realities'; that 'each of its elements is at the same time a living germ, in which the present involves the future'; and that 'in the finite the infinite exists potentially'.[4] Such men would be truly philosophic statesmen, philosopher guardians, uniquely qualified to govern the state in the light of its ultimate and ideal ends. 'The first man on whom the light of an idea dawned, did in that same moment receive the spirit and the credentials of a lawgiver. . . .'[5] To such a man, the science of realities contained in the Bible would be an open book. 'O what a mine of undiscovered treasures, what a new world of power and truth would the Bible promise to our future meditation, if in some gracious moment one solitary text of all its inspired contents should but dawn upon us in the pure untroubled brightness of an idea. . . .'[6]

Coleridge, said De Quincey, 'wanted better bread than can be made with wheat'. And certainly, to point the way out of the present discontents of 1816 by a programme for the Platonic instruction of Lords Liverpool, Castlereagh and Sidmouth, in the further hope that they would read their Bibles in the light of Christian-Platonism, was to say the least—a counsel of perfection. But if we set aside the Coleridgian optimism about his immediate purposes, if we disregard the

[1] S. T. Coleridge, *Church and State*, ch. VII, final paragraph.

[2] *Statesman's Manual*, p. 10.

[3] *Church and State*, ch. VII.

[4] *Statesman's Manual*, p. 28. [5] *Ibid.* p. 10. [6] *Ibid.* p. 29.

spiritual dialectic, if we decide that the Bible affords us no more—and no less—of the science of realities than the works of Shakespeare, or Dante, or Karl Marx; still, we are left with the poet's theory of mind—which was the principal contribution of the English romantic poets to both critical and constructive political thinking in their age. The significant characteristic of this theory of mind is not that it is romantic but that it is poetic. Not all the romantics possessed it in explicit, or philosophical, form. Wordsworth had it, as Coleridge said that Shakespeare had had it, implicitly rather than upon the tongue or the pen. For Wordsworth was, Coleridge insisted, like every great poet, a great philosopher.[1] Shelley had it more explicitly than Wordsworth and less completely than Coleridge, in his *Defence of Poetry*, where the doctrine of the creative imagination as the organ of moral truth is expressed with a passionate beauty of language second only to that of his great Platonic precursor, Sir Philip Sidney. Coleridge had described the function of poetry, as that of history, to be the conversion of a series into a whole, and had likened 'a poem to that image of God which we were created with, and which still seeks that unity, or revelation of the One in and by the Many . . .'.[2] So Shelley speaks of 'the creative faculty, which is the basis of all knowledge', and of a poem as

> the very image of life expressed in its eternal truth. . . . The great instrument of moral good is the imagination; and poetry administers to the effect by acting upon the cause. . . . Poetry strengthens the faculty which is the organ of the moral nature of man in the same manner as exercise strengthens a limb. . . .[3]

It is beside the point to describe this theory of mind as 'Romantic' or 'Idealist', Platonic or Kantian. It was, quite simply, poetic, and was the offspring of poetic experience. Without it, the poetic activity—indeed, the creative life of mankind in general—must remain unaccountable save in terms of the *legerdemain* of abnormal psychology. Coleridge himself,

[1] *Unpublished Letters*, vol. I, p. 266.

[2] *Ibid.* vol. II, pp. 128-9.

[3] *Defence of Poetry*, p. 202.

it is clear, arrived at what he calls 'the philosophy of life', as distinct from 'the philosophy of death' taught by Locke and the sensationalists, in an attempt to *understand* the poetry of Wordsworth. It was in 1796 that he heard Wordsworth read aloud his poem *Guilt and Sorrow*. The immediate impact was upon his feelings; but, being Coleridge, his understanding at once seized upon the intellectual problem thus presented. 'I no sooner felt than I sought to understand.' What he principally needed to understand was 'the original gift of spreading the tone, the atmosphere, and with it the depth and height of the ideal world around forms, incidents and situations, of which, for the common view, custom had bedimmed all the lustre, had dried up the sparkle and the dewdrops'.[1] This gift was Imagination—the soul in the body of creative activity. It is this shaping gift of Imagination, 'modifying' all else, that works the wonder of the whole and delivers the work of art. It is the power that transmutes that mass of multifarious and associative detail into which Professor Lowes has rendered down *The Ancient Mariner*. That poem, like any other work of genius, is not the mere sum of the impressions which the literary analyst can trace and track down from line to line, or from word to word. As Professor Lowes puts it: 'every impression . . . is what it now is in the completed poem . . . through its participation in a *whole*, foreseen as a whole in each integral part,—a whole which is the working out of a controlling, imaginative design.'[2] Whatever x may be, it is not a plus b plus c, etc. . . . 'On the contrary, the unity that has somehow come about is as integral as the union of seven colours which blend in a beam of white light.'[3] In Coleridge's own words, the series has become a whole, the straight line has assumed to our understandings 'a circular motion—the snake with its tail in its mouth'.[4] Fifteen years later, Coleridge was to refute John Locke on the unanswerable argument of poetic

[1] Coleridge, *Biographia Literaria*, ch. IV. See also Wordsworth, *The Prelude*, ed. Ernest de Selincourt, Book XII, pp. 357-65, and editor's note on these lines. [2] J. Livingston Lowes, *The Road to Xanadu*, p. 304.
[3] *Ibid.* p. 54. [4] See above, p. xiii, n. 1.

experience thus: 'Locke says four and five are nine. Now I say that four and five are not nine, but that they will make nine.'[1] But then Locke was no poet. That was the whole trouble.[2]

The philosophy of poetry, thus done into a philosophy of mind and nature, has come under fire from many quarters. 'Salvation through Poetry'—or the substitution of Art for Religion: these are the commonest watchwords of the attack. Romanticism, it is said, was the last phase of that humanistic subjectivism which would pass off the whims of the individual artist under the guise of objective truths. To be governed by the private visions of the artist, posturing as the eternal verities—in what, after all, would this be a superior condition of things to the dominion of our moral world by the infallibilities of priests, lawyers, scientists, psychologists, or any other intellectual oligarchy? Carlyle, Gladstone, Walter Pater, Mr G. M. Young—all have warned us against the tyranny of 'the bright thought' of subjective idealism. Dr Gerbrandy saw in the Kantian revolution the root of that 'ethical autonomy of man' which produced National Socialism.[3] As Professor D. G. James has put it, very recently, 'this is dangerous doctrine, and left the field to any crazy creatures of doubtful intuition who could shout loud enough'.

Two things should be said of this criticism. The first is, that in so far as the poets were Platonists they were safeguarded against the perils of ethical autonomy. 'A poet participates in the eternal, the infinite, and the one', Shelley asserted, against those who might suppose him bound by the temporal and provincial standards of his time, his country, his class; 'as far as relates to his conceptions, time and place and number are not.'[4] And in the second place, the poets believed that there could be no antagonism between truth as discovered by the creative imagination, and the essential truths of the Christian religion. Carlyle's caustic observation that this involved

[1] *Table Talk*, 24 August 1831.

[2] For Locke on poets and poetry, see the admirable discussion in Professor D. G. James's *English Augustans: The Life of Reason*, 1949, ch. 2.

[3] See Dr Gerbrandy's Taylorian Lecture, *National and International Stability*, Oxford, 1944.

[4] *Defence of Poetry*, p. 200.

'believing by "the reason" what "the understanding" had been obliged to find out as incredible'[1] bears an imputation of insincerity which could not be substantiated from the lives and characters of these men. Far from wishing to disparage the human understanding, the poets wished to redeem it. They were, all three of them, essentially strong and logical intellects, distrustful of vague intuitions and of the high-falutin' manners of the self-accredited 'mystic'. Coleridge's love of logic was almost a disease. 'Logic the most severe', De Quincey avowed, 'was as inalienable from his modes of thinking, as grammar from his language.'[2] Wordsworth was the only great genius that Coleridge had ever known who was '*all* man',[3] and it is scarcely necessary to insist upon the all-too-obtrusive element of the merely prosaic in his make-up. Mary Shelley's opinion that her husband possessed powers of analytical reasoning equal to his powers as a poet,[4] points to a truth about Shelley which is borne out by the sheer intellectual power that informs not only his doctrine of poetry but his poetry itself. It might be remembered, too, that both Coleridge and Shelley were amateur scientists, and fed their minds enthusiastically upon the great discoveries of science in their time.

Far from wishing to denigrate the physical sciences, these men wished to infect science itself with the creative spirit and thereby to redeem its purposes. The problem, as they saw it in their time, was one of balance. To Coleridge, the dialectic of man's attachment to subjective and objective truth was what history is about: he thought that in his own age, man's attach-

[1] Carlyle, *Life of Sterling*, ch. 8.

[2] Thomas De Quincey, *Recollections of the Lakes*. De Quincey's *Works*, vol. II, pp. 55-6.

[3] *Table Talk*, 17 March 1832: here Coleridge is known to have been referring to Wordsworth although his name does not appear in the record. Compare the reference in Allsop's *Letters, Conversations and Recollections of S. T. Coleridge*: 'Of all the men I ever knew, Wordsworth has the least femineity in his mind. He is *all* man.'

[4] Mary Shelley's Note on *The Revolt of Islam* (Poetical Works of Shelley, 1939): 'Shelley possessed two remarkable qualities of intellect—a brilliant imagination, and a logical exactness of reason.' The whole passage is important for the present discussion.

ment to outward things was atrophying his sense of value, that his concern for medial ends was obscuring ultimate ends, that technology was usurping the place of true science. 'We live', he exclaimed, after studying with awe and admiration a history of inventions,

> we live . . . under the dynasty of the understanding: and this is its golden age. It is the faculty of medial ends. . . . Sea, and land, rock, mountain, lake and moor, yea nature and all her elements sink before them, or yield themselves captive! But the *ultimate* ends? Where shall I seek for information concerning these? By what name shall I seek for the historiographer of REASON? Where shall I find the annals of *her* recent campaigns? . . .[1]

Wordsworth wrote in the same terms:

> While Mechanic Arts, Manufactures, Agriculture, Commerce . . . have, with the aid of Experimental Philosophy, been every day putting on more brilliant colours: the splendour of the Imagination has been fading . . . and still the Peasant or Artizan, their master, [may] be a slave in mind. . . .[2]

Shelley's passage in the same vein is more famous than either:

> The cultivation of poetry is never more to be desired than at periods when, from an excess of the selfish and calculating principle, the accumulation of the materials of external life exceed the quantity of the power of assimilating them to the internal laws of human nature. . . . The cultivation of those sciences which have enlarged the limits of the empire of man over the external world, has, for want of the poetical faculty, proportionally circumscribed those of the internal world; and man, having enslaved the elements, remains himself a slave.[3]

It is for this, their insight into the spiritual unbalance of their age—an age like our own, afflicted with what has been called 'cosmic impiety'—that the politics of the poets will remain of permanent importance. Had they been mere enemies of science, mental Luddites like some of their successors of the industrial epoch, or mere mourners for a departed age of peasant virtue and the simple life, they would have little to

[1] *Church and State*, ch. VI, concluding paragraphs.

[2] *Convention of Cintra*, pp. 182-3.

[3] *Defence of Poetry*, pp. 205-6.

say that men could not easily forget. As it is, they afford a constructive criticism of the world as we know it. The philosophy of the Imagination saved them alike from the bland excesses of idealism and the obtuse optimism of the materialist. The politics of the poet are the politics of organism, a source of perennial vitality.

4. The Present Discontents

At the deepest level, the politics of the poets are, of course, concerned with a life beyond both political institution and economic organization. They were all profoundly aware that the problem of their time—as of all times, indeed—was neither institutional nor economic, but spiritual. It was the problem of the dislocation of man's spiritual organism, a failure of integration. The terminology in which they treat of the problem may vary from man to man, but the problem itself is the same problem, and the remedies they propose possess a fundamental similarity. What Coleridge calls the usurpation of the insulated understanding at the expense of the reason, appears in Wordsworth as the over-growth of cold expediency at the expense of generous feeling, and in Shelley as the excess of the calculating faculty over the quality of the imagination. Taking the forms of social phenomena, these spiritual conflicts appear at the surface of society in diverse shapes. Coleridge identifies the usurpation of the Understanding, or the analytical faculty, with both the triumph of technology over science and the over-balance of the commercial spirit at the expense of the commonweal. Wordsworth concerns himself with the breakdown of the moral fibre of the nation *vis-a-vis* the enemies of liberty incarnate in Napoleonic France. Shelley saw the conflict in terms of social inequality: the excess of calculation and the enfeeblement of imagination had turned the achievements of science and industry into instruments of tyranny of man over man which 'exasperate at once the extremes of luxury and want. . . . The rich have become richer and the poor have become poorer; and the vessel of the state is driven between the

Scylla and Charybdis of anarchy and despotism. Such are the effects which must ever flow from an unmitigated exercise of the calculating faculty.'[1] The stress is laid differently, from one writer to another, but the diagnosis differs scarcely at all, and the remedies—even in the case of Shelley—differ far less than might be expected.

Coleridge's second *Lay Sermon* (1817) is the only one of these documents which (as its sub-title indicates) professes to deal with the present discontents in a comprehensive way. Coleridge intended this work for the Middle, as well as the Higher, classes; and it is, both in tone and in range of treatment, far plainer and more 'practical' than the first. 'My first I never dreamt would be understood (except in fragments) by the general reader,' he tells us; 'but of the second, I can scarcely discover any part or passage which would compel any man of common education and information, to read it a second time in order to understand it.' The style is, as he averred, as plain as the style of the first is stately.[2] After a laborious and off-putting 'Allegoric Vision' (omitted in the present text), and a brief appeal to the philosophic spirit of his readers, he addresses himself at once to the supposed causes of the discontents: the War, high taxation, sinecures and pensions. John Stuart Mill was to dismiss Coleridge's political economy as that of 'an arrant driveller', but anyone reading these passages today, with their very modern treatment of taxation as an instrument for the circulation of wealth, of the trade-cycle, and of the fallacies of *laissez-faire*,[3] will feel a good deal less confidence in that judgment than Mill's readers of the *Westminster Review* in 1840. Coleridge's views on the economic and social repercussions of war,[4] possess a relevance and insight which will hardly be missed by a twentieth-century reader. Nor is his lengthy analysis of the technique of political demagogy[5] one moment out of date in the present year of grace. The greater part of the essay, however, is given to an analysis of the deeper

[1] *Defence of Poetry*, p. 204. [2] *Unpublished Letters*, vol. II, p. 193.
[3] *Lay Sermon*, pp. 74, 101 and 102.
[4] *Ibid.* p. 75, and again p. 106. [5] *Ibid.* pp. 70-3.

causes of distress, and it is here that we come upon the philosophical content of *The Statesman's Manual* in its practical bearings upon the England of 1817.

The eclipse of 'the first philosophy' or 'a life-giving philosophy of ideas' by the pseudo-philosophy of sensation, or mechanistic materialism, which was described and deplored in Appendix B of *The Statesman's Manual*[1] is now to be found bearing its unnatural fruit in the over-balance of the commercial spirit. Not that a healthy commercial spirit is to be dispensed with in any progressive society: it is not the spirit itself that is at fault, but its excess, and its incursion into spheres where its operation is harmful to society—for example, in agriculture.[2] These excesses and illegitimate incursions are to to be accounted to the weakening of those counterforces which once held them in check: notably, the prevalence of the kind of philosophy which engages men's minds—and particularly the minds of statesmen and men of property—in a steady and comprehensive view of ultimate social purposes. Since the later seventeenth century, however, the minds of men, at any rate in England and France, had been increasingly dominated by 'that meretricious philosophy' associated with the name of John Locke: the philosophy of a dead nature, a mechanistic universe.[3] The triumph of this philosophy went hand in hand with low-church Protestantism, 'simplified religion', and (latterly) atheism—for 'no cement can keep together pious conclusions and atheistic premises'.[4] The consequence had been the fatal weakening of the power of religion to act as 'a countercharm to the sorcery of wealth'.

'Religion and the rise of Capitalism' was to become a central theme among historians of the twentieth century. Here, as in much else, Coleridge was a precursor. He was never a victim of that plausible superficiality which treats of this theme in terms of simple cause and effect. Protestantism was no necessary

[1] *Statesman's Manual*, pp. 45-8. Coleridge's letter to Lord Liverpool (see note 5, above) opens with a brief and lively summary of the illicit adventures of the Understanding in the century between 1688 and 1789.

[2] *Lay Sermon*, pp. 112-14.

[3] *Statesman's Manual*, pp. 49-50.

[4] Letter to Lord Liverpool, see note 5, above.

ally of capitalism. The way was made easy for the ubiquitous supremacy of capitalist, or commercial, values, not by the inherent characteristics of Protestantism itself, but by a decline in the philosophical quality of religious thinking in general. Men had been encouraged to believe that religion could be 'simplified' by the dissocation of religion from philosophy. They had been encouraged to think that religion requires but the application of common sense, that theological science is a waste of time, and that the philosophical content of a creed can be dispensed with in favour of a set of ethical maxims. A religion 'to be learnt *extempore* . . . a Christianity poured in on the *catechumen* all and all at once, as from a shower-bath . . .' has, for a busy commercial society, the advantage that it 'leaves the understanding vacant and at leisure for a thorough insight into present and temporal interests'. Is such a religion likely 'to reign in the thoughts of a man, and in the powers akin to thought'? Is it likely to engage the understanding and the reason, to demand 'the first-fruits' of the whole man? What degree of counterpoise to the spirit of commercial cupidity are we to expect from a religion which has 'parted company with that inquisitive and bookish theology which tends to defraud the student of his worldly wisdom, in as much as it diverts his mind from the accumulation of wealth by pre-occupying his thoughts in the acquisition of knowledge'?[1]

No more than he expected Lord Liverpool to take a course of Platonism did Coleridge expect Mr Gradgrind to set aside his ledger in favour of Hooker's *Ecclesiastical Polity*. The stewardship of philosophical religion had its officers in the clerisy, or in the National Church, that undenominational corporation of all the learned in all the arts and sciences. The nature and functions of this organ of scholarship, teaching and preaching, are not discussed in the present text.[2] But 'an accredited, learned and philosophic class' is declared to be 'an essential element in the composition of a civilized community',[3]

[1] *Lay Sermon*, pp. 85-97.
[2] See *Church and State*, ch. VI.
[3] *Lay Sermon*, p. 83, and p. 85.

and it is to this order of men that Coleridge looks for the formative influence in the neutralization of an excessive commercialism. The clerisy should be the leaven in the lump of society, exercising its permeative power through the written and the spoken word, through the schools and universities, through every intellectual and spiritual agency of the State. It was to this body, unfortunately because ambiguously called 'The National Church', that Coleridge looked for the larger hope of social rehabilitation. He looked to it far more hopefully than he looked to the institutional State, or to Parliament. A clerisy possessed of the 'dynamic theory of the eldest philosophy', would promote the study, and the reform, of social and political institutions in the light of their ideas, or ultimate ends. Possessed of the true idea of the State, it would secure the stewardship of landed property as a trust for society, and afford the true touchstone for legislative intervention on behalf of the rights of human personality.

5. National Regeneration

'Let us become a better people, and the reform of all the public (real or supposed) grievances, which we use as pegs whereon to hang our own errors and defects, will follow of itself.'[1] Thus Coleridge concluded his second *Lay Sermon*, and this is really the message of Wordsworth in *The Convention of Cintra*. 'The things with which we are primarily and mainly concerned are inward passions and not outward arrangements',[2] Wordsworth observes, mid-way through his discourse.

> Of . . . decay in the machine of government and . . . illegitimate forces which are checking and controlling its constitutional motions, I have not spoken, nor shall I now speak. . . . No *immediate* effect can be expected from the soundest and most unexceptionable doctrines which might be laid down for the correcting of this evil.[3]

He has spoken, and he will speak, not of mechanism but of men. *The Convention of Cintra* is a trumpet-call to moral

[1] *Lay Sermon*, p. 116. [2] *Convention of Cintra*, p. 180.
[3] *Ibid.* p. 168.

rearmament on the part of the nation, and perhaps the greatest blast sounded by English lips upon that often equivocal instrument since Milton. 'Moral rearmament', as a phrase, has a horrid sound in an age afflicted by small men looking for an alibi. With Wordsworth it has the grand sustained harmony of an embattled organ pealing forth from the towers of a beleaguered citadel. England was at war with despotism on behalf of liberty, fighting from a precarious Iberian foothold upon the mainland of Napoleonic Europe, shoulder to shoulder with the patriots of Spain and Portugal. The commanders in the field had given generous terms to an ungenerous enemy after a great victory. The blood spilt at Vimiero, and in the thousand cities and villages of the peninsula, cried for justice. Wordsworth took up his pen—the pen that had struck off the great sonnets of 1802, and wrote from a head and heart on fire with moral passion.

Coleridge[1] recognized in the work of his 'dear friend and house-mate . . . sentiments and principles matured in our understanding by common energies and twelve years' intercommunion'. It seemed to him, indeed, that *The Convention of Cintra* was 'almost a self-robbery from some great philosophical poem',—that great philosophical poem which, for many years, he urged Wordsworth to write in enunciation of the great moral and political truths which the two friends had wrested from the life of poetry. Coleridge did not go so far as to claim *The Convention* as a joint-production, but there can be no doubt that in it Wordsworth spoke from the union of their two hearts and heads over many years of common experience. Coleridge's appraisal of the work might almost be the utterance of its author's other, calmer, self. 'I have not often met with a book at once so profound and so eloquent', he said. Even its defects were but 'the overflowings of excellence'. Its influence, however, was unlikely to be very great because Wordsworth

[1] Coleridge's appraisal of the *Convention* is to be found in two letters: the first, written to Daniel Stuart on 13 June 1809 (*Letters of S. T. Coleridge*, ed. E. H. Coleridge, pp. 547-50); and the second, written to T. W. Smith on 22 June 1809 (*Unpublished Letters of S. T. Coleridge*, ed. Earl Leslie Griggs, vol. II, pp. 1-3).

was addressing himself to a public 'effeminated . . . by the unremitted action of great outward events daily soliciting and daily gratifying the appetite of curiosity'. Readers of sense and feeling, on the other hand, might well have reason to fear that the work would die of a 'plethora of the highest qualities of combined philosophic and poetic genius'. In fact, it was too great a work for its age. Even readers of sense and judgment might justly complain 'of a want of shade and background; that it is all fore-ground, all in hot tints; that the first note is pitched at the height of the instrument and never suffered to sink. . . .' It kept the reader's attention throughout 'at its utmost strain and stretch'. Wordsworth's style, Coleridge averred, 'represents the chain of his thoughts and the movements of his heart admirably for me and a few others'; but the system of punctuation (supplied by De Quincey) left the periods too long, sometimes immeasurable.

Coleridge's judgment says all that needs to be said. *The Convention of Cintra* is a *tour de force*. To read it is like swimming under water. But there are marvels in the great deep, priceless to the reader who is ready to chance his lungs. Even the surface beauties, from time to time, are of a surpassing splendour: for example, the passages on courage,[1] and on the glory and tragedy of human passions.[2] It is scarcely necessary, today, to concern ourselves with the occasion of this sublime essay on the soul of state. Coleridge feared that 'the long porch', as he called the opening sections on the Convention itself, might prevent readers from entering 'the Temple'. We may agree with Coleridge, likewise, that Wordsworth's account of the effects of national enthusiasm on the Spanish people 'is somewhat too much idealized'. Yet, to anthologize the work in order to exhibit only the passages of general relevance would be to emasculate it, for contemporary reference and universal reflection lie locked in close embrace. The sword should not lie between them but should unite them. It was Wordsworth's purpose to show that moral passion is invincible. The whole work is a threnody on his own immortal lines:

[1] *Convention of Cintra*, p. 162. [2] *Ibid.* pp. 191-2.

> The power of armies is a visible thing,
> Formal, and circumscribed in time and space;
> But who the limits of that power shall trace
> Which a brave people into light can bring
> Or hide, at will,—for freedom combating. . .[1]

'But from within proceeds a nation's health. . . .' *The Convention of Cintra* is a treatise on the springs of social union. It penetrates to the source of those forces of cohesion, permanence and creative power which determine the historic destiny of peoples. It starts from common ground with Coleridge, that man lives in, and by, ideas. Coleridge's famous assertion that universal and eternal truths 'alone can interest the undegraded human spirit deeply and enduringly, because these alone belong to its essence and will remain with it permanently. . . .'[2] is taken up by Wordsworth as the interpretative instrument for his reading of the whole struggle between the free peoples and Napoleon. Wordsworth, however, speaks less of ideas than of objects—ideas enshrined in moral ends or ideals. Mere riddance, mere safety, driving the French invader back to his own territory—could be no secure inspiration for effort or endurance, 'for the mind gains consciousness of its strength to undergo [i.e. to endure] only by exercise among materials which admit the impression of its power. . . .' Its objects must be of its own kind, for 'the vigour of the human soul is from without and from futurity'. It is from communion with those images, thoughts, and feelings which are the habitual concern of genius, and from communion with which 'proceeds originally all that is creative in art and science, and all that is magnanimous in virtue'—it is from these that the minds of men must, and will, in times of trial draw their strength.[3]

Wordsworth's passion mastered his intellect. *The Convention of Cintra* suffers by reason of an incomplete application of its philosophic principle. In his intemperate exhortation of the

[1] Wordsworth, *Poems dedicated to National Independence and Liberty*, 1811.

[2] *Statesman's Manual*, p. 21.

[3] *Convention of Cintra*, p. 162.

friends of freedom to adopt a posture of 'principled reposal on superior constancy and immutable resolve,' he forgets that the enemy had his ideas, and ideals, too. His was the error of his master, Burke, in the impassioned pages of his *Reflections on the Revolution*. It is a failure of dialectic. For, if God really does marshal men by a divine tactic within a dialectic of ideas, the political philosopher must look at both sides of the barricade. He may believe in a Gresham's law of ideas, operating in reverse, so that good ideas drive out bad ideas; but he must at any rate believe that the enemy acts upon conviction and not merely on perversity. Coleridge, with his despised dialectic, never fell into the error of denying, or even of underrating, the philosophical standing of his opponents. 'It is bad policy' he was writing in *The Friend*, in the very year of the Convention, 'it is bad policy . . . to represent a political system as having no charm but for robbers and assassins, and no natural origin but in the brains of fools or madmen, when experience has proved that the great danger of the system consists in the peculiar fascination it is calculated to exert on noble and imaginative spirits. . . .'[1] He was ready to avow that the system of the French revolutionaries (and, he would have added, of the French under Napoleon) 'had its golden side for the noblest minds. . . . Let it be remembered by both parties, and indeed by controversialists on all subjects, that every speculative error which boasts a multitude of advocates, has its golden as well as its dark side; that there is always some truth connected with it. . . .'[2] Napoleon himself was philosophically intelligible. He represented the human will in abstraction from reason and religion: 'satanic pride and rebellious self-idolatry in the relations of the spirit to itself, and remorseless despotism relatively to others.' He had dared to say: 'Evil, be thou my good.' Therein lay his initial advantage over the rest of mankind.[3]

Wordsworth adopted precisely this view of Bonaparte, and was even prepared to attribute to him the adoption of evil as a

[1] *The Friend*, Section I (Political Knowledge), Essay 4.
[2] *Op. cit.* Essays 5 and 6.
[3] *Statesman's Manual*, pp. 34-5.

principle.[1] But he seems to have had no answer to the questions why did the French people follow him? and why were they so successful in arms? He contents himself with a grudging reference to the efficiency of administration generated by the adoption of the principle of *la carrière ouverte aux talents*, and with hearty aspersions upon the imbecility of France's opponents.[2] The really extraordinary fact is that Wordsworth could not bring himself to apply his principle of nationality to the French people. He was ready to account on moral grounds for the valour of the Spaniards, and his great purpose in writing the *Convention* was to recall his own countrymen to self-knowledge in their springs of national virtue. Peoples thus regenerate were, he held, invincible. Yet the French, invincible on every field for so long, were but lucky victors by reason of the imbecility of others. The idea that the French might have beaten, and might for long continue to beat, their enemies by reason of a burning faith in a superior social system brought to birth under the banner of Liberty, Equality and Fraternity, seems to have eluded him. Chesterton once wrote of the English soldiers in the wars with Napoleon who:

> Lay in living ruins, firing, and fearing not
> The strange fierce face of the Frenchmen
> Who knew for what they fought. . . .[3]

They did, indeed. But Wordsworth did not. The failure in comprehension was, as so often with Wordsworth, a failure in philosophy. It was the measure of the triumph of feeling over intellectual grasp.

It will be observed that Wordsworth's appeal in *The Convention of Cintra* is made to the general body of his countrymen. Coleridge had always insisted that

> in the disclosal of opinion, it is our duty to consider the character of those to whom we address ourselves, their situations, and probable degree of knowledge. We should be bold in the avowal of political truth among those only whose minds are susceptible of reasoning: and never to the multitude, who, ignorant and needy,

[1] *Convention of Cintra*, p. 176. [2] *Ibid.* p. 175.
[3] G. K. Chesterton, *The Secret People*.

> must necessarily act from the impulse of inflamed passions. . . . Consequently we should plead *for* the oppressed, not *to* them.[1]

The Statesman's Manual is avowedly an appeal *ad clerum*; the second *Lay Sermon* opens with a similar delimitation of the author's audience. Indeed, Coleridge came to believe that the wretched condition of the reading public was likely, before long, to cause a revival of the esoteric doctrine among the learned.[2] Wordsworth had no such inhibitions. The *Convention* is actually an appeal to the people against their government. Wordsworth never departed from the Rousseauan persuasion of his youth that the heart of the people is sound. Indeed, the very essence of the *Convention* is to be discovered in its recourse to the supposedly simple virtues of common men in contrast to the soullessness of routine statesmen or 'men of affairs'. 'Worldly distinctions and offices of command do not lie in the path . . . of philosophy and virtue.'[3] It would be greatly to the advantage of social progress and the common good 'if Governors better understood the rudiments of nature as studied in the walks of common life; if they were men who had themselves felt every strong emotion . . . and could calculate upon the force of the grander passions.'[4] This, perhaps, is the nearest that Wordsworth comes to echoing Coleridge's appeal for philosophic statesmanship, and even this is attended by an *arrière pensée.* He questions whether it is

> so desirable as might at first sight be imagined, much less is it desirable as an absolute good, that men of comprehensive sensibility and tutored genius—either for the interests of mankind or for their own—should, in ordinary times, have vested in them political power. . . . Nothing but a strong spirit of love can counteract the consciousness of pre-eminence which ever attends pre-eminent intellectual power with correspondent attainments: and this spirit of love is best encouraged by humility and simplicity in mind, manners, and conduct of life. . . .[5]

[1] Coleridge, *Essays on His Own Times*, edited by His Daughter, 1850, vol. I, pp. 21, 29. It is interesting to note that these observations came not from the 'Tory' Coleridge of Highgate, but from the young 'Jacobin' editor of *The Watchman* (1795).

[2] *Unpublished Letters*, vol. II, p. 194.

[3] *Convention of Cintra*, p. 172.

[4] *Ibid.* p. 171.

[5] *Ibid.* pp. 171-2.

The appeal, then, of the *Convention* is to the inherent virtue of common men against the cowardice and equivocation of their leaders. 'All have a right to speak, and to make their voices heard, so far as they have power. . . . These are times also in which . . . the heads of the army, more than at any other period, stand in need of being taught wisdom by the voice of the people.'[1] Indeed, popular condemnation of the policy of the statesmen and soldiers is an 'inevitable consequence from the constitution of human nature'. Why wait for courts of judicature or commissions of enquiry? 'When the people speaks loudly, it is from being strongly possessed either by the Godhead or the Demon; and he, who cannot discover the true spirit from the false, hath no ear for profitable communion.'[2] And here again, at the crisis of his argument, Wordsworth allows his impassioned feelings to obscure the intellectual problem. It is all very well to assert that 'an ear for profitable communion' will qualify us for distinguishing between *vox dei* and *vox diaboli*, but whence does such an ear derive its power of discrimination? Coleridge, quoting the self-same reference to the voice of the people, was prepared to allow that 'the voice of ten millions of men calling for the same thing is a spirit', but he insisted that we can only know whether that spirit is of Heaven or Hell 'by trying the thing called for by the prescript of reason and God's will'.[3] Generally, he would allow, the feeling of the multitude will be in favour of something good; but common sense and experience told him that the multitude 'are always under the domination of some one feeling or view; whereas truth, and above all, practical wisdom, must be the result of a wide comprehension of the more and the less, the balance and the counter-balance'.[4] Coleridge spoke in the tradition of Burke in refuting the heresy that 'the opinions of even the greatest multitudes are the standard of rectitude'.[5]

It may be said, of course, that 'the prescript of reason and God's will' afford no more of an objective standard of judgment

[1] *Convention of Cintra*, p. 151. [2] *Ibid.* p. 161.
[3] *Table Talk*, 29 April 1832. [4] *Ibid.* 20 November 1831.
[5] Burke's Speech to his Bristol Constituents, 1780.

than anything else. That was, indeed, Bentham's opinion. But when the concept of reason has behind it a philosophy of mind and nature which gives to 'ideas' an objective as well as a subjective reality, as is the case with the philosophy of Coleridge, the argument has at any rate the respectability of belonging to an intellectual system. Wordsworth, however, contented himself with the assertion that the public voice—in this particular instance—had the 'unquestionable sound of inspiration' because it was associated with the 'passions of pity, love and gratitude . . . the sentiments of admiration and rivalry . . .', and this despite the fact that it was also associated with 'hatred, and anger, and vengeance'—these last passions being somehow transmuted by 'a mystery of nature'.[1] The voice of the people to which he appeals comes forth self-evidently from an edifice dedicated to Holiness and Truth. That a similar fine mixture of outraged virtue and righteous vengeance might come forth from 'The People's Courts' of a later day was mercifully veiled from him. Perhaps it is as well that he was incapable of intruding philosophical apparatus into an essay intended for a popular audience, in the Coleridgian manner; but it is unfortunate that the terms of that essay betray the absence of such an apparatus even from the author's mind. The defect is the more serious because the absence of considered philosophical reference could be made conducive to a theory of politics which Wordsworth would wish to repudiate. There seems no reason whatever why his conclusions, in these passages on the popular voice, should not refer to thoroughly Jacobinical premises,—premises which will not square for one moment with the theory of mind to which he appeals elsewhere. When Coleridge observed that 'the introductory part respecting the Convention of Cintra might with great advantage have been written in a more calm and argumentative *manner*',[2] there can be little doubt that he had detected the philosophical weakness here exposed.

[1] *Convention of Cintra*, p. 161.
[2] *Unpublished Letters*, vol. II, p. 2.

6. The Philosophy of Reform

If Wordsworth's appeal to the people, with its simple faith in the virtues of common men, and its accompanying distrust of 'moneyed worldlings' and routine statesmen, is characteristic of Romanticism—then neither Coleridge nor Shelley was a Romantic. Actually, it would be better to call it Rousseauan. It was bred of reaction, on the part of introspective and lonely souls, against the artificiality and the rather heartless urbanity of the *ancien règime*. After Rousseau, it belongs peculiarly to Wordsworth. To equate it with Romanticism is a profitless trifling with words and labels. To appeal from expert statesmanship to the infallibility of the popular voice had no part in the intention of Coleridge or even of Shelley. To them, the problem was either to make statesmen into philosophers, or to bring to bear directly the spirit of the creative imagination upon society as a whole. It would be foolish to attribute to Shelley a Coleridgian faith in a philosophic aristocracy. He was an aristocrat himself, and while he was prepared to admire a certain magnanimity of spirit in that order of society from which he himself sprang, as distinct from the 'set of pelting wretches' who had recently risen into their places from the ranks of stockjobbers and attornies, he still knew that 'at the bottom it is all trick'.[1] Shelley put his faith in no class: neither in a Platonic aristocracy nor in a republican peasantry. To him, the hope of the future lay in a universal participation in the spirit of poetry. The agents of man's amelioration are the poets, and poets belong to no class and to no age. They participate in the universal and the eternal, and, by awakening and nourishing the potential poet in all men, they alone can bring about the regeneration of the world.

Shelley's teaching on the imagination is, in all essentials, that of Coleridge, but it is brought to bear upon the human situation directly, without Coleridge's impedimenta of metaphysics and theology. While Coleridge seems often to equate the Imagina-

[1] *Philosophical View of Reform*, p. 235.

tion with the Reason, as the faculty by which man apprehends ultimate ends, or 'living, inborn, essential truths', and at the same time reduces the Understanding to the position of a 'subaltern faculty' concerned only with means, Shelley conceives of the Imagination as 'the great instrument of moral good'[1] and continues to accept the eighteenth-century conception of the Reason as 'the principle of analysis' or 'the calculating faculty'. Shelley's description of the Imagination as 'mind acting upon . . . thoughts so as to colour them with its own light',[2] recalls at once Coleridge's experience of the alchemic power of the Imagination in Wordsworth's poetry. The Platonic character of Shelley's conception is at once apparent when, at the beginning of *The Defence of Poetry*, he says of the Imagination that it 'has for its objects those forms which are common to universal nature and existence itself'. Its concern is with universals, with 'the similitudes of things'. It is the agent of ultimate truth, 'a principle within the human being' which harmonizes 'by an internal adjustment' the external impressions presented to it by the senses.[3]

Shelley's delight in Plato dates from his undergraduate days, but it was not to bear fruit until late in his short life. It has been suggested that he would have deserted Hume and the materialists much earlier had he not been driven into a fury of revolt against established authority by his expulsion from Oxford, by his experience of the Court of Chancery, and by his passionate sympathy with the sufferings of the English poor. Outraged by his personal experience of the machine of Church and State, and by the devastation of human values by the machines of the Industrial Revolution, he sought an adequate philosophy of revolution, and found it in Godwin's *Political Justice*. It was not until the last five years of his life that he discovered that the deepest radicalism of all was to be found in the philosophy of ideas of his earliest master. His political faith in Godwinian anarchism never weakened. Non-attachment, the necessity to hold aloof from party-politics and from all forms of violence; egalitarianism; ideal communism; these

[1] *Defence of Poetry*, p. 202. [2] *Ibid.* p. 199. [3] *Ibid.* p. 199.

remained cardinal doctrines in his creed. But the basic materialism was to be replaced by Platonic idealism, and the agency by which the Godwinian society was to be brought into being was to be the awakening of the ideal nature of man by the exercise of the Imagination through the operation of poetry. *The Defence of Poetry* and *A Philosophical View of Reform*, taken together, afford the materials for a synthesis of Plato and Godwin.

When Coleridge declared that 'the first man on whom the light of an idea dawned, did in that same moment receive the spirit and the credentials of a lawgiver',[1] he was saying in metaphysical terms what Shelley was to say in his most-quoted aphorism: 'Poets are the unacknowledged legislators of the world.'[2] What both men are really saying is that, no matter where political power may seem to reside in a society, the real government of society always lies, and must always lie, with those whom Shelley calls 'the hierophants of an unapprehended inspiration'[3]—or with its men of vision, its poets, its philosophers, all those who 'participate in the eternal, the infinite, and the one'.[4] Coleridge sees this essential governing force in society in institutional terms: the clerisy of his National Church will be its effective organ for the endless task of platonizing society, training up both governors and governed in the light of life-giving philosophy. Shelley never submitted the conception to the framework of an institution. He could accept neither a National Church nor a philosophic aristocracy as guardians and propagators of truth. To him, the poet is a free spirit operating upon free spirits; although, the nature of Imagination being what it is, he will be a Platonist, and a Platonic Guardian, *malgré lui*. Only once does Shelley suggest anything resembling concerted life and action by his 'unacknowledged legislators'. It is when, at the close of the *Philosophical View of Reform*, he is proposing ways and means of bringing to bear informed opinion for the reformation of Parliament. 'The poets, philosophers and artists ought to remonstrate, and the memorials

[1] See above, p. xvii, n. 5.
[2] *Defence of Poetry*, p. 206.
[3] *Ibid.* p. 206.
[4] *Ibid.* p. 200.

entitled their petitions might shew the universal conviction they entertain of the inevitable connection between national prosperity and freedom, and the cultivation of the imagination and the cultivation of scientific truth, and the profound development of moral and metaphysical enquiry.' The effect, he thought, must be 'radiant and irresistible'. Indeed, 'it would be Eternity warning Time'.[1]

The Defence of Poetry might be said to be Shelley's counterpart to *The Statesman's Manual*, in that it contains his profoundest, because his most philosophical, analysis of the human situation in his age. What Coleridge has to say of the 'usurpation of the Understanding' as the clue to modern man's disorders, finds expression again in Shelley's central passages on the necessity for the cultivation of poetry in an age of excessive attachment to 'the selfish and calculating principle'. What Coleridge calls the Understanding has given men a plethora of scientific and economical knowledge 'disproportioned to the presence of the creative faculty, which is the basis of all knowledge'. In fact, 'we have eaten more than we can digest'. Man has conquered the external world, but 'for the want of the poetical faculty . . . remains a slave'.[2] When comparison is made with Coleridge at this, the deepest point of their analysis, however, it will be noticed that Shelley at once carries the argument to the level of social justice. The excess of calculation over imagination is made responsible for the extremes of riches and poverty in society, for 'the abuse of all invention for abridging and combining labour to the exasperation of the inequality of mankind'. With this extremism in wealth and poverty has come extremism in government, so that the ship of state is driven between the Scylla and Charybdis of anarchy and despotism. The nearest that Coleridge came to stating the problem of spiritual unbalance in terms of social dislocation was in the second *Lay Sermon*, where the loss of philosophic religion is deplored as weakening the counterbalance to commercial cupidity. Shelley's social interpretation, while it is less extensive, is far bolder. In the *Philosophical View*

[1] *Philosophical View of Reform*, p. 259. [2] *Defence of Poetry*, pp. 205-6.

of Reform it is taken up in a thoroughly Socialistic programme for the equalizing of wealth, the abolition of unearned increment, and a more than Socialistic treatment of the National Debt.

Shelley's radical and democratic proposals are less important than the spirit in which they were proposed, and the remarkably statesmanlike caution with which he surrounds his suggestions for their accomplishment. He was as horrified as any so-called 'Tory-reactionary' among the lake-poets, at the near prospect of a *bellum servile*. He was anxious to recommend, while there was yet time (if there *was* yet time), that Parliament should reform itself; that the half-loaf of ratepayer suffrage should be accepted by peaceful contrivance rather than that the whole-loaf of universal suffrage should be gained by violence;[1] in fact, that 'general illumination should precede revolution . . .' —so that, in fact, revolution would be unnecessary. Nothing could serve better to correct the stock-portrait of Shelley the wild-eyed revolutionary than a perusal of the *Philosophical View of Reform*.

The philosophic view of reform, as proposed by the poets, is hardly to be discovered in Shelley's work of that title, but rather in the fully-fledged Platonism of Coleridge. What we have in Shelley's tract is a re-statement of the necessitarian philosophy of Godwin, and while it is true that Shelley never wholly rid himself of that attractive but superficial doctrine, it is no less true that he was finding his way, at the time of his death, to the political and social instrumentation of the spiritual voluntarism of his predecessors. In *A Defence of Poetry*, where his purpose is less to establish a political programme than to adumbrate a creative philosophy of mind, we get a fascinating glimpse of what he might have done for the furtherance of a creative politics had he lived to follow up the social and political implications of his poetic experience. Coleridge is known to have observed, after Shelley's death, that he regretted never having met him, because he felt that he could have helped him. Nor is there any reason to doubt that the younger man would have learnt from the 'mighty poet' whose mind was 'a

[1] *Philosophical View of Reform*, p. 259.

mist', and who yet possessed the central doctrine of *A Defence of Poetry*: the poet who, in *Peter Bell the Third*, ascribed to poetry—

> Heaven's light on earth—Truth's brightest beam. . . .[1]

The unifying force, beneath all the surface divergencies, of the poets here presented, is the theory of mind and nature at which they all, in greater or lesser degree, arrived as the consequence of their experience of the life of poetry, and from which they set out upon the tasks of social and political regeneration. It is by their success or failure in translating the philosophy of poetry into terms of a philosophy of society that their permanent importance must be judged.

[1] *Peter Bell the Third*, Part the Fifth.

BIBLIOGRAPHICAL NOTE

THE Coleridge tracts (generally referred to as *The Lay Sermons*) were first published by Messrs Gale and Fenner, London, in 1816 and 1817 respectively. The definitive edition may be said to be that published by Edward Moxon, London, in 1852, and edited by Derwent Coleridge 'with the author's last corrections and notes'. Otherwise, they have sometimes been republished along with more popular works of Coleridge, e.g. with a third edition of *The Constitution of Church and State*, and again with a re-issue of *Biographia Literaria* in 1866. For the present reprint, the text of the first edition has been used.

Wordsworth's *Convention of Cintra* was published in an edition of five hundred by Messrs Longman in 1809. It was not sold off, and 'many copies were disposed of by the publishers as waste paper, and went to the trunkmakers....' (*Memoirs of William Wordsworth*, vol. I, pp. 404-5.) Two short portions of the tract appeared originally in December and January 1808-9, in the *Courier* newspaper. Copies of the tract are exceedingly rare. It was included in *The Prose Works of William Wordsworth*, edited by the Rev. Alexander B. Grosart, 3 vols., in 1876, occupying pp. 31-174 of the first volume. It is to be found also in Volume I of *The Prose Works of William Wordsworth*, edited by William Knight, in 1896. The late A. V. Dicey republished the tract, with an Introduction, in 1915. Grosart's text has been used for the present reprint.

A Defence of Poetry was originally conceived as the first part of an essay in answer to Thomas Love Peacock's *Four Ages of Poetry* (1820). It was intended for *Ollier's Literary Miscellany*, where Peacock's work had appeared, but the magazine ceased publication, and Shelley's essay was first published by Mrs Shelley in her edition of her husband's *Essays, etc.* in 1840. The various extant versions of the essay were collated by H. Buxton Forman for his edition of *The Prose Works of Shelley* (4 vols., London), in 1880. Forman's text (vol. 3, pp. 99-144) has been used in selecting the passages reprinted here.

A Philosophical View of Reform remained unpublished for nearly a century. The manuscript comprises a notebook which passed from Lady Shelley, the poet's daughter-in-law, to her friend the Rev.

Stopford A. Brooke, at whose death in 1916 it passed to his daughter, the wife of T. W. Rolleston, Esq., who transcribed and edited it for publication by the Oxford Press in 1920. This slender, finely-printed volume is now very scarce. Permission to include the text as transcribed by the late Mr Rolleston has been kindly given by his daughter, Mrs Honor Drysdale, of Park End, Radley. Thanks are also due to Geoffrey Cumberlege, Esq. for assistance in tracing the copyright in this transcription. Shelley's original MS was sold to Mr Rosenbach of the United States.

The purpose of the present volume is to provide a manageable text for students of political thought, and to this end certain editorial procedures have been adopted. None of the original texts, with the exception of *A Philosophical View of Reform* has been reprinted *in extenso*. Merely repetitive passages (particularly in *The Convention of Cintra*), and passages bearing little obvious reference to politics (notably certain theological passages in *The Statesman's Manual*), have been omitted, the omissions being indicated thus . . . . Many footnotes (especially in the Coleridge tracts) have also been omitted, but where a footnote either helped to clarify or to support the argument, or added something of obvious value, it has been retained with a proper indication of its authorship. The purpose of the end-notes supplied by the present editor is two-fold: to explicate references to persons or events, and to supply cross-reference to the treatment of the same point by other writers represented. Each text is prefaced by a synopsis, which is intended as a guide to the reader and as a substitute for an index. The fullness of the synopsis varies in direct ratio to the difficulty of the text. It has been found by experience that the problem presented by the political writings of the English 'Romantics' is not so much the inaccessibility of their writings (although that is considerable) as the elucidation of their meaning. Only in two instances has the editor taken the liberty of re-arrangement of the original text. *The Statesman's Manual*, as Coleridge wrote it, began at page 10 of the present text, with the paragraph beginning 'If our whole knowledge. . . .' The passages on the nature of the reading public and on education (pp. 1-9) are actually embedded in the middle of the tract (pp. 40-7 in Derwent Coleridge's edition of 1852). These reflections seemed so obviously introductory in character, that they have been transposed to the beginning. The other change concerns the appendices to *The Statesman's Manual*. Coleridge's 'Appendix A' and 'Appendix

C' have no political reference, and are omitted here. This has involved altering the lettering of the remainder, so that Coleridge's 'Appendix B' now becomes 'A', while his 'D' and 'E' have been united to form 'B'. It is always dangerous, by the very nature of his thought to assert that anything Coleridge wrote was 'unpolitical', and any re-arrangement for the sake of simplification must run the risk of misrepresenting him. It is hoped, however, that the avowed purpose of the present volume may exempt the editor from the charge of too severe man-handling of difficult material in the interests of accessibility. He wishes to express grateful thanks to two members of his College, Dr W. L. Cuttle and Mr James Stevenson, for their assistance in checking Coleridge's Latin and Greek.

R. J. WHITE

Downing College,
Cambridge

THE STATESMAN'S MANUAL

OR

THE BIBLE THE BEST GUIDE TO POLITICAL SKILL AND FORESIGHT:

A LAY SERMON
Addressed to the Higher Classes of Society,
With an Appendix, Containing
Comments and Essays Connected with the
Study of the Inspired Writings

BY

S. T. COLERIDGE, Esq.

'Ad isthoec quoeso vos, qualiacunque primo videantur aspectu, ut qui vobis forsan insanire videar, saltem quibus insaniam rationibus cognoscatis.'

LONDON
1816

D

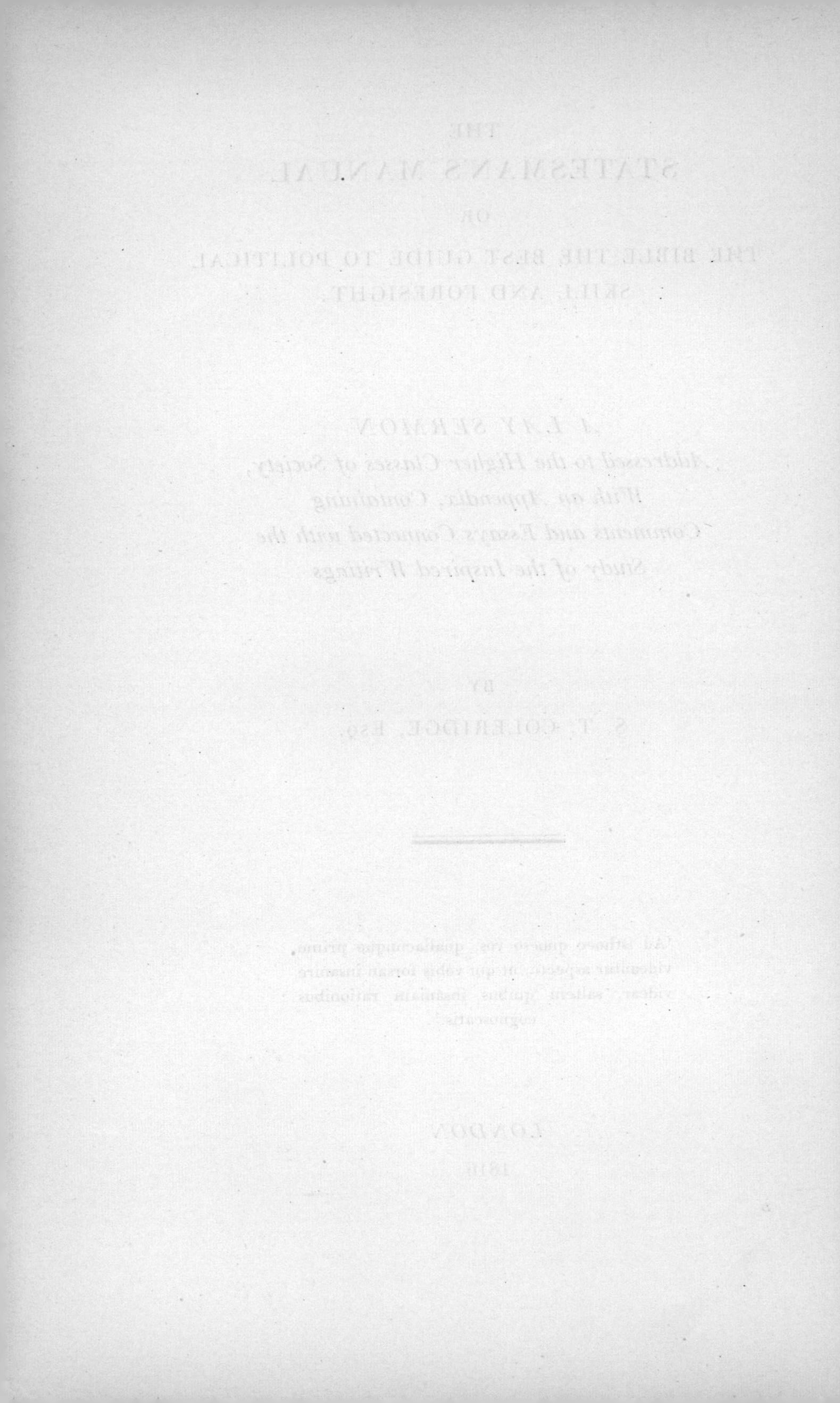

SUMMARY OF CONTENTS

APPENDIX

THE BIBLE
THE STATESMAN'S MANUAL
A LAY SERMON, &c.

The author and the reading public

WHEN I named this essay a sermon, I sought to prepare the inquirers after it for the absence of all the usual softenings suggested by worldly prudence, of all compromise between truth and courtesy. But not even as a sermon would I have addressed the present discourse to a promiscuous audience; and for this reason I likewise announced it in the title-page as exclusively *ad clerum*; i.e., (in the old and wide sense of the word) to men of clerkly acquirements, of whatever profession. I would that the greater part of our publications could be thus directed, each to its appropriate class of readers. But this cannot be. For among other odd burrs and kecksies, the misgrowth of our luxuriant activity, we have now a reading public, [1] as strange a phrase, methinks, as ever forced a splenetic smile on the staid countenance of meditation; and yet no fiction! For our readers have, in good truth, multiplied exceedingly, and have waxed proud. It would require the intrepid accuracy of a Colquhoun [2] to venture at the precise number of that vast company only, whose heads and hearts are dieted at the two public ordinaries of literature, the circulating libraries and the periodical press. But what is the result? Does the inward man thrive on this regimen? Alas! if the average health of the consumers may be judged by the articles of largest consumption; if the secretions may be conjectured from the ingredients of the dishes that are found best suited to their palates; from all that I have seen, either of the banquet or the guests, I shall utter my profaccia with a desponding sigh. From a popular philosophy and a philosophic populace, good sense deliver us!

An appeal ad clerum

At present, however, I am to imagine for myself a very different audience. I appeal exclusively to men from whose station and opportunities I may dare anticipate a respectable portion of that 'sound book learnedness' into which our old public schools still continue to initiate their pupils. [3] I appeal to men in whom I may hope to find, if not philosophy, yet occasional impulses at least to philosophic thought. And here, as far as my own experience extends, I can announce one favourable symptom. The notion of our measureless superiority in good sense to our ancestors, so general at the commencement of the French Revolution and for some years before it, is out of fashion. We hear, at least, less of the jargon of this enlightened age. After fatiguing itself as performer or spectator in the giddy figure-dance of political changes, Europe has seen the shallow foundations of its self-complacent faith give way; and among men of influence and property, we have now more reason to apprehend the stupor of despondence than the extravagances of hope unsustained by experience, or of self-confidence not bottomed on principle.

Popular education

In this rank of life the danger lies, not in any tendency to innovation, but in the choice of the means for preventing it. And here my apprehensions point to two opposite errors, each of which deserves a separate notice. The first consists in a disposition to think that, as the peace of nations has been disturbed by the diffusion of a false light, it may be re-established by excluding the people from all knowledge and all prospect of amelioration. O! never, never! Reflection and stirrings of mind, with all their restlessness and all the errors that result from their imperfection, from the too much, because too little, are come into the world. The powers that awaken and foster the spirit of curiosity are to be found in every village: books are in every hovel. The infant's cries are hushed with picture-books; and the cottager's child sheds his first bitter tears over pages, which render it impossible for the man to be treated or governed as a child. Here, as in so many other cases, the inconveniences that have arisen from a thing's having become too general, are best removed by making it universal.

The other and contrary mistake proceeds from the assumption

that a national education will have been realized whenever the people at large have been taught to read and write. Now, among the many means to the desired end, this is doubtless one, and not the least important. But neither is it the most so. Much less can it be held to constitute education, which consists in educing the faculties and forming the habits; the means varying according to the sphere in which the individuals to be educated are likely to act and become useful. I do not hesitate to declare that whether I consider the nature of the discipline adopted, [4] or the plan of poisoning the children of the poor with a sort of potential infidelity under the 'liberal idea' of teaching those points only of religious faith in which all denominations agree, [5] I cannot but denounce the so-called Lancastrian schools as pernicious beyond all power of compensation by the new acquirement of reading and writing. But take even Dr Bell's original and unsophisticated plan, [6] which I myself regard as an especial gift of Providence to the human race; and suppose this incomparable machine, this vast moral steam-engine, to have been adopted and in free motion throughout the empire; it would yet appear to me a most dangerous delusion to rely on it as if this of itself formed an efficient national education. We cannot, I repeat, honour the scheme too highly as a prominent and necessary part of the great process; but it will neither supersede, nor can it be substituted for, sundry other measures that are at least equally important. And these are such measures, too, as unfortunately involve the necessity of sacrifices on the side of the rich and powerful, more costly, and far more difficult, than the yearly subscription of a few pounds!—such measures as demand more self-denial than the expenditure of time in a committee or of eloquence in a public meeting.

Undenominational instruction

Nay, let Dr Bell's philanthropic end have been realized, and the proposed modicum of learning universal: yet convinced of its insufficiency to stem up against the strong currents set in from an opposite point, I dare not assure myself, that it may not be driven backward by them and become confluent with the evils it was intended to preclude.

Re-education of the governing class

What other measures I had in contemplation, it has been my endeavour to explain elsewhere. But I am greatly deceived, if one preliminary to an efficient education of the labouring classes be not the recurrence to a more manly discipline of the intellect on the part of the learned themselves, in short, a thorough recasting of the moulds, in which the minds of our gentry, the characters of our future land-owners, magistrates and senators, are to receive their shape and fashion. [7] O what treasures of practical wisdom would be once more brought into open day by the solution of this problem! Suffice it for the present to hint the master-thought. The first man on whom the light of an idea dawned, did in that same moment receive the spirit and the credentials of a lawgiver: [8] and as long as man shall exist, so long will the possession of that antecedent knowledge (the maker and master of all profitable experience) which exists only in the power of an idea, be the one lawful qualification of all dominion in the world of the senses. Without this, experience itself is but a Cyclops walking backwards, under the fascination of the past: and we are indebted to a lucky coincidence of outward circumstances and contingencies, least of all things to be calculated on in times like the present, if this one-eyed experience does not seduce its worshipper into practical anachronisms. [9]

But alas! the halls of old philosophy have been so long deserted, that we circle them at shy distance as the haunt of phantoms and chimeras. The sacred grove of Academus is held in like regard with the unfoodful trees in the shadowy world of Maro that had a dream attached to every leaf. The very terms of ancient wisdom are worn out, or, far worse, stamped on baser metal: [10] and whoever should have the hardihood to reproclaim its solemn truths must commence with a glossary....

If our whole knowledge and information concerning the Bible had been confined to the one fact of its immediate derivation from God, we should still presume that it contained rules and assistances for all conditions of men under all circumstances; and therefore for communities no less than for individuals. . . . The humblest and least educated of our countrymen must have wilfully neglected the inestimable privileges, secured to all alike, if he has not himself found, if he has not from his own personal experience discovered, the sufficiency of the Scriptures in all knowledge requisite for a right performance of his duty as a man and a Christian. Of the labouring classes, who in all countries form the great majority of the inhabitants, more than this is not demanded, more than this is not perhaps generally desirable—'They are not sought for in public counsel, nor need they be found where politic sentences are spoken. It is enough if everyone is wise in the working of his own craft; so best will they maintain the state of the world.'

Intellectual responsibilities of the upper classes

But you, my friends, to whom the following pages are more particularly addressed, as to men moving in the higher class of society—You will, I hope, have availed yourselves of the ampler means entrusted to you by God's providence, to a more extensive study and a wider use of His revealed will and word. From you we have a right to expect a sober and meditative accommodation to your own times and country of those important truths declared in the inspired writings 'for a thousand generations', and of the awful examples, belonging to all ages, by which those truths are at once illustrated and confirmed. Would you feel yourselves conscious that you had shown yourselves unequal to your station in society—would you stand degraded in your own eyes, if you betrayed an utter want of information respecting the acts of human sovereigns and legislators? And should you not much rather be both ashamed and afraid to know yourselves inconversant with the acts and constitutions of God, whose law executeth itself, and whose word is the foundation, the power, and the life of the universe? Do you hold it a requisite of your rank to show yourselves inquisitive concerning the expectations and plans of statesmen and state-councillors? Do you excuse it as natural curiosity, that you lend a listening ear to the guesses of state-gazers, to the dark hints and open revilings of our self-inspired state fortune-tellers, 'the wizards that peep and mutter' and forecast, alarmists by trade, and malcontents for their bread? And should you not feel a deeper interest in predictions which are permanent prophecies, because they are at the same time eternal truths? Predictions which in containing the grounds of fulfilment involve the principles of foresight, and teach the science of the future in its perpetual elements?. . . [11]

Past and present

If there be any antidote to that restless craving for the wonders of the day, which in conjunction with the appetite for publicity is spreading like an efflorescence on the surface of our national character; if there exist means for deriving resignation from general discontent, means of building up with the very materials of political gloom that stedfast frame of hope which affords the only certain shelter from the throng of self-realizing alarms, at the same time that it is the natural home and workshop of all the active virtues; that antidote and these means must be sought for in the collation of the present with the past, in the habit of thoughtfully assimilating the events of our own age to those of the time before us. If this be a moral advantage derivable from history in general, rendering its study therefore a moral duty for such as possess the opportunities of books, leisure and education, it would be inconsistent even with the name of believers not to recur with pre-eminent interest to events and revolutions, the records of which are as much distinguished from all other history by their especial claims to divine authority, as the facts themselves were from all other facts by especial manifestation of divine interference. 'Whatsoever things', saith St Paul (Romans xv. 4), 'were written aforetime, were written for our learning; that we through patience and comfort of the Scriptures might have hope'. [12]

Miracles as educative against superstition

In the infancy of the world, signs and wonders were requisite in order to startle and break down that superstition, idolatrous in itself and the source of all other idolatry, which tempts the natural man to seek the true cause and origin of public calamities in outward circumstances, persons and incidents: in agents, therefore, that were themselves but surges of the same tide, passive conductors of the one invisible influence, under which the total host of billows, in the whole line of successive impulse, swell and roll shoreward; there finally, each in its turn, to strike, roar, and be dissipated.

But with each miracle worked there was a truth revealed, which thenceforward was to act as its substitute: and if we think the Bible less applicable to us on account of the miracles, we degrade ourselves into mere slaves of sense and fancy, which are indeed the appointed medium between earth and heaven, but for that very cause stand in a desirable relation to spiritual truth then only, when, as a mere and passive medium, they yield a free passage to its light. It was only to overthrow the usurpation exercised in and through the senses, that the senses were miraculously appealed to. Reason and religion are their own evidence. The natural Sun is in this respect a symbol of the spiritual. Ere he is fully arisen, and while his glories are still under veil, he calls up the breeze to chase away the usurping vapours of the night season, and thus converts the air itself into the minister of its own purification: not surely in proof or elucidation of the light from heaven, but to prevent its interception.

Wherever, therefore, similar circumstances co-exist with the same moral causes, the principles revealed, and the examples recorded, in the inspired writings render miracles superfluous: and if we neglect to apply truths in expectation of wonders, or under pretext of the cessation of the latter, we tempt God and merit the same reply which our Lord gave to the Pharisees on a like occasion. 'A wicked and an adulterous generation seeketh after a sign, and there shall no sign be given to it, but the sign of the prophet Jonas': that is, a threatening call to repentance. Equally applicable and prophetic will the following verses be: 'The men of Nineveh shall rise in judgment with this generation and shall condemn it, because they repented at the preaching of Jonas, and behold, a greater than Jonas is here. The queen of the south shall rise up in the judgment with this generation, and shall condemn it: for she came from the uttermost parts of the earth to bear the wisdom of Solomon, and behold a greater than Solomon is here.' For have we not divine assurance that Christ is with His church, even to the end of the world? And what could the queen of the south, or the men of Nineveh have beheld, that could enter into competition with the events of our own times, in importance, in splendour, or even in strangeness and significancy?

How to learn from history

The true origin of human events is so little susceptible of that kind of evidence which can compel our belief; so many are the disturbing forces which in every cycle or ellipse of changes modify the motion given by the first projection; and every age has, or imagines it has, its own circumstances which render past experience no longer applicable to the present case; that there will never be wanting answers, and explanations, and specious flatteries of hope to persuade a people and its government that the history of the past is inapplicable to their case. And no wonder, if we read history for the facts instead of reading it for the sake of the general principles, [13] which are to the facts as the root and sap of a tree to its leaves: and no wonder, if history so read should find a dangerous rival in novels, nay, if the latter should be preferred to the former on the score even of probability. I well remember, that when the examples of former Jacobins, as Julius Caesar, Cromwell, and the like, were adduced in France and England at the commencement of the French Consulate, it was ridiculed as pedantry and pedant's ignorance to fear a repetition of usurpation and military despotism at the close of the enlightened eighteenth century! Even so, in the very dawn of the late tempestuous day, when the revolutions of Corcyra, the proscriptions of the Reformers, Marius, Caesar, &c., and the direful effects of the levelling tenets in the Peasants' War in Germany (differenced from the tenets of the first French constitution only by the mode of wording them, the figures of speech being borrowed in the one instance from theology, and in the other from modern metaphysics), were urged on the Convention, and its vindicators; the Magi of the day, the true citizens of the world, the *plusquam-perfecti* of patriotism, gave us set proofs that similar results were impossible, and that it was an insult to so philosophical an age, to so enlightened a nation, to dare direct the public eye towards them as to lights of warning! Alas! like lights in the stern of a vessel they illumined the path only that had been passed over!

Historical causation

The politic Florentine [14][1] has observed, that there are brains of three races. The one understands of itself; the other understands as much as is shown it by others; the third neither understands of itself, not what is shown it by others. In our times there are more perhaps who belong to the third class from vanity and acquired frivolity of mind, than from natural incapacity. It is no uncommon foible with those who are honoured with the acquaintance of the great, to attribute national events to particular persons, particular measures, to the errors of one man, to the intrigues of another, to any possible spark of a particular occasion, rather than to the true proximate cause (and which alone deserves the name of a cause), the predominant state of public opinion. And still less are they inclined to refer the latter to the ascendancy of speculative principles, and the scheme or mode of thinking in vogue. I have known men, who with significant nods and the pitying contempt of smiles, have denied all influence to the corruptions of moral and political philosophy, and with much solemnity have proceeded to solve the riddle of the French Revolution by anecdotes! Yet it would not be difficult, by an unbroken chain of historic facts, to demonstrate that the most important changes in the commercial relations of the world had their origin in the closets or lonely walks of uninterested theorists—that the mighty epochs of commerce, that have changed the face of empires, nay, the most important of those discoveries and improvements in the mechanic arts, which have numerically increased our population beyond what the wisest statesmen of Elizabeth's reign deemed possible, and again doubled this population virtually; the most important, I say, of those inventions that in their results

——————— best uphold
War by her two main nerves, iron and gold

[1] Sono di tre generazioni cervelli: l'uno in tende per se; l'altro intende quanto da altri gli e mostro; e il terzo non intende né per se stesso né per dimostrazione d'altri.
Machiavelli.

had their origin not in the cabinets of statesmen, or in the practical insight of men of business, but in the closets of uninterested theorists, in the visions of recluse genius. [15] To the immense majority of men, even in civilized countries, speculative philosophy has ever been, and must ever remain, a *terra incognita*. Yet it is not the less true, that all the epoch-forming revolutions of the Christian world, the revolutions of religion and with them the civil, social, and domestic habits of the nations concerned, have coincided with the rise and fall of metaphysical systems. [16] So few are the minds that really govern the machine of society, and so incomparably more numerous and more important are the indirect consequences of things than their foreseen and direct effects.

Abstract ideas govern men in times of tumult

It is with nations as with individuals. In tranquil moods and peaceable times we are quite practical. Facts only and cool common sense are then in fashion. But let the winds of passion swell, and straightway men begin to generalize; to connect by remotest analogies; to express the most universal positions of reason in the most glowing figures of fancy; in short, to feel particular truths and mere facts, as poor, cold, narrow, and incommensurate with their feelings. [17]

The Apostle of the Gentiles quoted from a Greek comic poet. Let it not then be condemned as unseasonable or out of place, if I remind you that in the intuitive knowledge of this truth, and with his wonted fidelity to nature, our own great poet has placed the greater number of his profoundest maxims and general truths, both political and moral, not in the mouths of men at ease, but of men under the influence of passion, when the mighty thoughts over-master and become the tyrants of the mind that has brought them forth. In his Lear, Othello, Macbeth, Hamlet, principles of deepest insight and widest interest fly off like sparks from the glowing iron under the loud anvil. It seems a paradox only to the unthinking, and it is a fact that none but the unread in history will deny, that in periods of popular tumult and innovation the more abstract a notion is, the more readily has it been found to combine, the closer has appeared its affinity, with the feelings of a people and with all their immediate impulses to action. At the commencement of the French Revolution, in the remotest villages every tongue was employed in echoing and enforcing the almost geometrical abstractions of the physiocratic politicians and economists. The public roads were crowded with armed enthusiasts disputing on the inalienable sovereignty of the people, the imprescriptible laws of the pure reason, and the universal constitution, which, as rising out of the nature and rights of man as man, all nations alike were under the obligation of adopting. Turn over the fugitive writings, that are still extant, of the age of Luther; peruse the pamphlets and loose sheets that came out in flights during the reign of Charles the First and the Republic; and you will find in these one continued comment on the aphorism of Lord Chancellor Bacon (a man assuredly sufficiently acquainted with the extent of secret and personal influence), that the knowledge of the speculative principles of men in general between the age of twenty and thirty, is the one great source of political prophecy. And Sir Philip Sidney regarded the adoption of one set of principles in the Netherlands as a proof of the divine agency and the fountain of all the events and successes of that revolution. [18]

A calm and detailed examination of the facts justifies me to my own mind in hazarding the bold assertion, that the fearful blunders of the late dread revolution, and all the calamitous mistakes of its opponents, from its commencement even to the era of loftier principles and wiser measures (an era that began with, and ought to be named from, the war of the Spanish and Portuguese insurgents), every failure with all its gloomy results, may be unanswerably deduced from the neglect of some maxim or other that had been established by clear reasoning and plain facts in the writings of Thucydides, Tacitus, Machiavel, Bacon, or Harrington. These are red-letter names even in the almanacs of worldly wisdom: and yet I dare challenge all the critical benches of infidelity to point out any one important truth, any one efficient, practical direction or warning, which did not pre-exist, and for the most part in a sounder, more intelligible, and more comprehensive form, in the Bible.

Peculiar claims of Hebrew historians to our attention: their prescripts flow direct from universal principles of reason

In addition to this, the Hebrew legislator, and the other inspired poets, prophets, historians and moralists of the Jewish church have two immense advantages in their favour. First, their particular rules and prescripts flow directly and visibly from universal principles, as from a fountain: they flow from principles and ideas that are not so properly said to be confirmed by reason as to be reason itself. Principles, in act and procession, disjoined from which, and from the emotions that inevitably accompany the actual intuition of their truth, the widest maxims of prudence are like arms without hearts, [19] muscles without nerves. Secondly, from the very nature of these principles, as taught in the Bible, they are understood in exact proportion as they are believed and felt. The regulator is never separated from the main spring. For the words of the apostle are literally and philosophically true: We (that is, the human race) live by faith. Whatever we do or know, that in kind is different from the brute creation, has its origin in a determination of the reason to have faith and trust in itself. This, its first act of faith is scarcely less than identical with its own being. *Implicité*, it is the copula—it contains the possibility—of every position, to which there exists any correspondence in reality. It is itself, therefore, the realizing principle, the spiritual substratum of the whole complex body of truths. This primal act of faith is enunciated in the word, GOD: a faith not derived from experience, but its ground and source, and without which the fleeting chaos of facts would no more form experience, than the dust of the grave can of itself make a living man. [20] The imperative and oracular form of the inspired Scripture is the form of reason itself in all things purely rational and moral. If it be the word of Divine Wisdom, we might anticipate that it would in all things be distinguished from other books, as the Supreme Reason, whose knowledge is creative, and antecedent to the things known, is distinguished from the understanding, or creaturely mind of the individual, the acts of which are posterior to the things it records and arranges. Man alone was created in the image of God: a position groundless and inexplicable, if the reason in man do not differ from the understanding. [21] For this the inferior animals (many at least) possess in degree: and assuredly the divine image or idea is not a thing of degrees.

Hence it follows that what is expressed in the inspired writings, is implied in all absolute science. The latter whispers what the former utter as with the voice of a trumpet. [22] As sure as God liveth, is the pledge and assurance of every positive truth, that is asserted by the reason. The human understanding musing on many things, snatches at truth, but is frustrated and disheartened by the fluctuating nature of its objects; its conclusions therefore are timid and uncertain, and it hath no way of giving permanence to things but by reducing them to abstractions: hardly (saith the author of the *Wisdom of Solomon*, of whose words the preceding sentence is a paraphrase), hardly do we guess aright at things that are upon earth, and with labour do we find the things that are before us; but all certain knowledge is in the power of God, and a presence from above. So only have the ways of men been reformed, and every doctrine that contains a saving truth, and all acts pleasing to God (in other words, all actions consonant with human nature, in its original intention) are through wisdom: this is the rational spirit of man.

Knowing and becoming

This, then, is the prerogative of the Bible; this is the privilege of its believing students. With them the principle of knowledge is likewise a spring and principle of action. [23] And as it is the only certain knowledge, so are the actions that flow from it the only ones on which a secure reliance can be placed. The understanding may suggest motives, may avail itself of motives, and make judicious conjectures respecting the probable consequences of actions. But the knowledge taught in the Scriptures produces the motives, involves the consequences; and its highest formula is still: As sure as God liveth, so will it be unto thee! Strange as this position will appear to such as forget that motives can be causes only in a secondary and improper sense, inasmuch as the man makes the motive, not the motive the man; and that the same thought shall be a motive to one man and no motive to his neighbour; (a sufficient

Proximate and ultimate causes

proof that the motives themselves are effects, the principle of which, good or evil, lies far deeper)—matter for scorn and insult though this position will furnish to those, who think (or try to think) every man out of his senses who has not lost his reason (or alienated it by wilful sophistry, demanding reasons for reason itself), yet all history bears evidence to its truth. The sense of expediency, the cautious balancing of comparative advantages, the constant wakefulness to the *cui bono*?—in connection with the quid mihi?—all these are in their places in the routine of conduct, by which the individual provides for himself the real or supposed wants of today and tomorrow: and in quiet times and prosperous circumstances a nation presents an aggregate of such individuals, a busy ant-hill in calm and sunshine. By the happy organization of a well-governed society, the contradictory interests of ten millions of such individuals may neutralize each other, and be reconciled in the unity of the national interest. But whence did this happy organization first come?—Was it a tree transplanted from Paradise, with all its branches in full fruitage?—Or was it sowed in sunshine—Was it in vernal breezes and gentle rains that it fixed its roots, and grew and strengthened? Let history answer these questions! With blood was it planted—it was rocked in tempests—the goat, the ass, and the stag gnawed it—the wild boar has whetted his tusks on its bark. The deep scars are still extant on its trunk, and the path of the lightning may be traced among its higher branches. And even after its full growth, in the season of its strength, 'when its height reached to the heaven, and the sight thereof to all the earth', the whirlwind has more than once forced its stately top to touch the ground: it has been bent like a bow, and sprung back like a shaft. Mightier powers were at work than expediency ever yet called up!—yea, mightier than the mere understanding can comprehend! One confirmation of the latter assertion you may find in the history of our country, written by the same Scotch philosopher, [24] who devoted his life to the undermining of the Christian religion; and expended his last breath in a blasphemous regret that he had not survived it!—by the same

Hume's History *as evidence of inadequacy of the unredeemed understanding as the governing faculty of the historian*

heartless sophist who, in this island, was the main pioneer of that atheistic philosophy, which in France transvenomed the natural thirst of truth into the hydrophobia of a wild and homeless scepticism; the Elias of that Spirit of Antichrist, which

> ———still promising
> Freedom, itself too sensual to be free,
> Poisons life's amities and cheats the soul
> Of faith, and quiet hope and all that lifts
> And all that soothes the spirit!

This inadequacy of the mere understanding to the apprehension of moral greatness we may trace in this historian's cool systematic attempt to steal away every feeling of reverence for every great name by a scheme of motives, in which as often as possible the efforts and enterprises of heroic spirits are attributed to this or that paltry view of the most despicable selfishness. But in the majority of instances this would have been too palpably false and slanderous: and therefore the founders and martyrs of our church and constitution, of our civil and religious liberty, are represented as fanatics and bewildered enthusiasts. But histories incomparably more authentic than Mr Hume's (nay, spite of himself even his own history) confirm by irrefragable evidence the aphorism of ancient wisdom, that nothing great was ever achieved without enthusiasm. [25] For what is enthusiasm but the oblivion and swallowing-up of self in an object dearer than self, or in an idea more vivid?—How this is produced in the enthusiasm of wickedness, I have explained in the first comment annexed to this discourse. [26] But in the genuine enthusiasm of morals, religion, and patriotism, this enlargement and elevation of the soul above its mere self attest the presence, and accompany the intuition of ultimate principles alone. These alone can interest the undegraded human spirit deeply and enduringly, because these alone belong to its essence, and will remain with it permanently. [27]

Enthusiasm

The seminal power of ideas

Notions, the depthless abstractions of fleeting phenomena, the shadows of sailing vapours, the colourless repetitions of rainbows, have effected their utmost when they have added to the distinctness of our knowledge. For this very cause they are of themselves adverse to lofty emotion, and it requires the influence of a light and warmth, not their own, to make them crystallize into a semblance of growth. But every principle is actualized by an idea; and every idea is living, productive, partaketh of infinity, and (as Bacon has sublimely observed) containeth an endless power of semination. [28] Hence it is, that science, which consists wholly in ideas and principles, is power. Scientia et potentia (saith the same philosopher) in idem coincidunt. Hence too it is, that notions, linked arguments, reference to particular facts and calculations of prudence, influence only the comparatively few, the men of leisurely minds who have been trained up to them: and even these few they influence but faintly. But for the reverse, I appeal to the general character of the doctrines which have collected the most numerous sects, and acted upon the moral being of the converts, with a force that might well seem supernatural! The great principles of our religion, the sublime ideas spoken out everywhere in the Old and New Testament, resemble the fixed stars, which appear of the same size to the naked as to the armed eye; the magnitude of which the telescope may rather seem to diminish than to increase. At the annunciation of principles, of ideas, the soul of man awakes, and starts up, as an exile in a far distant land at the unexpected sounds of his native language, when after long years of absence, and almost of oblivion, he is suddenly addressed in his own mother-tongue. [29] He weeps for joy, and embraces the speaker as his brother. How else can we explain the fact so honourable to Great Britain, that the poorest amongst us will contend with as much enthusiasm as the richest for the rights of property? These rights are the spheres and necessary conditions of free agency. [30] But free agency contains the idea of the free will; and in this he intuitively knows the sublimity, and the infinite hopes, fears, and capabilities of his own nature. [31] On what other ground but the cognateness of ideas and principles to man as man, does the nameless soldier rush to the combat in defence of the liberties or the honour of his country? Even men wofully neglectful of the precepts of religion will shed their blood for its truth.

Mistaken notion that we already 'know' the scriptures

Alas!—the main hindrance to the use of the Scriptures, as your manual, lies in the notion that you are already acquainted with its contents. Something *new* must be presented to you, wholly new and wholly out of yourselves; [32] for whatever is within us must be as old as the first dawn of human reason. Truths of all others the most awful and mysterious and at the same time of universal interest, are considered as so true as to lose all the powers of truth and lie bedridden in the dormitory of the soul, side by side, with the most despised and exploded errors. But it should not be so with you! The pride of education, the sense of consistency, should preclude the objection: for would you not be ashamed to apply it to the works of Tacitus, or of Shakespeare? Above all, the rank which you hold, the influence you possess, the powers you may be called to wield give a special unfitness to this frivolous craving for novelty. To find no contradiction in the union of old and new, to contemplate the Ancient of Days, His words and His works, with a feeling as fresh as if they were now first springing forth at His fiat—this characterizes the minds that feel the riddle of the world and may help to unravel it! This, most of all things, will raise you above the mass of mankind, and therefore will best entitle and qualify you to guide and control them! You say, you are already familiar with the Scriptures. With the words, perhaps, but in any other sense you might as wisely boast of your familiar acquaintance with the rays of the sun, and under that pretence turn away your eyes from the light of Heaven.

Great statesmen of the past were habitually concerned with 'Ideas'

Or would you wish for authorities?—for great examples? You may find them in the writings of Thuanus, or Lord Clarendon, of Sir Thomas More, of Raleigh; and in the life and letters of the heroic Gustavus Adolphus. But these, though eminent statesmen, were Christians, and might lie under the thraldom of habit and prejudice. I will refer you then . . . to the man whose works have been in all ages deemed the models of good sense, and are still the pocket companions of those who pride themselves on uniting the scholar with the gentleman. This accomplished man of the world has given an account of the subjects of conversation between the illustrious statesmen who governed, and the brightest luminaries who then adorned, the empire of the civilized world:

> Sermo oritur non de villis domibusve aliensis
> Nec, male, necne Lepus saltet. Sed quod magis ad nos
> Pertinet, et nescire malum est, agitamus: utrumne
> Divitiis homines, an sint virtute beati?
> Et quod sit natura boni? summumque quid ejus?
>
> HORAT. SERMON. L. II. *Sat. 6, v. 71.*[1]

Berkeley indeed asserts, and is supported in his assertion by the great statesmen, Lord Bacon and Sir Walter Raleigh, that without an habitual interest in these subjects a man may be a dexterous intriguer, but never can be a statesman. . . . [33]

Scriptural history free from modern 'hollowness of abstractions'

In nothing is Scriptural history more strongly contrasted with the histories of highest note in the present age, than in its freedom from the hollowness of abstractions. While the latter present a shadow-fight of things and quantities, the former gives us the history of men, and balances the important influence of individual minds with the previous state of the national morals and manners, in which, as constituting a specific susceptibility, it presents to us the true cause both of the influence itself, and of the weal or woe that were its consequents.

This because it is a product of reason, not understanding

How should it be otherwise? The histories and political economy of the present and preceding century partake in the general contagion of its mechanic philosophy, and are the product of an unenlivened generalizing understanding. In the Scriptures they are the living educts of the imagination; of that reconciling and mediatory power, which, incorporating the reason in images of the sense, and organizing (as it were) the

[1] *Translation:* Conversation arises not concerning the country seats of families of strangers in a neighbourhood, or whether the dancing hare performed well or ill. But we discuss what more nearly concerns us, and which it is an evil not to know: whether men are made happy by wealth or by virtue? in what consists the nature of good? And what is the supreme good, and to be our ultimate aim?

flux of the senses by the permanence and self-circling energies of the reason, gives birth to a system of symbols, harmonious in themselves, and consubstantial with the truths of which they are the conductors. . . . Its contents present to us the stream of time continuous as life and a symbol of eternity, inasmuch as the past and the future are virtually contained in the present. [34] According therefore to our relative position on its banks, the Sacred History becomes prophetic, the Sacred Prophecies historical, while the power and substance of both inhere in its laws, its promises, and its comminations. In the Scriptures therefore both facts and persons must of necessity have a two-fold significance, a past and a future, a temporary and a perpetual, a particular and a universal application. They must be at once portraits and ideals.

Prophetic power of scriptural history arises from its symbolism: past and future are contained in the historic present

Eheu! paupertina philosophia in paupertinam religionem ducit:—A hunger-bitten and idealess philosophy naturally produces a starveling and comfortless religion. It is among the miseries of the present age that it recognizes no medium between literal and metaphorical. Faith is either to be buried in the dead letter, or its name and honours usurped by a counterfeit product of the mechanical understanding, which in the blindness of self-complacency confounds symbols with allegories. Now an allegory is but a translation of abstract notions into a picture-language, which is itself nothing but an abstraction from objects of the senses; the principal being more worthless even than its phantom proxy, both alike unsubstantial, and the former shapeless to boot. On the other hand a symbol (ὁ ἔστιν ἀεὶ ταυτηγόρικον)[1] is characterized by a translucence of the special in the individual, or of the general in the especial, or of the universal in the general. Above all by the translucence of the eternal through and in the temporal. It always partakes of the reality which it renders intelligible; and while it enunciates the whole, abides itself as a living part in that unity, of which it is the representative. The other are but empty echoes which the fancy arbitrarily associates with apparitions of matter, less beautiful but not less shadowy than the sloping orchard or

Symbols partake of the reality which they make intelligible

[1] Coleridge's accentuation has been retained. Ed.

hill-side pasture-field seen in the transparent lake below. Alas for the flocks that are to be led forth to such pastures! 'It shall even be as when the hungry dreameth, and behold! he eateth; but he waketh and his soul is empty: or as when the thirsty dreameth, and behold he drinketh; but he awaketh and is faint!' (Isaiah xxix. 8). O! that we would seek for the bread which was given from heaven, that we should eat thereof and be strengthened! O that we would draw at the well at which the flocks of our forefathers had living water drawn for them, even that water which, instead of mocking the thirst of him to whom it is given, becomes a well within himself springing up to life everlasting!

Necessity and free-will are reconciled Scriptural history

When we reflect how large a part of our present knowledge and civilization is owing, directly or indirectly, to the Bible; when we are compelled to admit, as a fact of history, that the Bible has been the main lever by which the moral and intellectual character of Europe has been raised to its present comparative height; we should be struck, methinks, by the marked and prominent difference of this book from the works which it is now the fashion to quote as guides and authorities in morals, politics, and history. I will point out a few of the excellencies by which the one is distinguished, and shall leave it to your own judgment and recollection to perceive and apply the contrast to the productions of highest name in these latter days. In the Bible every agent appears and acts as a self-subsisting individual: each has a life of its own, and yet all are one life. The elements of necessity and free-will are reconciled in the higher power of an omnipresent Providence, that predestinates the whole in the moral freedom of the integral parts. [35] Of this the Bible never suffers us to lose sight. The root is never detached from the ground. It is God everywhere: and all creatures conform to His decrees, the righteous by performance of the law, the disobedient by the sufferance of the penalty.

Threefold necessity

Suffer me to inform or remind you that there is a threefold necessity. There is a logical and there is a mathematical necessity; but the latter is always hypothetical, and both subsist formally only, not in any ıeal object. Only by the intuition and immediate spiritual consciousness of the idea of God, as the One and Absolute, at once the Ground and the Cause, who alone containeth in Himself the ground of His own nature, and therein of all natures, do we arrive at the third, which alone is a real objective necessity. Here the immediate consciousness decides: the idea is its own evidence, and is insusceptible of all other. It is necessarily groundless and indemonstrable; because it is itself the ground of all possible demonstration. [36] The reason hath faith in itself, in its own revelations. Ὁ λόγος ἔφη. Ipse dixit! So it is: for it is so! All the necessity of casual relations (which the mere understanding reduces, and must reduce, to co-existence and regular succession in the objects of which they are predicated, and to habit and association in the mind predicating) depends on or rather inheres in, the idea of the omnipresent and absolute: for this it is, in which the possible is one and the same with the real and the necessary. Herein the Bible differs from all the books of Greek philosophy, and in a twofold manner. It doth not affirm a Divine Nature only, but a God: and not a God only, but the living God. Hence, in the Scriptures alone is the *Jus divinum*, or direct relation of the state and its magistracy to the Supreme Being, taught as a vital and indispensable part of all moral and of all political wisdom, even as the Jewish alone was a true theocracy.

Causes of the French Revolution

But I refer to the demand. Were it my object to touch on the present state of public affairs in this kingdom, or on the prospective measures in agitation respecting our sister island, I would direct your most serious meditations to the latter period of the reign of Solomon, and to the revolutions in the reign of Rehoboam, his successor. But I should tread on glowing embers. I will turn to a subject on which all men of reflection are at length in agreement—the causes of the revolution and fearful chastisement of France. We have learned to trace them back to the rising importance of the commercial and manufacturing class, and its incompatibility with the old feudal privileges and prescriptions; to the spirit of sensuality and ostentation, which from the court had spread through all the towns and cities of the empire; to the predominance of a presumptuous and irreligious philosophy; [37] to the extreme overrating of the knowledge and power given by the improvements of the arts and sciences, especially those of astronomy, mechanics, and a wonder-working chemistry; to an assumption of prophetic power, and the general conceit that states and governments might be and ought to be constructed as machines, every movement of which might be foreseen and taken into previous calculation; to the consequent multitude of plans and constitutions, of planners and constitution-makers, and the remorseless arrogance with which the authors and proselytes of every new proposal were ready to realize it, be the cost what it might in the established rights, or even in the lives, of men; in short, to restlessness, presumption, sensual indulgence, and the idolatrous reliance on false philosophy in the whole domestic, social, and political life of the stirring and effective part of the community: these all acting at once and together on a mass of materials supplied by the unfeeling extravagance and oppressions of the government, which 'showed no mercy, and very heavily laid its yoke'. Turn then to the chapter from which the last words were cited, and read the following seven verses: and I am deceived if you will not be compelled to admit that the prophet Isaiah revealed the true philosophy of the French Revolution more than two thousand years before it became a sad irrevocable truth of history. . .

Revealed by the prophet Isaiah

The Bible alone contains a science of realities; and therefore each of its elements is at the same time a living germ, in which the present involves the future, and in the finite the infinite exists potentially. That hidden mystery in every, the minutest form of existence, which, contemplated under the relations of time, presents itself to the understanding retrospectively as an infinite ascent of causes, and prospectively as an interminable progression of effects—that which contemplated in space is beheld intuitively as a law of action and re-action, continuous and extending beyond all bound—this same mystery freed from the phenomena of time and space, and seen in the depth of real beings, reveals itself to the pure reason as the actual

Historical causation belongs to time and space: scriptural history shows also the immanence of all in each—the timeless and non-spatial life of ideas

Scriptural history transcends historical causation

immanence of all in each. Are we struck with admiration at beholding the cope of heaven imaged in a dew-drop? The least of the animalcula to which that drop would be an ocean contains in itself an infinite problem of which God omnipresent is the only solution. The slave of custom is roused by the rare and the accidental alone; but the axioms of the unthinking [38] are to the philosopher the deepest problems as being the nearest to the mysterious root, and partaking at once of its darkness and its pregnancy.

O what a mine of undiscovered treasures, what a new world of power and truth would the Bible promise to our future meditation, if in some gracious moment one solitary text of all its inspired contents should but dawn upon us in the pure untroubled brightness of an idea, that most glorious birth of the God-like within us, which even as the light, its material symbol, reflects itself from a thousand surfaces, and flies homeward to its parent mind enriched with a thousand forms, itself above form, and still remaining in its own simplicity and identity! O for a flash of that same light, in which the first position of geometric science that ever loosed itself from the generalizations of a groping and insecure experience, did, for the first time, reveal itself to a human intellect, in all its evidence and all its fruitfulness, transparence without vacuum, and plenitude without opacity! O that a single gleam of our own inward experience would make comprehensible to us the rapturous Eureka, and the grateful hecatomb, of the philosopher of Samos! or that vision which, from the contemplation of an arithmetical harmony, rose to the eye of Kepler, presenting the planetary world, and all its orbits in the divine order of their ranks and distances: or which, in the falling of an apple, revealed to the ethereal intuition of our own Newton the constructive principle of the material universe. [39] The promises which I have ventured to hold forth concerning the hidden treasures of the Law and the Prophets will neither be condemned as paradox nor as exaggeration, by the mind that has learnt to understand the possibility, that the reduction of the sands of the sea to number should be found a less stupendous problem by Archimedes than the simple conception of the Parmenidean One. What however is achievable by the human understanding without this light, may be comprised in the epithet, κενόσπουδοι: and a melancholy comment on that phrase would the history of human cabinets and legislators for the last thirty years furnish! The excellent Barrow, the last of the disciples of Plato and Archimedes among our modern mathematicians, shall give the description and state the value: and in his words I shall conclude.

Aluid agere, to be impertinently busy, doing that which conduceth to no good purpose, is in some respects worse than to do nothing. Of such industry we may understand that of the Preacher, 'The labour of the foolish wearieth every one of them.'

APPENDIX

containing

COMMENTS AND ESSAYS

(A). Reason, Understanding, and Religion

Reason and understanding

Reason and religion differ only as a twofold application of the same power. But if we are obliged to distinguish, we must ideally separate. In this sense I affirm that reason is the knowledge of the laws of the whole considered as one: and as such it is contra-distinguished from the understanding, which concerns itself exclusively with the quantities, qualities, and relations of particulars in time and space. The understanding, therefore, is the science of phenomena, and their subsumption under distinct kinds and sorts (genus and species). Its functions supply the rules and constitute the possibility of experience; but remain mere logical forms, except as far as materials are given by the senses or sensations. The reason, on the other hand, is the science of the universal, having the ideas of oneness and allness as its two elements or primary factors. In the language of the old schools,

$$\text{Unity} + \text{Omneity} = \text{Totality}$$

Man's mind can rest only in the whole and infinite

The reason first manifests itself in man by the tendency to the comprehension of all as one. We can neither rest in an infinite that is not at the same time a whole, nor in a whole that is not infinite. Hence the natural Man is always in a state either of resistance or of captivity to the understanding and the fancy, which cannot represent totality without limit: and he either loses the one in the striving after the infinite, (i.e. atheism with or without polytheism), or the infinite in the striving after the one (i.e. anthropomorphic monotheism).

Evil of reason in abstraction

The rational instinct, therefore, taken abstractedly and unbalanced, did in itself ('Ye shall be as gods!' Gen. iii. 5), and in its consequences (the lusts of the flesh, the eye, and the understanding, as in verse the sixth), form the original temptation, through which man fell: and in all ages has continued to originate the same, even from Adam, in whom we all fell, to the atheist who deified the human reason in the person of a harlot during the earlier period of the French Revolution.

Religion corrects this by particularity

To this tendency, therefore, religion, as the consideration of the particular and individual (in which respect it takes up and identifies with itself the excellence of the understanding) but, of the individual, as it exists and has its being in the universal (in which respect it is one with the pure *reason*),—to this tendency, I say, religion assigns the due limits, and is the echo of the 'voice of the Lord God walking in the garden'. Hence in all the ages and countries of civilization Religion has been the parent and fosterer of the Fine Arts, as of Poetry, Music, Painting, &c., the common essence of which consists in a similar union of the Universal and the Individual. In this union, moreover, is contained the true sense of the ideal. Under the old law the altar, the curtains, the priestly vestments, and whatever else was to represent the beauty of holiness, had an ideal character: and the Temple itself was a masterpiece of ideal beauty. [40]

Human mind is a tri-unity of reason, religion, and the will

There exists in the human being, at least in man fully developed, no mean symbol of Tri-unity, in reason, religion, and the will. For each of the three, though a distinct agency, implies and demands the other two, and loses its own nature at the moment that from distinction it passes into division or separation. The perfect frame of a man is the perfect frame of a state: and in the light of this idea we must read Plato's *Republic*. For, if I judge rightly, this celebrated work is to *The History of the Town of Man-soul*, what Plato was to John Bunyan.

Reason in abstraction is visionariness

The comprehension, impartiality, and far-sightedness of reason (the legislative of our nature), taken singly and exclusively, becomes mere visionariness in intellect, and indolence or hard-heartedness in morals. It is the science of cosmopolitism without country, of philanthropy without neighbourliness or consanguinity, in short, of all the impostures of that philosophy of the French Revolution, which would sacrifice each to the shadowy idol of all. For Jacobinism [41] is *monstrum hybridum*, made up in part of despotism, and in part of abstract reason misapplied to objects that belong entirely to experience and the understanding. Its instincts and mode of action are in strict correspondence with its origin. In all places, Jacobinism betrays its mixed parentage and nature, by applying to the brute passions and physical force of the multitude (that is, to man as a mere animal), in order to build up government and the frame of society on natural rights instead of social privileges, on the universals of abstract reason instead of positive institutions, the lights of specific experience, and the modifications of existing circumstances. Right in its most proper sense is the creature of law and statute, and only in the technical language of the courts has it any substantial and independent sense. In morals, right is a word without meaning except as the correlative of duty. [42]

Jacobinism

From all this it follows, that reason as the science of all as the whole, must be interpenetrated by a power, that represents the concentration of all in each—a power that acts by contraction of universal truths into individual duties, as the only form in which those truths can attain life and reality. Now this is religion, which is the executive of our nature, and on this account the name of highest dignity, and the symbol of sovereignty.

This is corrected by Religion, which contracts universal truths into individual duties

Yet this again—yet even religion itself, if ever in its too exclusive devotion to the specific and individual it neglects to interpose the contemplation of the universal, changes its being into superstition, and becoming more and more earthly and servile, as more and more estranged from the one in all, goes wandering at length with its pack of amulets, bead-rolls, periapts, fetisches, and the like pedlary, on pilgrimages to Loretto, Mecca, or the temple of Jaggernaut, arm-in-arm with sensuality on one side and self-torture on the other, followed

Religion in abstraction is superstition

by a motley group of friars, pardoners, faquirs, gamesters, flagellants, mountebanks, and harlots.

The will: sustaining, coercive and ministerial power

But neither can reason nor religion exist or co-exist as reason and religion, except as far as they are actuated by the Will (the platonic θυμὸς), which is the sustaining, coercive and ministerial power, the functions of which in the individual correspond to the officers of war and police in the ideal Republic of Plato. In its state of immanence (or indwelling) in reason and religion, the Will appears indifferently, as wisdom or as love: two names of the same power, the former more intelligential, the latter more spiritual, the former more frequent in the Old, the latter in the New Testament. But in its utmost abstraction and consequent state of reprobation, the Will becomes satanic pride and rebellious self-idolatry in the relations of the spirit to itself, and remorseless despotism relatively to others; the more hopeless as the more obdurate by its subjugation of sensual impulses, by its superiority to toil and pain and pleasure; in short, by the fearful resolve to find in itself alone the one absolute motive of action, under which all other motives from within and from without must be either subordinated or crushed.

The will in abstraction= self-idolatry and despotism

E.g. Satan and Bonaparte

This is the character which Milton has so philosophically as well as sublimely embodied in the Satan of his Paradise Lost. Alas! too often has it been embodied in real life! Too often has it given a dark and savage grandeur to the historic page! And wherever it has appeared, under whatever circumstances of time and country, the same ingredients have gone to its composition; and it has been identified by the same attributes. Hope in which there is no cheerfulness; stedfastness within and immovable resolve, with outward restlessness and whirling activity; violence with guile; temerity with cunning; and, as the result of all, interminableness of object with perfect indifference of means; these are the qualities that have constituted the commanding genius! these are the marks that have characterized the masters of mischief, the liberticides and mighty hunters of mankind, from Nimrod to Napoleon. And from inattention to the possibility of such a character as well as from ignorance of its elements, even men of honest intentions too frequently become fascinated. Nay, whole nations have been so far duped by this want of insight and reflection as to regard with palliative admiration, instead of wonder and abhorrence, the Molochs of human nature, who are indebted for the far larger portion of their meteoric success to their total want of principle, and who surpass the generality of their fellow-creature in one act of courage only, that of daring to say with their whole heart, 'Evil, be thou my good!' All system so far is power; and a systematic criminal, self-consistent and entire in wickedness, who entrenches villany within villany, and barricadoes crime by crime, has removed a world of obstacles by the mere decision, that he will have no obstacles but those of force and brute matter. [43]

The conscience

I have only to add a few sentences in completion of this note, on the conscience and on the understanding. The conscience is neither reason, religion, nor will, but an experience (*sui generis*) of the coincidence of the human will with reason and religion. It might, perhaps, be called a spiritual sensation; but that there lurks a contradiction in the terms, and that it is often deceptive to give a common or generic name to that, which being unique, can have no fair analogy. Strictly speaking, therefore, the conscience is neither a sensation nor a sense; but a testifying state, best described in the words of our liturgy, as *the peace of God that passeth all understanding*.

The understanding: its inappropriateness to the modes and laws of spiritual experience

Of this latter faculty considered in and of itself the peripatetic aphorism, *nihil in intellectu quod non prius in sensu*, is strictly true, as well as the legal maxim, *de rebus non apparentibus et non existentibus eadem est ratio*. The eye is not more inappropriate to sound, than the mere understanding to the modes and laws of spiritual existence. In this sense I have used the term; and in this sense I assert that 'the understanding or experiential faculty, unirradiated by the reason and the spirit, has no appropriate object but the material world in relation to our worldly interests. The far-sighted prudence of man, and the more narrow but at the same time far less fallible cunning of the fox, are both no other than a nobler substitute for salt, in order that the hog may not putrefy before its destined hour!!' (*The Friend.*)

The healthy man uses his understanding as the tool of his reason

It must not, however, be overlooked, that this insulation of the understanding is our own act and deed. [44] The man of healthful and undivided intellect uses his understanding in this state of abstraction only as a tool or organ: even as the arithmetician uses numbers, that is, as the means not the end of knowledge. Our Shakespeare in agreement both with truth and the philosophy of his age, names it 'discourse of reason', as an instrumental faculty belonging to reason: and Milton opposes the discursive to the intuitive, as the lower to the higher,

Differing but in degree, in *kind* the same!

Limitations of the understanding

Of the discursive understanding, which forms for itself general notions and terms of classification for the purpose of comparing and arranging phenomena, the characteristic is clearness without depth. It contemplates the unity of things in their limits only, and is consequently a knowledge of superficies without substance. So much so indeed, that it entangles itself in contradictions, in the very effort of comprehending the idea of substance. The completing power which unites clearness with depth, the plenitude of the sense with the comprehensibility of the understanding, is the imagination, impregnated with which the understanding itself becomes intuitive, and a living power. [45] The reason (not the abstract reason, not the reason as the mere organ of science, or as the faculty of scientific principles and schemes a priori; but reason), as the integral spirit of the regenerated man, reason substantiated and vital, 'one only, yet manifold, overseeing all, and going through all understanding; the breath of the power of God, and a pure influence from the glory of the Almighty; which remaining in itself regenerateth all other powers, and in all ages entering into holy souls maketh them friends of God and prophets' (Wisdom of Solomon vii.); this reason without being either the sense, the understanding, or the imagination, contains all three within itself, even as the mind contains its thoughts and is present in and through them all; or as the expression pervades

Reason = the integral spirit of the regenerated man

the different features of an intelligent countenance. Each individual must bear witness of it to his own mind, even as he describes life and light: and with the silence of light it describes itself and dwells in *us* only as far as we dwell in it. It cannot in strict language be called a faculty, much less a personal property, of any human mind! He, with whom it is present, can as little appropriate it, whether totally or by partition, as he can claim ownership in the breathing air, or make an inclosure in the cope of heaven. . . .

Reason not a personal property

O! if as the plant to the orient beam, we would but open out our minds to that holier light, which 'being compared with light is found before it, more beautiful than the sun, and above all the order of stars' (Wisdom of Solomon vii. 29), ungenial, alien, and adverse to our very nature would appear the boastful wisdom which, beginning in France, gradually tampered with the taste and literature of all the most civilized nations of Christendom, seducing the understanding from its natural allegiance, and therewith from all its own lawful claims, titles, and privileges. It was placed as a ward of honour in the courts of faith and reason; but it chose to dwell alone, and became a harlot by the wayside. The commercial spirit, and the ascendancy of the experimental philosophy which took place at the close of the seventeenth century, though both good and beneficial in their own kinds, combined to foster its corruption. Flattered and dazzled by the real or supposed discoveries which it had made, the more the understanding was enriched, the more did it become debased; till science itself put on a selfish and sensual character, [46] and immediate utility, in exclusive reference to the gratification of the wants and appetites of the animal, the vanities and caprices of the social, and the ambition of the political, man was imposed as the test of all intellectual powers and pursuits. Worth was degraded into a lazy synonym of value; and value was exclusively attached to the interest of the senses. But though the growing alienation and self-sufficiency of the understanding was perceptible at an earlier period, yet it seems to have been about the middle of the last century, under the influence of Voltaire, D'Alembert, Diderot,

Brief history of the wanton adventures of the insulated understanding in modern times

say generally of the so-called encyclopaedists, and alas! of their crowned proselytes and disciples, Frederick, Joseph, and Catharine, that the human understanding, and this too in its narrowest form, was tempted to throw off all show of reverence to the spiritual and even to the moral powers and impulses of the soul; and, usurping the name of reason, openly joined the banners of Antichrist, at once the pander and the prostitute of sensuality; and whether in the cabinet, laboratory, the dissecting-room, or the brothel, alike busy in the schemes of vice and irreligion. Well and truly might it, thus personified in our fancy, have been addressed in the words of the evangelical prophet, which I have once before quoted: 'Thou hast said, none is my overseer!—thy wisdom and thy knowledge, it hath perverted thee!—and thou hast said in thy heart, I am, and there is none beside me!' (Isaiah xlvii. 10.)

Mechanic philosophy is the philosophy of a dead nature

Prurient, bustling, and revolutionary, this French wisdom has never more than grazed the surfaces of knowledge. As political economy, in its zeal for the increase of food, it habitually overlooked the qualities and even the sensations of those that were to feed on it. As ethical philosophy, it recognized no duties which it could not reduce into debtor and creditor accounts on the ledgers of self-love, [47] where no coin was sterling which could not be rendered into agreeable sensations. And even in its height of self-complacency as chemical art, greatly am I deceived if it has not from the very beginning mistaken the products of destruction, *cadavera rerum*, for the elements of composition: and most assuredly it has dearly purchased a few brilliant inventions at the loss of all communion with life and the spirit of nature. As the process, such the result!—a heartless frivolity alternating with a sentimentality as heartless—an ignorant contempt of antiquity—a neglect of moral self-discipline—a deadening of the religious sense, even in the less reflecting forms of natural piety—a scornful reprobation of all consolations and secret refreshings from above—and as the *caput mortuum* of human nature evaporated, a French nature of rapacity, levity, ferocity and presumption. [48]

Man of understanding, canst thou command the stone to lie,

canst thou bid the flower bloom, where thou hast placed it in thy classification? Canst thou persuade the living or the inanimate to stand separate even as thou hast separated them? And do not far rather all things spread out before thee in glad confusion and heedless intermixture, even as a lightsome chaos on which the Spirit of God is moving? Do not all press and swell under one attraction, and live together in promiscuous harmony, each joyous in its own kind, and in the immediate neighbourhood of myriad others that in the system of thy understanding are distant as the poles? If to mint and to remember names delight thee, still arrange and classify and pore and pull to pieces, and peep into death to look for life, as monkeys put their hands behind a looking-glass! Yet consider, in the first sabbath which thou imposest on the busy discursion of thought, that all this is at best little more than a technical memory: that like can only be known by like: that as truth is the correlative of being, so is the act of being the great organ of truth: that in natural no less than in moral science, *quantum sumus, scimus*.

Vital philosophy is a philosophy of a living nature and creative mind

That which we find in ourselves is (*gradu mutato*) the substance and the life of all our knowledge. Without this latent presence of the 'I am', all modes of existence in the external world would flit before us as coloured shadows, with no greater depth, root, or fixture, than the image of a rock hath in a gliding stream, or the rainbow on a fast-sailing rainstorm. The human mind is the compass, in which the laws and actuations of all outward essences are revealed as the dips and declinations. (The application of geometry to the forces and movements of the material world is both proof and instance.) The fact, therefore, that the mind of man, in its own primary and constituent forms, represents the laws of nature, is a mystery which of itself should suffice to make us religious: for it is a problem of which God is the only solution—God, the One before all, and of all, and through all! True natural philosophy is comprised in the study of the science and language of symbols. The power delegated to nature is all in every part: and by a symbol I mean, not a metaphor or allegory or any other figure of speech or form of fancy, but an actual and essential part of that, the whole of which it represents. Thus our Lord speaks symbolically when He says that 'the eye is the light of the body'. The genuine naturalist is a dramatic poet in his own line: and such as our myriad-minded Shakespeare is, compared with the Racines and Metastasios, such and by a similar process of self-transformation would the man be, compared with the doctors of the mechanic school, who should construct his physiology on the heaven-descended, Know thyself. [49]

Dreams

Even 'the visions of the night' speak to us of powers within us that are not dreamt of in their day-dream of philosophy. The dreams which we most often remember are produced by the nascent sensations and inward Motiunculoe (the fluxions) of the waking state. Hence, too, they are more capable of being remembered, because, passing more gradually into our waking thoughts, they are more likely to associate with our first perceptions after sleep. Accordingly, when the nervous system is approaching to the waking state, a sort of under-consciousness blends with our dreams, that in all we imagine as seen or heard, our own self is the ventriloquist, and moves the slides in the magic-lanthorn. We dream about things!

To dream about things

But there are few persons of tender feelings and reflecting habits who have not, more or less often in the course of their lives, experienced dreams of a very different kind, and during the profoundest sleep that is compatible with after-recollection-states of which it would be scarcely too bold to say that we dream the things themselves; so exact, minute, and vivid beyond all power of ordinary memory is the portraiture, so marvellously perfect is our brief metempsychosis into the very being, as it were, of the person who seems to address us. If I may be allowed to quote from myself (*The Friend*), 'the dullest wight is at times a Shakespeare in his dreams'. Not only may we expect that men of strong religious feelings, but little religious knowledge, will occasionally be tempted to regard such occurrences as supernatural visitations; but it ought not to surprise us if such dreams should sometimes be confirmed

And to dream the things themselves

Divination

by the event, as though they had actually possessed a character of divination. For who shall decide how far a perfect reminiscence of past experience (of many perhaps that had escaped our reflex consciousness at the time)—who shall determine to what extent this reproductive imagination, unsophisticated by the will, and undistracted by intrusions from the senses, may or may not be concentred and sublimed into foresight and presentiment? There would be nothing herein either to foster superstition, on the one hand, or to justify contemptuous disbelief, on the other. Incredulity is but credulity seen from behind, bowing and nodding assent to the habitual and the fashionable. . . .

Two ways of emancipation from superstition

The feeling that, in point of fact, chiefly influenced me in the preceding half apology for the supposition of a divining power in the human mind, arose out of the conviction that an age or nation may become free from certain prejudices, beliefs, and superstitious practices, in two ways. It may have really risen above them; or it may have fallen below them, and become too bad for their continuance. 'The rustic would have little reason to thank the philosopher who should give him true conceptions of ghosts, omens, dreams, and presentiments, at the price of abandoning his faith in Providence, and in the continued existence of his fellow-creatures after their death. The teeth of the old serpent sowed by the Cadmuses of French literature under Louis XV produced a plenteous crop of such philosophers and truth-trumpeters in the reign of his ill-fated successor. They taught many facts, historical, political, physiological, and ecclesiastical, diffusing their notions so widely that the very ladies and hair-dressers of Paris became fluent encyclopaedists; and the sole price which their scholars paid for these treasures of new light, was to believe Christianity an imposture, the Scriptures a forgery, the worship of God superstition, hell a fable, heaven a dream, our life without Providence, and our death without hope. What can be conceived more natural than the result: that self-acknowledged beasts should first act, and next suffer themselves to be treated, as beasts?' (*The Friend.*) [50]

Exit of superstition no proof of entry of good sense

Thank heaven!—notwithstanding the attempts of Thomas Payne and his compeers, it is not so bad with us. Open infidelity has ceased to be a means even of gratifying vanity: for the leaders of the gang themselves turned apostates to Satan, as soon as the number of their proselytes became so large, that atheism ceased to give distinction. Nay, it became a mark of original thinking to defend the Belief and the Ten Commandments: so the strong minds veered round, and religion came again into fashion. But still I exceedingly doubt, whether the superannuation of sundry superstitious fancies to be the result of any real diffusion of sound thinking in the nation at large. For instance, there is now no call for Picus Mirandola to write seven books against astrology. It might seem indeed, that a single fact like that of the loss of Kempenfeldt and his crew, or the explosion of the L'Orient, would prove to the common sense of the most ignorant, that even if astrology could be true, the astrologers must be false: for if such a science were possible it could be a science only for gods. Yet Erasmus, the prince of sound common sense, is known to have disapproved of his friend's hardihood, and did not himself venture beyond scepticism; and the immortal Newton, to whom more than to any other human being, Europe owes the purification of its general notions concerning the heavenly bodies, studied astrology with much earnestness, and did not reject it till he had demonstrated the falsehood of all its pretended grounds and principles. The exit of two or three superstitions is no more a proof of the entry of good sense, than the strangling of a despot at Algiers or Constantinople is a symptom of freedom. If therefore not the mere disbelief, but the grounds of such disbelief, must decide the question of our superior illumination, I confess that I could not from my own observations on the books and conversation of the age vote for the affirmative without much hesitation. As many errors are despised by men from ignorance as from knowledge. . . .

Limitations of modern 'enlightenment'

I fear that the decrease in our feelings of reverence towards mankind at large, and our increasing aversion to every opinion not grounded in some appeal to the senses, have a larger share in this our emancipation from the prejudices of Socrates and Cicero than reflection, insight, or a fair collation of the facts and arguments. For myself, I would far rather see the English people believe somewhat too much than merely just enough, if the latter is to be produced, or must be accompanied, by a contempt or neglect of the faith and intellect of their forefathers. For not to say what yet is most certain, that a people cannot believe just enough, and that there are errors which no wise man will treat with rudeness, while there is a probability that they may be the refraction of some great truth as yet below the horizon; [51] it remains most worthy of our serious consideration, whether a fancied superiority to their ancestors' intellects must not be speedily followed in the popular mind by disrespect for their ancestors' institutions. And assuredly it is not easy to place any confidence in a form of church or state, of whose founders we have been taught to believe, that their philosophy was jargon, and their feelings and notions rank superstition. Yet are we never to grow wiser? Are we to be credulous by birthright, and take ghosts, omens, visions, and witchcraft, as an heirloom? God forbid! A distinction must be made, and such a one as shall be equally availing and profitable to men of all ranks. Is this practicable? Yes! it exists. It is found in the study of the Old and New Testament, if only it be combined with a spiritual partaking of the Redeemer's Blood, of which mysterious as the symbol may be, the sacramental wine is no mere or arbitrary memento. This is the only certain, and this is the universal preventive, of all debasing superstitions. . . . Indeed, a Christian will as little think of informing himself concerning the future by dreams or presentiments, as of looking for a distant object at broad noon-day with a lighted taper in his hand.

True progress is increase of consciousness: to become what we know

But whatever of good and intellectual nature worketh in us, it is our appointed task to render gradually our own work. For all things that surround us, and all things that happen unto us, have (each doubtless its own providential purpose, but) all one common final cause; namely, the increase of consciousness, in such wise, that whatever part of the *terra incognita* of our nature the increased consciousness discovers, our will may conquer and bring into subjection to itself under the sovereignty of reason.

Differences between mechanical and vital philosophy

The leading differences between mechanic and vital philosophy may all be drawn from one point; namely, that the former demanding for every mode and act of existence real or possible visibility, knows only of distance and nearness, composition (or rather juxta-position) and decomposition, in short the relations of unproductive particles to each other; so that in every instance the result is the exact sum of the component quantities, as in arithmetical addition. This is the philosophy of death, and only of a dead nature can it hold good. In life, much more in spirit, and in a living and spiritual philosophy, the two component counterpowers actually interpenetrate each other, and generate a higher third, including both the former, *ita tamen ut sit alia et major*.

Religion based on the understanding is only a theory—a generalization

To apply this to the subject of the present essay. The elements (the factors, as it were) of religion are reason and understanding. If the composition stopped in itself, an understanding thus rationalized would lead to the admission of the general doctrines of natural religion, the belief of a God, and of immortality; and probably to an acquiescence in the history and ethics of the Gospel. But still it would be a speculative faith, and in the nature of a theory; as if the main object of religion were to solve difficulties for the satisfaction of the intellect. Now this state of mind, which alas! is the state of too many among our self-entitled rational religionists, is a mere balance or compromise of the two powers, not that living and generative interpenetration of both which would give being to essential religion—to the religion, at the birth of which 'we receive the spirit of adoption, whereby we cry, Abba, Father; the spirit itself bearing witness with our spirit, that we are the children of God' (Rom. viii. 15, 16). In religion there is no abstraction. To the unity and infinity of the Divine Nature, of which it is the partaker, it adds the fulness, and to the fulness the grace and the creative overflowing. That which intuitively it at once beholds and adores, praying always, and rejoicing always—that doth it tend to become. In all things, and in each

Religion based on interpenetration of reason and understanding is a concrete and living reality

thing—for the Almighty goodness does not create generalities or abide in abstractions—in each, the meanest, object it bears witness to a mystery of infinite solution. Thus 'beholding as in a glass the glory of the Lord, it is changed into the same image from glory to glory' (2 Cor. iii. 18). . . .

Join with me, reader, in the fervent prayer, that we may seek within us, what we can never find elsewhere; that we may find within us what no words can put there; that one only true religion, which elevateth knowing into being, which is at once the science of being, and the being and the life of all genuine science. [52]

(B). Present State and Prospects of Philosophy

Modern contempt for ancient and traditional wisdom

In all ages of the Christian Church, and in the later period of the Jewish (that is, as soon as from their acquaintance first with the Oriental and afterwards with the Greek philosophy, the precursory and preparative influences of the gospel began to work), there have existed individuals—Laodiceans in spirit, Minims in faith, and Nominalists in philosophy—who mistake outlines for substance, and distinct images for clear conceptions; with whom therefore not to be a thing, is the same as not to be all. The contempt in which such persons hold the works and doctrines of all theologians before Grotius, and of all philosophers before Locke and Hartley (at least before Bacon and Hobbes), is not accidental, nor yet altogether owing to that epidemic of a proud ignorance occasioned by a diffused sciolism, which gave a sickly and hectic showiness to the latter half of the last century. It is a real instinct of self-defence acting offensively by anticipation. For the authority of all the greatest names of antiquity is full and decisive against them; and man, by the very nature of his birth and growth, is so much the creature of authority, that there was no way of effectually resisting it but by undermining the reverence for the past *in toto*. Thus the Jewish prophets have, forsooth, a certain degree of antiquarian value, as being the only specimens extant of the oracles of a barbarous tribe; the Evangelists are to be interpreted with a due allowance for their superstitious prejudices concerning evil spirits, and St Paul never suffers them to forget that he had been brought up at the feet of a Jewish Rabbi! The Greeks indeed were a fine people in works of taste; but as to their philosophers! the writings of Plato are smoke and flash from the witch's cauldron of a disturbed imagination! Aristotle's works a quickset hedge of fruitless and thorny distinctions! and all the philosophers before Plato and Aristotle fablers and allegorisers!

Signs of a better spirit

But these men have had their day: and there are signs of the times clearly announcing that that day is verging to its close. Even now there are not a few, on whose convictions it will not be uninfluencive to know, that the power by which men are led to the truth of things, instead of the appearances, was deemed and entitled the living and substantial Word of God by the soundest of the Hebrew doctors; that the eldest and most profound of the Greek philosophers demanded assent to their doctrine, mainly as σοφία θεοπαράδοτος, i.e. a traditionary wisdom that had its origin in inspiration; that these men referred the same power to the πῦρ ἀείζωον ὑπὸ διοικοῦντος ΛΌΓΟΥ; and that they were scarcely less express than their scholar Philo Judæus in their affirmations of the Logos, as no mere attribute or quality, no mode of abstraction, no personification, but literally and mysteriously *Deus alter et idem.* [53]

When education has disciplined the minds of our gentry for austerer study; when educated men will be ashamed to look abroad for truths that can be only found within; within themselves they will discover, intuitively will they discover, the distinctions between 'the light that lighteth every man that cometh into the world', and the understanding, which forms the peculium of each man, as different in extent and value from another man's understanding as his estate may be from his neighbour's estate. The words of St John, from the 7th to the 12th verse of his first chapter, are in their whole extent interpretable of the understanding, which derives its rank and mode of being in the human race (that is, as far as it may be contrasted with the instinct of the dog or elephant, in all which constitutes it human understanding) from the universal light. This light, therefore, comes as to its own. Being rejected, it leaves the understanding to a world of dreams and darkness: for in it alone is life, and the life is the light of men. What then but apparitions can remain to a philosophy which strikes death through all things visible and invisible; satisfies itself then only when it can explain those abstractions of the outward senses, which by an unconscious irony it names indifferently facts and phenomena, mechanically that is, by the laws of death; and brands with the name of mysticism every solution grounded in life, or the powers and intuitions of life?

On the other hand, if the light be received by faith, to such understandings it delegates the privilege (ἐξουσίαν) to become sons of God, expanding while it elevates, even as the beams of the sun incorporate with the mist, and make its natural darkness and earthly nature the bearer and interpreter of their own glory.... Ἐὰν μὴ πιστεύσητε, οὐ μὴ συνῆτε....

Modern debasement of the term 'idea'

An idea is equidistant in its signification from sensation, image, fact and notion... it is the antithesis, not the synonyme of εἴδωλον. The magnificent son of Como was wont to discourse with Ficino, Politian, and the princely Mirandula on the ideas of will, God and immortality. The accomplished author of the Arcadia, the star of serenest brilliance in the glorious constellation of Elizabeth's court, our England's Sir Philip Sidney! He, the paramount gentleman of Europe, the poet, warrior, and statesman, held high converse with Spenser on the idea of supersensual beauty; on all 'earthly fair and amiable', as the symbol of that idea; and on music and poesy as its living educts. With the same genial reverence did the younger Algernon commune with Harrington and Milton on the idea of a perfect state; and in what sense it is true, that the men (i.e. the aggregate of the inhabitants of a country at any one time) are made for the state, not the state for the men. [54] But these lights shine no longer, or for a few. Exeunt: and enter in their stead Holofernes and Costard, [55] masked as Metaphysics and Commonsense. And these, too, have *their* ideas! The former has an idea, that Hume, Hartley, and Condillac [56] have exploded all ideas but those of sensation; he has an idea that he was particularly pleased with the fine *idea* of the last-named philosopher, that there is no absurdity in asking what colour virtue is of? inasmuch as the proper philosophic answer would be black, blue, or bottle-green, according as the coat, waistcoat, and small-clothes might chance to be of the person the series of whose motions had excited the sensations which formed our idea of virtue. The latter has no idea of a better-flavoured haunch of venison than he dined off at the Albion: he admits that the French have an excellent idea of cooking in general, but holds that their best cooks have no more idea of dressing a turtle than the gourmands themselves, at Paris, have of the true taste and colour of the fat!

The philosophy of an age and its theology

It is not impossible that a portion of the high value attached of late years to the dates and margins of our old folios and quartos, may be transferred to their contents. Even now there exists a shrewd suspicion in the minds of reading men, that not only Plato and Aristotle, but even Scotus Erigena, and the schoolmen from Peter Lombard to Duns Scotus, are not such mere blockheads as they pass for with those who have never perused a line of their writings. [57] What the results may be should this ripen into conviction, I can but guess. But all history seems to favour the persuasion I entertain, that in every age the speculative philosophy in general acceptance, the metaphysical opinions that happen to be predominant, will influence the theology of that age. . . . Now it is not denied that the framers of our Church Liturgy, Homilies and Articles, entertained metaphysical opinions irreconcilable in their first principles with the system of speculative philosophy which has been taught in this country, and only not universally received, since the asserted and generally believed defeat of the Bishop of Worcester (the excellent Stillingfleet) in his famous controversy with Mr Locke. . . . [58] I repeat the question then: Is it likely that the faith of our ancestors will be retained when their philosophy is rejected? rejected *a priori*, as baseless notions not worth inquiring into, as obsolete errors which it would be slaying the slain to confute? . . .

How and why the Lockeian philosophy came to capture the European mind

We have attached a portion even of our national glory (not only to the system itself, that system of disguised and decorous Epicureanism, which has been the only orthodox philosophy of the last hundred years; but also, and more emphatically) to the name of the assumed father of the system, who raised it to its present 'pride of place', and almost universal acceptance throughout Europe. And how was this effected? Extrinsically, by all the causes, consequences, and accompaniments of the Revolution in 1688: by all the opinions, interests, and passions which counteracted by the sturdy prejudices of the malcontents with the Revolution; qualified by the compromising character of its chief conductors; not more propelled by the spirit of enterprise and hazard in our commercial towns, than held in check by the characteristic *vis inertiœ* of the peasantry and landholders; both parties cooled and lessoned by the equal failure of the destruction, and of the restoration, of monarchy; it was effected extrinsically, I say, by the same influences, which (not in and of themselves, but with all these and sundry other modifications) combined under an especial control of Providence to perfect and secure the majestic temple of the British Constitution!—But the very same which in France, without this providential counterpoise, overthrew the motley fabric of feudal oppression to build up in its stead the madhouse of Jacobinism! Intrinsically, and as far as the philosophic scheme itself is alone concerned, it was effected by the mixed policy and bonhomie with which the author contrived to retain in his celebrated work whatever the system possesses of soothing for the indolence, and of flattering for the vanity, of men's average understandings: while he kept out of sight all its darker features that outraged the instinctive faith and moral feelings of mankind, ingeniously threading on the dried and shrivelled, yet still wholesome and nutritious fruits, plucked from the rich grafts of ancient wisdom, to the barren and worse than barren fig-tree of the mechanic philosophy. Thus the sensible Christians, 'the angels of the church of Laodicea', with the numerous and mighty sect of their admirers, delighted with the discovery that they could purchase the decencies and the creditableness of religion at so small an expenditure of faith, extolled the work for its pious conclusions: while the infidels, wiser in their generation than the children (at least than these nominal children) of light, eulogized it with no less zeal for the sake of its principles and assumptions, and with the foresight of those obvious and only legitimate conclusions that might and would be deduced from them. Great at all times and almost incalculable are the influences of party spirit in exaggerating contemporary reputation; but never perhaps 'from the first syllable of recorded time' were they exerted under such a concurrence and conjunction of fortunate accidents, of helping and furthering events and circumstances, as in the instance of Mr Locke.

Impossibility of reconciling traditional principles in church and state with Lockeian philosophy of mind

I am most fully persuaded, that the principles both of taste, morals, and religion, taught in our most popular compendia of moral and political philosophy, natural theology, evidences of Christianity, &c., are false, injurious, and debasing. But I am likewise not less deeply convinced, that all the well-meant attacks on the writings of modern infidels and heretics, in support either of the miracles or of the mysteries of the Christian religion, can be of no permanent utility, while the authors themselves join in the vulgar appeal to common sense as the one infallible judge in matters which become subjects of philosophy only, because they involve a contradiction between this common sense and our moral instincts, and require therefore an arbiter, which containing both (*eminenter*) must be higher than either. We but mow down the rank of misgrowth instead of cleansing the soil, as long as we ourselves protect and manure, as the pride of our garden, a tree of false knowledge, which looks fair and showy and variegated with fruits not its own, that hang from the branches which have at various times been ingrafted on its stem; but from the roots of which underground the runners are sent off, that shoot up at a distance and bring forth the true and natural crop. I will speak plainly, though in so doing I must bid defiance to all the flatterers of the folly and foolish self-opinion of the half-instructed many. The articles of our Church, and the true principles of government and social order, will never be effectually and consistently maintained against their antagonists till the champions have themselves ceased to worship the same Baal with their enemies, till they have cast out the common idol from the recesses of their own convictions, and with it the whole service and ceremonial of idolism. While all parties agree in their abjuration of Plato and Aristotle, and in their contemptuous neglect of the Schoolmen and the scholastic logic, without which the excellent Selden (that genuine English mind whose erudition, broad, deep, and manifold as it was, is yet less remarkable than his robust healthful common sense) affirms it (see his *Table Talk*) [59] impossible for a Divine thoroughly to comprehend or reputably to defend the whole undiminished and unadulterated scheme of Catholic faith: while all alike pre-assume, with Mr Locke, that the mind contains only the relics of the senses, and therefore proceed with him to explain the substance from the shadow, the voice from the echo: they can but detect each the other's inconsistencies. The champion of orthodoxy will victoriously expose the bald and staring incongruity of the Socinian scheme with the language of Scripture and with the final causes of all revealed religion:—the Socinian will retort on the orthodox the incongruity of a belief in mysteries, with his own admissions concerning the origin and nature of all tenable ideas, and as triumphantly expose the pretences of believing in a form of words, to which the believer himself admits that he can attach no consistent meaning. Lastly, the godless materialist, as the only consistent because the only consequent reasoner, will secretly laugh at both. If these sentiments should be just, the consequences are so important that every well-educated man who has given proofs that he has at least partially studied the subject, deserves a patient hearing. Had I not the authority of the greatest and noblest intellects for at least two thousand years on my side, yet from the vital interest of the opinions themselves, and their natural, unconstrained, and (as it were) spontaneous coalescence with the faith of the Catholic Church (they being, moreover, the opinions of its most eminent Fathers), I might appeal to all orthodox Christians, whether they adhere to the faith only, or both to the faith and forms of the Established Church, in the words of my motto: Ad isthœc quœ so vos, qualiacunque primo videantur aspectu, attendite ut qui vobis forsan insanire videar, saltem quibus insaniam rationibus cognoscatis. [60]

There are still a few, however, young men of loftiest minds, and the very stuff out of which the sword and shield of truth and honour are to be made, who will not withdraw all confidence from the writer, although

> Tis true, that, passionate for ancient truths
> And honouring with religious love the great
> Of elder times, he hated to excess,
> With an unquiet and intolerant scorn,
> The hollow puppets of a hollow age,
> Ever idolatrous, and changing ever
> Its worthless idols!

a few there are, who will still less be indisposed to follow him in his milder mood, whenever their Friend,

> Piercing the long-neglected holy Cave,
> The haunt obscure of Old Philosophy,
> Shall bid with lifted torch its starry walls
> Sparkle, as erst they sparkled to the flame
> Of odorous lamps tended by saint and sage!

Glossary of terms of true philosophy

I have hinted above at the necessity of a glossary, and I will conclude these supplementary remarks with a nomenclature of the principal terms that occur in the elements of speculative philosophy, in their old and rightful sense, according to my belief; at all events, the sense in which I have myself employed them. The most general term (*genus summum*) belonging to the speculative intellect, as distinguished from acts of the will, is representation, or (still better) presentation.

A conscious presentation, if it refers exclusively to the subject as a modification of his own state of being is = sensation.

The same if it refers to an object is = perception.

A perception, immediate and individual, is = an intuition.

The same, mediate, and by means of a character or mark common to several things, is = a conception.

A conception, extrinsic and sensuous, is = a fact, or a cognition.

The same, purely mental and abstracted from the forms of the understanding itself, = a notion.

A notion may be realized, and becomes cognition; but that which is neither a sensation or a perception, that which is neither individual (i.e. a sensible intuition) nor general (i.e. a conception), which neither refers to outward facts, nor yet is abstracted from the forms of perception contained in the understanding, but which is an educt of the imagination actuated by the pure reason, to which there neither is nor can be an adequate correspondent in the world of the senses—this and this alone is = an idea. Whether ideas are regulative only, according to Aristotle and Kant; or likewise constitutive, and one with the power and life of Nature, according to Plato and Plotinus (ἐν λόγῳ ζωὴ ἦν, καὶ ἡ ζωὴ ἦν τὸ φῶς τῶν ἀνθρώπων), is the highest *problem* of philosophy, and not part of its nomenclature. [61]

'Blessed are ye that sow beside all waters!'

A LAY SERMON

ADDRESSED TO THE

HIGHER AND MIDDLE CLASSES

ON THE EXISTING

DISTRESSES AND DISCONTENTS

BY

S. T. COLERIDGE, Esq.

HERACLITUS apud Theodoret, vol. iv. p. 716.

'If ye do not hope, ye will not find: for in despairing ye block up the mine at its mouth! ye extinguish the torch, even when ye are already in the shaft.'

LONDON

1817

SUMMARY OF CONTENTS

A LAY SERMON

The Introduction

Intellectual responsibility of the upper classes

FELLOW-COUNTRYMEN! You, I mean, who fill the higher and middle stations of society! The comforts, perchance the splendours, that surround you designate your rank, but cannot constitute your moral and personal fitness for it. Be it enough for others to know, that you are its legal—but by what mark shall you stand accredited to your own consciences as its worthy—possessors? Not by common sense or common honesty; for these are equally demanded of all classes, and therefore mere negative qualifications in your rank of life, or characteristic only by the aggravated ignominy consequent on their absence. Not by genius or splendid talent: for these, as being gifts of nature, are objects of moral interest for those alone to whom they have been allotted. Nor yet by eminence in learning; for this supposes such a devotion of time and thought, as would in many cases be incompatible with the claims of active life. Erudition is, doubtless, an ornament that especially beseems a high station: but it is professional rank only that renders its attainment a duty.

The mark in question must be so far common, that we may be entitled to look for it in you from the mere circumstance of your situation, and so far distinctive that it must be such as cannot be expected generally from the inferior classes. Now, either there is no such criterion in existence, or the desideratum is to be found in an habitual consciousness of the ultimate principles to which your opinions are traceable. The least that can be demanded of the least favoured among you, is an earnest endeavour to walk in the light of your own knowledge; and not, as the mass of mankind, by laying hold on the skirts of custom. . . . Your habits of reflection should at least be equal to your opportunities of leisure, and to that which is itself a species of leisure—your immunity from bodily labour, from the voice and lash of the imperious ever-recurring this day! Your attention to the objects that stretch away below you in the living landscape of good and evil, and your researches into their existing or practicable bearings on each other, should be proportional to the elevation that extends and diversifies your prospect. If you possess more than is necessary for your own wants, more than your own wants ought to be felt by you as your own interests. You are pacing on a smooth terrace, which you owe to the happy institutions of your country—a terrace on the mountain's breast. To what purpose, by what moral right, if you continue to gaze only on the sod beneath your feet? Or if, converting means into ends, and with all your thoughts and efforts absorbed in selfish schemes of climbing cloudward, you turn your back on the wide landscape, and stoop the lower the higher you ascend?

Value of contemplating particulars in the light of universal laws

The remedial and prospective advantages that may be rationally anticipated from the habit of contemplating particulars in their universal laws; its tendency at once to fix and to liberalize the morality of private life, at once to produce and enlighten the spirit of public zeal and, let me add, its especial utility in recalling the origin and primary purport of the term generosity to the heart and thoughts of a populace tampered with by sophists and incendiaries of the revolutionary school; these advantages I have felt it my duty and have made it my main object to press on your serious attention during the whole period of my literary labours from earliest manhood to the present hour. Whatever may have been the specific theme of my communications, and whether they related to criticism, politics, or religion, still principles, their subordination, their connection and their application in all the divisions of our tastes, duties, rules of conduct and schemes of belief, have constituted my chapter of contents. [1]

Opinions without principle, and unprincipled opinions

It is an unsafe partition, that divides opinions without principle from unprincipled opinions. If the latter are not followed by correspondent actions, we are indebted for the escape, not to the agent himself, but to his habits of education, to the sympathies of superior rank, to the necessity of character, often, perhaps to the absence of temptation from providential circumstances or the accident of a gracious nature. These, indeed, are truths of all times and places; but I seemed to see especial reason for insisting on them in our own times. A long and attentive observation has convinced me, that formerly men were worse than their principles, but that at present the principles are worse than the men. [2]

Advantages of being Englishmen

Few are sufficiently aware how much reason most of us have, even as common moral livers, to thank God for being Englishmen. It would furnish grounds both for humility towards Providence and for increased attachment to our country, if each individual could but see and feel how large a part of his innocence he owes to his birth, breeding, and residence in Great Britain. The administration of the laws; the almost continual preaching of moral prudence; the number and respectability of our sects; the pressure of our ranks on each other, with the consequent reserve and watchfulness of demeanour in the superior ranks, and the emulation in the subordinate; the vast depth, expansion, and systematic movements of our trade; and the consequent interdependence, the arterial or nerve-like network of property, which make every deviation from outward integrity a calculable loss to the offending individual himself from its mere effects, as obstruction and irregularity; and lastly, the naturalness of doing as others do:—these and the like influences, peculiar, some in the kind and all in the degree, to this privileged island, are the buttresses on which our foundationless well-doing is upheld, even as a house of cards, the architecture of our infancy, in which each is supported by all.

Taking root downwards in order to grow upwards

Well then may we pray, Give us peace in our time, O Lord! Well for us if no revolution or other general visitation betray the true state of our national morality! But, above all, well will it be for us if even now we dare disclose the secret to our own souls! Well will it be for as many of us as have duly reflected on the Prophet's assurance, that we must take root downwards if we would bear fruit upwards; if we would bear fruit, and continue to bear fruit, when the foodful plants that stand straight, only because they grow in company, or whose slender surface-roots owe their whole stedfastness to their intertanglement, have been beaten down by the continued rains, or whirled aloft by the sudden hurricane! Nor have we far to seek for whatever it is most important that we should find. The wisdom from above has not ceased for us: 'The principles of the oracles of God' (Hebrews v. 12) are still uttered from before the altar! Oracles, which we may consult without cost! Before an altar, where no sacrifice is required, but of the vices which unman us! no victims demanded, but the unclean and animal passions, which we may have suffered to house within us, forgetful of our baptismal dedication—no victim but the spiritual sloth, or goat, or fox, or hog, which lay waste the vineyard that the Lord had fenced and planted for Himself.

The Bible the Statesman's Manual

I have endeavoured in my previous discourse to persuade the more highly gifted and educated part of my friends and fellow-Christians, that as the New Testament sets forth the means and conditions of spiritual convalescence, with all the laws of conscience relative to our future state and permanent being, so does the Bible present to us the elements of public prudence, instructing us in the true causes, the surest preventives, and the only cures of public evils. The authorities of Raleigh, Clarendon, and Milton must at least exempt me from the blame of singularity if, undeterred by the contradictory charges of paradoxy from one party and of adherence to vulgar and old-fashioned prejudices from the other, I persist in avowing my conviction, that the inspired poets, historians, and sententiaries of the Jews are the clearest teachers of political economy: in short, that their writings are the Statesman's best manual, not only as containing the first principles and ultimate grounds of state-policy, whether in prosperous times or in those of danger and distress, but as supplying likewise the details of their application, and as being a full and spacious repository of precedents and facts in proof.

Well therefore (again and again I repeat to you)—well will it be for us if we have provided ourselves from this armoury while 'yet the day of trouble and of treading down and of perplexity' appears at far distance only 'in the valley of Vision', if we have humbled ourselves and have confessed our thin and unsound state, even while 'from the uttermost parts of the earth we were hearing songs of praise and glory to the upright nation'. (Isaiah xxii. 5; xxiv. 16.)

Our example to Europe should be intellectual as well as material

But if, indeed, the day of treading down is present, it is still in our power to convert it into a time of substantial discipline for ourselves, and of enduring benefit to the present generation and to posterity. The splendour of our exploits during the late war is less honourable to us than the magnanimity of our views, and our generous confidence in the victory of the better cause. Accordingly, we have obtained a good name, so that the nations around us have displayed a disposition to follow our example and imitate our institutions—too often, I fear, even in parts where, from the difference of our relative circumstances, the imitation had little chance of proving more than mimicry. But it will be far more glorious, and to our neighbours incomparably more instructive, if, in distresses to which all countries are liable, we bestir ourselves in remedial and preventive arrangements which all nations may more or less adopt; inasmuch as they are grounded on principles intelligible to all rational and obligatory on all moral beings; inasmuch as, having been taught by God's word, exampled by God's providence, commanded by God's law, and recommended by promises of God's grace, they alone can form the foundations of a Christian community. Do we love our country? These are the principles by which the true friend of the people is contra-distinguished from the factious demagogue. They are at once the rock and the quarry. On these alone and with these alone is the solid welfare of a people to be built. Do we love our own souls? These are the principles, the neglect of which writes hypocrite and suicide on the brow of the professing Christian. For these are the keystone of that arch on which alone we can cross the torrent of life and death with safety on the passage; with peace in the retrospect; and with hope shining upon us from the cloud toward which we are travelling. . . . [3]

The Sermon

They have healed the hurt of the daughter of my people slightly, saying, Peace, peace, when there is no peace. We looked for peace, but no good came: for a time of health, and behold—trouble! The harvest is past, the summer is ended; and we are not saved. Is there no balm in Gilead? Is there no physician? Why then is not the health of the daughter of my people recovered? JEREMIAH, viii. 11, 15, 20, 22.

The peace that was no peace

. . . Peace has come without the advantages expected from peace, and, on the contrary, with many of the severest inconveniences usually attributable to war. . . . The inference therefore contained in the preceding verse is unavoidable. Where war has produced no repentance, and the cessation of war has brought neither concord nor tranquility, we may safely cry aloud with the Prophet: 'They have healed the hurt of the daughter of my people slightly, saying, Peace, peace, when there is no peace.' The whole remaining subject therefore may be comprised in the three questions implied in the last of the verses recited to you; in three questions, and in the answers to the same. First, who are they who have hitherto prescribed for the case, and are still tampering with it? What are their qualifications? What has been their conduct? Second, what is the true seat and source of the complaint—the ultimate causes as well as the immediate occasions? And lastly, what are the appropriate medicines? Who and where are the true physicians?

Political empirics

And first, then, of those who have been ever loud and foremost in their pretensions to a knowledge both of the disease and the remedy. In a preceding part of the same chapter from which I extracted the line prefixed, the Prophet Isaiah enumerates the conditions of a nation's recovery from a state of depression and peril, and among these, one condition which he describes in words that may be without any forced or overrefined interpretation unfolded into an answer to the present question. The vile person, he tells us, must no more be called liberal, nor the churl be said to be bountiful. For the vile person will speak villany, and his heart will work iniquity to practise hypocrisy, and to utter error against the Lord; to make empty the soul of the needy: and he will cause the drink of the thirsty to fail. The instruments also of the churl are evil: he deviseth wicked devices to destroy the poor with lying words, even when the needy speaketh aright. But the liberal deviseth liberal things, and by liberal things shall he stand. (Isaiah xxxii. 5, 6, 7, 8.)

Such are the political empirics, mischievous in proportion to their effrontery, and ignorant in proportion to their presumption, the detection and exposure of whose true characters the inspired statesman and patriot represents as indispensable to the re-establishment of the general welfare, while his own portrait of these impostors whom in a former chapter (ix. 15, 16) he calls, 'the tail of the nation', and in the following verse, demagogues 'that cause the people to err', affords to the intelligent believer of all ages and countries the means of detecting them, and of undeceiving all whose own malignant passions have not rendered them blind and deaf and brutish. For these noisy and calumnious zealots, whom (with an especial reference indeed to the factious leaders of the populace who under this name exercised a tumultuary despotism in Jerusalem, at once a sign and a cause of its approaching downfall) St John beheld in the Apocalyptic vision as a compound of locust and scorpion, are not of one place or of one season. They are the perennials of history: and though they may disappear for a time, they exist always in the egg, and need only a distempered atmosphere and an accidental ferment to start up into life and activity.

It is worth our while, therefore, or rather it is our duty, to examine with a more attentive eye this representative portrait drawn for us by an infallible master, and to distinguish its component parts, each by itself, so that we may combine without confusing them in our memory; till they blend at length into one physiognomic expression, which, whenever the counterpart is obtruded on our notice in the sphere of our own experience, may be at once recognized, and enable us to convince ourselves of the identity by a comparison of feature with feature.

Their character—or lack of it

The passage commences with a fact, which to the inexperienced might well seem strange and improbable: but which, being a truth nevertheless of our own knowledge, is the more striking and characteristic. Worthless persons of little or no estimation for rank, learning, or integrity, not seldom profligates, with whom debauchery has outwrestled rapacity, easy because unprincipled, and generous because dishonest, are suddenly cried up as men of enlarged views and liberal sentiments, our only genuine patriots and philanthropists: and churls, that is, men of sullen tempers and surly demeanour; men tyrannical in their families, appressive and troublesome to their dependents and neighbours, and hard in their private dealings between man and man; men who clench with one hand what they have grasped with the other;—these are extolled as public benefactors, the friends, guardians, and advocates of the poor! Here and there, indeed, we may notice an individual of birth and fortune

(For great estates enlarge not narrow minds)

who has been duped into the ranks of incendiaries and mobsycophants by an insane restlessness, and the wretched ambition of figuring as the triton of the minnows. Or we may find perhaps a professional man of showy accomplishments, but of a vulgar taste and shallow acquirements, who in part from vanity and in part as a means of introduction to practice, will seek notoriety by an eloquence well calculated to set the multitude agape, and excite gratis to overt acts of sedition or treason which he may afterwards be fee'd to defend! These, however, are but exceptions to the general rule. Such as the Prophet has described, such is the sort of men; and in point of historic fact it has been from men of this sort that profaneness is gone forth into all the land. (Jeremiah xxiii. 15.)

Their methods

In harmony with the general character of these false prophets are the particular qualities assigned to them. First, a passion for vague and violent invective, an habitual and inveterate predilection for the language of hate and rage and contumely, an ungoverned appetite for abuse and defamation! The vile will talk villany.

But the fetid flower will ripen into the poisonous berry, and the fruits of the hand follow the blossoms of the slanderous lips. His heart will work iniquity. That is, he will plan evil, and do his utmost to carry his plans into execution. . . . Whether in spoken or in printed addresses, whether in periodical journals or in yet cheaper implements of irritation, the ends are the same, the process is the same, and the same is their general line of conduct. On all occasions, but most of all and with a more bustling malignity whenever any public distress inclines the lower classes to turbulence, and renders them more apt to be alienated from the government of their country—in all places and at every opportunity pleading to the poor and ignorant—nowhere and at no time are they found actually pleading for them. [4] Nor is this the worst. They even plead against them. Yes; sycophants to the crowd, enemies of the individuals, and well-wishers only to the continuance of their miseries, they plead against the poor and afflicted, under the weak and wicked pretence that we are to do nothing of what we can, because we cannot do all that we would wish. Or if this sophistry of sloth (*sophisma pigri*) should fail to check the bounty of the rich, there is still the sophistry of slander in reserve to chill the gratitude of the poor. If they cannot dissuade the liberal from devising liberal things, they will at least blacken the motives of his beneficence. If they cannot close the hand of the giver, they will at least embitter the gift in the mouth of the receivers. Is it not as if they had said within their hearts, the sacrifice of charity has been offered indeed in despite of us; 'but with bitter herbs shall it be eaten.' (Exodus xii. 8.) Imagined wrongs shall make it distasteful. We will infuse vindictive and discontented fancies into minds already irritable and suspicious from distress: till the fever of the heart shall coat the tongue with gall and spread wormwood on the palate.

However angrily our demagogues may disclaim all intentions of this kind, such has been their procedure, and it is susceptible of no other interpretation. We all know that the shares must be scanty where the dividend bears no proportion to the number of the claimants. Yet He who satisfied the multitude in the wilderness with a few loaves and fishes, is still present to His Church. Small as the portions are, if they are both given and taken in the spirit of His commands, a blessing will go with each; and the handful of meal shall not fail, until the day when the Lord bringeth back plenty on the land. But no blessing can enter where envy and hatred are already in possession; and small good will the poor man have of the food prepared for him by his more favoured brother, if he have been previously taught to regard it as a mess of pottage given to defraud him of his birthright.

If then to promise medicine and to administer poison; if to flatter in order to deprave; if to affect love to all and show pity to none; if to exaggerate and misderive the distress of the labouring classes in order to make them turbulent, and to discourage every plan for their relief in order to keep them so; if to skulk from private infamy in the mask of public spirit, and make the flaming patriot privilege the gamester, swindler, or adulterer; if to seek amnesty for a continued violation of the laws of God by an equal pertinacity in outraging the laws of the land;—if these characterize the hypocrite, we need not look far back or far round for faces wherein to recognize the third striking feature of this prophetic portrait! When, therefore the verifying facts press upon us in real life; when we hear persons, the tyranny of whose will is the only law in their families, denouncing all law as tyranny in public—persons, whose hatred of power in others is in exact proportion to their love of it for themselves; when we behold men of sunk and irretrievable characters, to whom no man would entrust his wife, his sister, or his purse, having the effrontery to propose that we should entrust to them our religion and our country; when we meet with patriots, who aim at an enlargement of the rights and liberties of the people by inflaming the populace to acts of madness that necessitate fetters—pretended heralds of freedom and actual pioneers of military despotism;—we will call to mind the words of the Prophet Isaiah, and say to ourselves, this is no new thing under the sun! We have heard it with our own ears, and it was declared to our fathers, and in the old time before them, that one of the main characteristics of demagogues in all ages is, to practise hypocrisy.

Demagogues the enemies of liberty

Such, I assert, has been the general line of conduct pursued by the political empirics of the day: and your own recent experience will attest the truth of the assertion. It was affirmed likewise at the same time, that as the conduct, such was the process: and I will seek no other support of this charge, I need no better test both of the men and their works, than the plain question: Is there one good feeling, to which they do—is there a single bad passion, to which they do not—appeal? If they are the enemies of liberty in general, inasmuch as they tend to make it appear incompatible with public quiet and personal safety, still more emphatically are they the enemies of the liberty of the PRESS in particular; and therein of all the truths, human and divine, which a free press [5] is the most efficient and only commensurate means of protecting, extending, and perpetuating. The strongest, indeed the only plausible, arguments against the education of the lower classes, are derived from the writings of these incendiaries; and if for our neglect of the light that hath been vouchsafed to us beyond measure, the land should be visited with a spiritual dearth, it will have been in no small degree occasioned by the erroneous and wicked principles which it is the trade of these men to propagate. Well, therefore, has the Prophet made it the fourth mark of these misleaders of the multitude, not alone to utter error, but to utter error against the Lord, to make empty the soul of the hungry! Alas! it is a hard and a mournful thing, that the press should be constrained to call out for the harsh curb of the law against the press! for how shall the law predistinguish the ominous screech owl from the sacred notes of augury, from the auspicious and friendly birds of warning? And yet will we avoid this seeming injustice, we throw down all fence and bulwark of public decency and public opinion. Already has political calumny joined hands with private slander, and every principle, every feeling, that binds the citizen to his country, the spirit to its Creator, is in danger of being undermined; not by reasoning, for from that there is no danger, but by the mere habit of hearing them reviled and scoffed at with impunity. Were we to contemplate the evils of a rank and unweeded press only in its effects on the manners of a people, and on the general tone of thought and conversation, the greater love we bore to literature, and to all the means and instruments of human improvement, the more anxiously should we wish for some Ithuriel spear that might remove from the ear of the ignorant and half-learned, and expose in their own fiendish shape those reptiles which, inspiring venom and forging illusions as they list,

> . . . . . thence raise,
> At least distemper'd discontented thoughts,
> Vain hopes, vain aims, inordinate desires.
>
> PARADISE LOST

I feel, my friends, that even the strong and painful interest which the peculiar state of the times, and almost the occurrences of the hour, create, can scarcely counterbalance the wearisome aversion inspired by the deformity and palpableness of the subject itself. As the plan originates in the malignant restlessness of desperate ambition or desperate circumstances, so are its means and engines a drag-net of fraud and delusion. The instruments also of the churl are evil; he deviseth wicked devices with lying words. He employs a compound poison, of which the following are the main ingredients, the porportions varying as the case requires or the wit of the poisoner suggests. It will be enough rapidly to name and number the components, as in a catalogue. 1. Bold, warm, and earnest assertions, it matters not whether supported by facts or no, nay, though they should involve absurdities, and demonstrable impossibilities: ex. gr. that the amount of the sinecure places given by the executive power would suffice to remove all distress from the land. He is a bungler in the trade, and has been an indocile scholar of his dark master, the father of lies, who cannot make an assertion pass for a fact with an ignorant multitude. The natural generosity of the human heart, which makes it an effort to doubt; the confidence which apparent courage inspires; and

Analysis of Demagogic methods

the contagion of animal enthusiasm, will ensure the belief. Even in large assemblies of men highly educated, it is too often sufficient to place impressive images in juxta-position; and the constitutive forms of the mind itself aided by the power of habit will supply the rest. For we all think by causal connections. 2. Startling particular facts, which, dissevered from their context, enable a man to convey falsehood while he says truth. 3. Arguments built on passing events, and deriving an undue importance from the feelings of the moment. The mere appeal, however, to the auditors whether the arguments are not such that none but an idiot or an hireling could resist, is an effective substitute for any argument at all. For mobs have no memories. They are in nearly the same state as that of an individual when he makes (what is termed) a bull. The passions, like a fused metal, fill up the wide interstices of thought, and supply the defective links: and thus incompatible assertions are harmonized by the sensation, without the sense, of connection. 4. The display of defects without the accompanying advantages, or vice versa. 5. Concealment of the general and ultimate result behind the scenery of local and particular consequences. 6. Statement of positions that are true only under particular conditions, to men whose ignorance or fury make them forget that these conditions are not present, or lead them to take for granted that they are. 7. Chains of questions, especially of such questions as the persons best authorized to propose are ever the slowest in proposing; and objections intelligible of themselves, the answers to which require the comprehension of a system. 8. Vague and commonplace satire, stale as the wine in which flies were drowned last summer, seasoned by the sly tale and important anecdote of but yesterday, that came within the speaker's own knowledge! 9. Transitions from the audacious charge, not seldom of as signal impudence 'as any thing was ever carted for', to the lie pregnant and interpretative: the former to prove the orator's courage, and that he is neither to be bought or frightened; the latter to flatter the sagacity of the audience: . . . . δῆλός ἐστιν αὐτόθεν | ἐν πανουργίᾳ τε καὶ θράσει καὶ κοβαλικεύμασιν. 10. Jerks of style, from the lunatic trope, ῥήμαθ' ἱπποβάμονα, πολλάς τε ἀλινδήθρας ἐπῶν, to the buffoonery and 'red-lattice phrases' of the canaglia, Σκῶρ συσκεδῶν βόρβορον τε πόλυν καὶ κακίας καὶ συκοφαντίας; the one in ostentation of superior rank and acquirements (for where envy does not interfere, man loves to look up); the other in pledge of heartiness and good fellowship. 11. Lastly, and throughout all, to leave a general impression of something striking, something that is to come of it, and to rely on the indolence of men's understandings and the activity of their passions for their resting in this state, as the brood-warmth fittest to hatch whatever serpent's egg opportunity may enable the deceiver to place under it. Let but mysterious expressions[1] be aided by significant looks and tones, and you may cajole a hot and ignorant audience to believe any thing by saying nothing, and finally to act on the lie, which they themselves have been drawn in to make. This is the Pharmacopœia of political empirics, here and everywhere, now and at all times! These are the drugs administered, and the tricks played off by the mountebanks and zanies of patriotism; drugs that will continue to poison as long as irreligion secures a predisposition to their influence; and artifices that, like stratagems in war, are nevertheless successful for having succeeded a hundred times before. 'They bend their tongues as a bow! they shoot out deceits as arrows: they are prophets of the deceit of their own hearts: they cause the people to err by their dreams and their lightness: they make the people vain, they feed them with wormwood, they give them the water of gall for drink: and the people love to have it so. And what is the end thereof?' (Jeremiah *passim.*)

The Prophet answers for me in the concluding words of

[1] *Vide* North's *Examen*, p. 20; and *The Knights of Aristophanes.* A version of this comedy, abridged and modernised, would be a most seasonable present to the public. The words quoted above from this play and *The Frogs*, may be rendered freely in the order in which they occur: thus—

1. Thence he is illustrious, as a man of all waters, a bold fellow, and one who knows how to tickle the populace.
2. Phrases on horseback, curvetting and careering words.
3. Scattering filth and dirt, malice and sycophantic tales.

the description—To destroy the poor, even when the needy speaketh aright—that is, to impel them to acts that must end in their ruin by inflammatory falsehoods and by working on their passions till they lead them to reject the prior convictions of their own sober and unsophisticated understandings. As in all the preceding features so in this, with which the prophetic portrait is completed, our own experience supplies both proof and example. The ultimate causes of the present distress and stagnation are, in the writer's opinion, complex and deeply seated; but the immediate occasion is too obvious to be overlooked but by eyes at once red and dim through the intoxication of factious prejudice, the maddening spirit which pre-eminently deserves the title of *vinum dœmonum* applied by an ancient father of the Church to a far more innocent phrenzy. It is demonstrable that taxes, the product of which is circulated in the country from which they are raised, can never injure a country directly by the mere amount; but either from the time or circumstances under which they are raised, or from the injudicious mode in which they are levied, or from the improper objects to which they are applied. The sun may draw up the moisture from the river, the morass, and the ocean, to be given back in general showers to the garden, the pasture, and the cornfield; but it may likewise force upward the moisture from the fields of industry to drop it on the stagnant pool, the saturated swamp, or the unprofitable sand-waste. The corruptions of a system can be duly appreciated by those only who have contemplated the system in that ideal state of perfection exhibited by the reason: the nearest possible approximation to which under existing circumstances it is the business of the prudential understanding to realize. Those, on the other hand, who commence the examination of a system by identifying it with its abuses or imperfections, degrade their understanding into the pander of their passions, and are sure to prescribe remedies more dangerous than the disease. [6] Alas! there are so many real evils, so many just causes of complaint in the constitutions and administration of all governments, our own not excepted, that it becomes the imperious duty of the true

How to examine the corruptions of a system

patriot to prevent, as much as in him lies, the feelings and efforts of his fellow-countrymen from losing themselves on a wrong scent.

Taxation is circulation of wealth

If then we are to master the ideal of a beneficent and judicious system of finance as the preliminary to all profitable insight into the defects of any particular system in actual existence, we could not perhaps find an apter illustration than the gardens of southern Europe would supply. The tanks or reservoirs would represent the capital of a nation: while the hundred rills hourly varying their channels and directions, under the gardener's spade, would give a pleasing image of the dispersion of that capital through the whole population by the joint effect of taxation and trade. For taxation itself is a part of commerce, and government may be fairly considered as a great manufacturing-house, carrying on in different places, by means of its partners and overseers, the trades of the ship-builder, the clothier, the iron-founder, &c. &c. As long as a balance is preserved between the receipts and the returns of government in their amount, quickness, and degree of dispersion, as long as the due proportion obtains in the sums levied to the mass in productive circulation, so long as does the wealth and circumstantial prosperity of the nation (its wealth, I say, not its real welfare; its outward prosperity, but not necessarily its happiness) remain unaffected, or rather they will appear to increase in consequence of the additional stimulus given to the circulation itself by the reproductive action of all large capitals, and through the check which taxation, in its own nature, gives to the indolence of the wealthy in its continual transfer of property to the industrious and enterprising. If different periods be taken, and if the comparative weight of the taxes at each be calculated, as it ought to be, not by the sum levied in each individual, but by the sum left in his possession, the settlement of the account will be in favour of the national wealth, to the amount of all the additional productive labour sustained or excited by the taxes during the intervals between their efflux and their re-absorption.

But, on the other hand, in a direct ratio to this increase will be the distress produced by the disturbance of this balance, by the loss of this porportion; and the operation of the distress will be at least equal to the total amount of the difference between the taxes still levied, and the quantum of aid withdrawn from individuals by the abandonment of others, and of that which the taxes that still remain have ceased to give by the altered mode of their re-dispersion. But to this we must add the number of persons raised and reared in consequence of the demand created by the preceding state of things, and now discharged from their occupations: whether the latter belong exclusively to the executive power, as that of soldiers, &c. or from those in which the labourers for the nation in general are already sufficiently numerous. Both these classes are thrown back on the public, and sent to a table where every seat is pre-occupied. The employment lessens as the number of men to be employed is increased; and not merely in the same, but from additional causes and from the indirect consequences of those already stated, in a far greater ratio. For it may easily happen, that the very same change, which had produced this depression at home, may from equivalent causes have embarrassed the countries in commercial connection with us. At one and the same time the great customer at home wants less, and our customers abroad are able to buy less. The conjoint action of these circumstances will furnish, for a mind capable of combining them, a sufficient solution of the melancholy fact. They cannot but occasion much distress, much obstruction, and these again in their reaction are sure to be more than doubled by the still greater and universal alarm, and by the consequent check of confidence and enterprise, which they never fail to produce.

Economic stimulus of the war—

Now it is a notorious fact, that these causes did all exist to a very extraordinary degree, and that they all worked with united strength, in the late sudden transition from war to peace. It was one among the many anomalies of the late war, that it acted, after a few years, as a universal stimulant. We almost monopolized the commerce of the world. The high wages of our artisans and the high prices of agricultural produce inter-circulated. Leases of no unusual length not seldom enabled the provident and thrifty farmer to purchase the estate he had rented. Everywhere might be seen roads, railways, docks, canals, made, making, and projected; villages swelling into towns, while the metropolis surrounded itself, and became, as it were, set with new cities. Finally, in spite of all the waste and havoc of a twenty years' war, the population of the empire was increased by more than two millions! The efforts and war-expenditure of the nation, and the yearly revenue, were augmented in the same proportion: and to all this we must add a fact of the utmost importance in the present question, that the war did not, as was usually the case in former wars, die away into a long-expected peace, by gradual exhaustion and weariness on both sides, but plunged to its conclusion by a concentration, we might almost say by a spasm of energy, and consequently by an anticipation of our resources. We conquered by compelling reversionary power into alliance with our existing and natural strength. The first intoxication of triumph having passed over, this, our 'agony of glory,' was succeeded, of course, by a general stiffness and relaxation. The antagonist passions came into play; financial solicitude was blended with constitutional and political jealousies, and both, alas! were exacerbated by personal imprudences, the chief injury of which consisted in their own tendency to disgust and alienate the public feeling. And with all this, the financial errors and prejudices even of the more educated classes, in short, the general want or imperfection of clear views and a scientific insight into the true effects and influences of taxation, and the mode of its operation, became now a real misfortune, and opened an additional source of temporary embarrassment. Retrenchment could no longer proceed by cautious and calculated steps; but was compelled to hurry forward, like one who crossing the sands at too late an hour finds himself threatened by the inrush of the tide. Nevertheless, it was a truth susceptible of little less than mathematical demonstration, that the more, and the more suddenly, the revenue was diminished by the abandonment of the war-taxes, [7] the greater

And the dislocation caused by its sudden cessation

would be the disturbance of the balance: so that the agriculturist, the manufacturer, or the tradesman (all in short but annuitants and fixed stipendiaries) who during the war having paid as five and fifteen, would shortly have less than ten after having paid but two and a half.

Seasonal fluctuation of employment

But there is yet another circumstance which we dare not pass by unnoticed. In the best of times—or what the world calls such—the spirit of commerce will occasion great fluctuations, some falling while others rise, and therefore in all times there will be a large sum of individual distress. Trades likewise have their seasons, and at all times there is a very considerable number of artificers who are not employed on the average more than seven or eight months in the year: and the distress from this cause is great or small in proportion to the greater or less degree of dissipation and improvidence prevailing among them. But besides this, that artificial life and vigour of trade and agriculture which was produced or occasioned by the direct or indirect influences of the late war, proved by no means innoxious in its effects. Habit and the familiarity with outward advantages, which takes off their dazzle; sense of character; and above all, the counterpoise of intellectual pursuits and resources; are all necessary preventives and antidotes to the dangerous properties of wealth and power with the great majority of mankind. It is a painful subject: and I leave to your own experience and recollection the assemblage of folly, presumption and extravagance that followed in the procession of our late unprecedented prosperity; the blind practices and blinding passions of speculation in the commercial world, with the shoal of ostentatious fooleries and sensual vices which the sudden influx of wealth let in on our farmers and yeomanry. [8] Now though the whole mass of calamity consequent on these aberrations from prudence should in all fairness be attributed to the sufferer's own conduct; yet when there supervenes some one common cause or occasion of distress which pressing hard on many furnishes a pretext to all, this too will pass muster among its actual effects, and assume the semblance and dignity of national calamity. . . . The change of the moon will not

Effect of war-time prosperity on morals and manners

produce a change of weather except in places where the atmosphere has from local and particular causes been predisposed to its influence. But the former is one, placed aloft and conspicuous to all men; the latter are many and intricate, and known to few. Of course it is the moon that must bear the entire blame of wet summers and scanty crops. All these, however, whether they are distresses common to all times alike, or though occasioned by the general revolution and stagnation, yet really caused by personal improvidence or misconduct, combine with its peculiar and inevitable effects in making the cup overflow. The latter class especially, as being in such cases always the most clamorous sufferers, increase the evil by swelling the alarm. [9]

Demagogues decline to admit evils due to war

The principal part of the preceding explication, the main causes of the present exigencies, are so obvious, and lie so open to the common sense of mankind, that the labouring classes saw the connection of the change in the times with the suddenness of the peace as clearly as their superiors, and, being less heated with speculation, were in the first instance less surprised at the results. To a public event of universal concern there will often be more attributed than belongs to it; but never in the natural course of human feelings will there be less. That the depression began with the peace would have been of itself a sufficient proof with the many, that it arose from the peace. But this opinion suited ill with the purposes of sedition. The truth, that could not be precluded, must be removed; and 'when the needy speaketh aright' the more urgent occasion is there for the 'wicked device' and the 'lying words'. Where distress is felt, tales of wrong and oppression are readily believed, to the sufferer's own disquiet. Rage and revenge make the cheek pale and the hand tremble worse than even want itself: and the cup of sorrow overflows by being held unsteadily. On the other hand, nothing calms the mind in the hour of bitterness so efficaciously as the conviction that it was not within the means of those above us, or around us, to have prevented it. An influence, mightier than fascination, dwells in the stern eye of necessity, when it is fixed steadily on a man: for together with the power of resistance, it takes away its agitations likewise. This is one mercy that always accompanies the visitations of the Almighty when they are received as such. If therefore the sufferings of the lower classes are to supply air and fuel to their passions, and are to be perverted into instruments of mischief, they must be attributed to causes that can be represented as removeable; either to individuals who had been previously rendered unpopular, or to whole classes of men, according as the immediate object of their seducers may require. What though nothing should be more remote from the true cause? What though the invidious charge should be not only without proof, but in the face of strong proof to the contrary? What though the pretended remedy should have no possible end but that of exasperating the disease? All will be of little or no avail if these truths have not been administered beforehand. When the wrath is gone forth, the plague is already begun (Numbers xvi. 46). Wrath is cruel, and where is there a deafness like that of an outrageous multitude? For as the matter of the fire is, so it burneth. Let the demagogue but succeed in maddening the crowd, he may bid defiance to demonstration, and direct the madness against whom it pleaseth him. A slanderous tongue has disquieted many, and driven them from nation to nation; strong cities hath it pulled down, and overthrown the houses of great men. (Ecclesiasticus xxviii. 14.)

Pensions and sinecures

We see in every promiscuous public meeting the effect produced by the bold assertion that the present hardships of all classes are owing to the number and amount of pensions and sinecures. Yet from the unprecedented zeal and activity in the education of the poor, of the thousands that are inflamed by, and therefore give credit to, these statements, there are few without a child at home who could prove their impossibility by the first and simplest rules of arithmetic; there is not one perhaps who, taken by himself and in a cooler mind, would stand out against the simple question, whether it was not folly to suppose that the lowness of his wages or his want of employment could be occasioned by the circumstance that a sum (the whole of which, as far as it is raised by taxation, cannot take a yearly penny from him) was dispersed and returned into the general circulation by annuitants of the treasury instead of annuitants of the bank, by John instead of Peter, however blameable the regulation might be in other respects? What then? the hypothesis allows of a continual reference to persons, and to all the uneasy and malignant passions which personalities are of all means the best fitted to awaken. The grief itself, however grinding it may be, is of no avail to this end; it must first be converted into a grievance. Were the audience composed chiefly of the lower farmers and the peasantry, the same circumstance would, for the same reason, have been attributed wholly to the clergy and the system of tithes; as if the corn would be more plentiful if the farmers paid their whole rent to one man, instead of paying nine parts to the landlords and the tenth to the tithe-owners! But let the meeting be composed of the manufacturing poor, and then it is the machinery of their employers that is devoted to destruction: though it would not exceed the truth if I affirmed that to the use and perfection of this very machinery the majority of the poor deluded destroyers owe their very existence, owe to it that they ever beheld the light of heaven!

Social function of capitalists

Even so it is with the capitalists and storekeepers, who, by spreading the dearness of provisions over a larger space and time, prevent scarcity from becoming real famine, the frightful lot at certain and not distant intervals of our less commercial forefathers. These men, by the mere instinct of self-interest, are not alone birds of warning that prevent waste, but, as the raven of Elijah, they bring supplies from afar. But let the incendiary spirit have rendered them birds of ill omen, and it is well if the deluded malcontents can be restrained from levelling at them missiles more alarming than the curse of the unwise that alighteth not. 'There be three things (says the wise son of Sirach) that mine heart feareth, the slander of a city, the gathering together of an unruly multitude, and a false accusation: all these are worse than death.' But all these are the arena, and the chosen weapons of demagogues. Wretches! they would without remorse detract the hope that is the subliming and expanding warmth of public credit, destroy the public credit that is the vital air of national industry, convert obstruction into stagnation, and make grass grow in the exchange and the market-place; if so they might but goad ignorance into riot, and fanaticism into rebellion! They would snatch the last morsel from the poor man's lips to make him curse the government in his heart—alas! to fall at length either ignominiously beneath the strength of the outraged law, or (if God in His anger, and for the punishment of general depravity, should require a severer and more extensive retribution) to perish still more lamentably among the victims of its weakness.

Thus, then, I have answered at large to the first of the three questions proposed as the heads and divisions of this address. I am well aware that our demagogues are not the only empirics who have tampered with the case. But I felt unwilling to put the mistakes of sciolism, or even those of vanity and self-interest, in the same section with crime and guilt. What is omitted here will find its place elsewhere, the more readily that, having been tempted by the foulness of the ways to turn for a short space out of my direct path, I have encroached already on the second question; that, namely, which respects the ultimate causes and immediate occasions of the complaint.

The latter part of this problem I appear to myself to have solved fully and satisfactorily. To those who deem any further or deeper research superfluous, I must content myself with observing that I have never heard it denied that there is more than a sufficiency of food in existence. I have, at least, met with no proof that there is or has been any scarcity either in the materials of all necessary comforts, or any lack of strength, skill, and industry to prepare them. If we saw a man in health pining at a full table because there was not 'the savoury meat there which he loved' and had expected, the wanton delay or negligence of the messenger would be a complete answer to our inquiries after the occasion of this sullenness or inappetence; but the cause of it we should be tempted to seek in the man's own undisciplined temper, or habits of self-indulgence. So far from agreeing therefore with those who find the causes in the occasions, I think the half of the question already solved of very unequal importance with that which yet remains for solution.

The deeper causes of distress

The immediate occasions of the existing distress may be correctly given with no greater difficulty than would attend any other series of known historic facts; but towards the discovery of its true seat and sources I can but offer a humble contribution. They appear to me, however, resolvable into the overbalance [10] of the commercial spirit in consequence of the absence or weakness of the counter-weights; this overbalance considered as displaying itself, 1, in the commercial world itself; 2, in the agricultural; 3, in the government; and, 4, in the combined influence of all three on the more numerous and labouring classes.

Decline of natural counter-forces to the spirit of trade:

(1) *Respect for rank and ancestry*

Of the natural counter-forces to the impetus of trade, the first that presents itself to my mind is the ancient feeling of rank and ancestry, compared with our present self-complacent triumph over these supposed prejudices. Not that titles and the rights of precedence are pursued by us with less eagerness than by our fore-fathers. The contrary is the case; and for this very cause, because they inspire less reverence. In the old times they were valued by the possessors and revered by the people as distinctions of nature, which the crown itself could only ornament, but not give. Like the stars in heaven, their influence was wider and more general, because for the mass of mankind there was no hope of reaching, and therefore no desire to appropriate them. That many evils as well as advantages accompanied this state of things I am well aware: and likewise that many of the latter have become incompatible with far more important blessings. It would, therefore, be sickly affectation to suspend the thankfulness due for our immunity from the one, in an idle regret for the loss of the other. But however true this may be, and whether the good or the evil preponderated, still it acted as a counterpoise to the grosser superstition of wealth. Of the efficiency of this counter-influence we can offer negative proof only: and for this we need only look back on the deplorable state of Holland in respect of patriotism and public spirit at and before the commencement of the French Revolution.

(2) *Eclipse of philosophy by empiricism*

The limits and proportions of this address allow little more than a bare reference to this point. The same restraint I must impose on myself in the following. For under this head I include the general neglect of all the austerer studies; the long and ominous eclipse of philosophy; the usurpation of that venerable name by physical and psychological empiricism; and the non-existence of a learned and philosophic public, [11] which is perhaps the only innoxious form of an imperium in imperio, but at the same time the only form which is not directly or indirectly encouraged. So great a risk do I incur of malignant interpretation, and the assertion itself is so likely to appear paradoxical even to men of candid minds, that I should have passed over this point, most important as I know it to be, but that it will be found stated more at large, with all its proofs, in a work on the point of publication. [12] The fact is simply this. We have—lovers shall I entitle them?— or must I not rather hazard the introduction of their own phrases, and say, amateurs or dilettanti, as musicians, botanists, florists, mineralogists, and antiquarians? Nor is it denied that these are ingenuous pursuits, and such as become men of rank and fortune. Neither in these nor in any other points do I complain of any excess in the pursuits themselves; but of that which arises from the deficiency of the counterpoise. The effect is the same. Every work which can be made use of either to immediate profit or immediate pleasure; every work which falls in with the desire of acquiring wealth suddenly, or which can gratify the senses, or pamper the still more degrading appetite for scandal and personal defamation, is sure of an appropriate circulation. But neither philosophy nor theology, in the strictest sense of the words, can be said to have even a public existence among us. I feel assured that if Plato himself were to return and renew his sublime lucubrations in the metropolis of Great Britain, a handicraftsman from a laboratory, who had just succeeded in disoxydating an earth, would be thought far the more respectable, nay, the more illustrious, person of the two. Nor will it be the least drawback from his honours that he had never even asked himself what law of universal being nature uttered in his phenomenon: while the character of a visionary would be the sole remuneration of the man who, from the insight into that law, had previously demonstrated the necessity of the fact. [13] As to that which passes with us under the name of metaphysics, philosophic elements, and the like, I refer every man of reflection to the contrast between the present times and those shortly after the restoration of ancient literature. In the latter we find the greatest men of the age, statesmen, warriors, monarchs, architects, in closest intercourse with philosophy. I need only mention the names of Lorenzo the Magnificent, Picus, Count Mirandola, Ficinus, and Politian; the abstruse subjects of their discussion, and the importance attached to them, as the requisite qualifications of men placed by Providence as guides and governors of their fellow-creatures. If this be undeniable, equally notorious is it that at present the more effective a man's talents are, and the more likely he is to be useful and distinguished in the highest situations of public life, the earlier does he show his aversion to the metaphysics and the books of metaphysical speculation which are placed before him: though they come with the recommendation of being so many triumphs of modern good sense over the schools of ancient philosophy. Dante, Petrarch, Spenser, Sir Philip Sidney, Algernon Sidney, Milton, and Barrow, were Platonists. But all the men of genius with whom it has been my fortune to converse, either profess to know nothing of the present systems or to despise them. It would be equally unjust and irrational to seek the solution of this difference in the men; and if not, it can be found only in the philosophic systems themselves. And so in truth it is. The living of former ages communed gladly with a life-breathing philosophy. The living of the present age wisely leave the dead to take care of the dead. [14]

Statesmen of earlier ages were concerned with ideas

But whatever the causes may be, the result is before our eyes. An excess in our attachment to temporal and personal objects can be counteracted only by a pre-occupation of the intellect and the affections with permanent, universal, and eternal truths. Let no man enter, said Plato, who has not previously disciplined his mind by geometry. He considered

Chief check upon attachment to temporal and personal objects in the preoccupation of the intellect with universal truths

this science as the first purification of the soul, by abstracting the attention from the accidents of the senses. We too teach geometry; but that there may be no danger of the pupil's becoming too abstract in his conceptions, it has been not only proposed, but the proposal has been adopted, that it should be taught by wooden diagrams! It pains me to remember with what applause a work, that placed the inductions of modern chemistry in the same rank with the demonstrations of mathematical science, was received even in a mathematical university. I must not permit myself to say more on this subject, desirous as I am of showing the importance of a philosophic class, and of evincing that it is of vital utility, and even an essential element in the composition of a civilized community. [15] It must suffice that it has been explained in what respect the pursuit of truth for its own sake, and the reverence yielded to its professors, has a tendency to calm or counteract the pursuit of wealth; and that therefore a counter-force is wanting wherever philosophy is degraded in the estimation of society. What are you (a philosopher was once asked) in consequence of your admiration of these abstruse speculations? He answered: What I am, it does not become me to say; but what thousands are who despise them, and even pride themselves on their ignorance, I see—and tremble!

(3) *Decline of intellectually based religion*

There is a third influence, alternately our spur and our curb, without which all the pursuits and desires of man must either exceed or fall short of their just measure. Need I add that I mean the influence of religion? I speak of that sincere, that entire interest in the undivided faith of Christ which demands the first-fruits of the whole man, his affections no less than his outward acts, his understanding equally with his feelings. For be assured, never yet did there exist a full faith in the divine Word (by whom not immortality alone, but light and immortality, were brought into the world) which did not expand the intellect while it purified the heart; which did not multiply the aims and objects of the mind, while it fixed and simplified those of the desires and passions. If acquiescence without insight; if warmth without light; if an immunity from doubt given and guaranteed by a resolute ignorance; if the habit of taking for granted the words of a catechism, remembered or forgotten; if a sensation of positiveness substituted, I will not say for certainty, but for that calm assurance the very means and conditions of which it supersedes; if a belief that seeks the darkness, and yet strikes no root, immovable as the limpet from its rock, and like the limpet fixed there by mere force of adhesion;—if these suffice to make us Christians, in what intelligible sense could our Lord have announced it as the height and consummation of the signs and miracles which attested His divinity that the Gospel was preached to the poor? In what sense could the Apostle affirm that believers have received, not indeed the wisdom of this world that comes to nought, but the wisdom of God, that we might know and comprehend the things that are freely given to us of God? or that every Christian, in proportion as he is indeed a Christian, has received the Spirit that searcheth all things, yea the deep things of God himself?—on what grounds could the Apostle denounce even the sincerest fervour of spirit as defective, where it does not bring forth fruits in the understanding?[1] Or again, if to believe were enough, why are we commanded by another Apostle that, 'besides this, giving all diligence we should add to our faith manly energy, and to manly energy knowledge'? Is it not especially significant that, in the divine economy as revealed to us in the New Testament, the peculiar office of Redemption is attributed to the Word, that is, to the intellectual wisdom which from all eternity is with God, and is God? that in *Him* is life, and the life is the *light* of men?

'Plain and simple' Christianity ineffective

In the present day we hear much, and from men of various creeds, of the plainness and simplicity of the Christian religion: [16] and a strange abuse has been made of these words, often indeed with no ill intention, but still oftener by men who would fain transform the necessity of believing in Christ into a recommendation to believe Him. . . . It is the interest of those men to speak of the Christian religion as comprised in a few plain

[1] Brethren, be not children in understanding: howbeit, in malice be ye children, but in understanding be men.

doctrines, and containing nothing not intelligible, at the first hearing, to men of the narrowest capacities. . . . Religion and politics, they tell us, require but the application of a common sense, which every man possesses, to a subject in which every man is concerned. 'To be a musician, an orator, a painter, or even a good mechanician, presupposes genius; to be an excellent artisan or mechanic requires more than an average degree of talent; but to be a legislator or a theologian, or both at once, demands nothing but common sense.' Now we willingly admit that nothing can be necessary to the salvation of a Christian which is not in his power. For such, therefore, as have neither the opportunity nor the capacity of learning more, sufficient, doubtless, will be the belief of those plain truths, and the fulfilment of those commands, which to be incapable of understanding is to be a man in appearance only. But ever to this scanty creed the disposition of faith must be added: and let it not be forgotten that, though nothing can be easier than to understand a code of belief, four-fifths of which consists in avowals of disbelief, and the remainder in truths concerning which (in this country at least) a man must have taken pains to learn to have any doubt; yet it is by no means easy to reconcile this code of negatives with the declarations of the Christian Scriptures. On the contrary, it requires all the resources of verbal criticism, and all the perverse subtlety of special pleading, to work out a plausible semblance of correspondency between them. It must, however, be conceded, that a man may consistently spare himself the trouble of the attempt, and leave the New Testament unread, after he has once thoroughly persuaded himself that it can teach him nothing of any real importance that he does not already know. St Paul indeed thought otherwise. For though he too teaches us, that in the religion of Christ there is milk for babes; yet he informs us at the same time that there is meat for strong men! and to the like purpose one of the Fathers has observed, that in the New Testament there are shallows where the lamb may ford, and depths where the elephant must swim. The Apostle exhorts the followers of Christ to the continual study of the new religion, on the ground that in the mystery of Christ which in other ages was not made known to the sons of men, and in the riches of Christ, which no research could exhaust, there were contained all the treasures of knowledge and wisdom. Accordingly, in that earnestness of spirit which his own personal experience of the truth inspired, he prays with a solemn and a ceremonious fervour that, being 'strengthened with might in the inner man, they may be able to comprehend with all saints what is the breadth and length and depth and height' of that living principle, at once the giver and the gift! of that anointing faith, which in endless evolution 'teaches us of all things, and is truth!' For all things are but parts and forms of its progressive manifestation, and every new knowledge but a new organ of sense and insight into this one all-inclusive verity, which, still filling the vessel of the understanding, still dilates it to a capacity of yet other and yet greater truths, and thus makes the soul feel its poverty by the very amplitude of its present, and the immensity of its reversionary, wealth. All truth indeed is simple, and needs no extrinsic ornament. And the more profound the truth is, the more simple: for the whole labour and building-up of knowledge is but one continued process of simplification. But I cannot comprehend in what ordinary sense of the words the properties of plainness and simplicity can be applied to the Prophets, or to the writings of St John, or to the epistles of St Paul; or what can have so marvellously improved the capacity of our laity beyond the same class of persons among the primitive Christians; who, as we are told by a fellow apostle, found in the writings last-mentioned many passages hard to be understood, which the unlearned, as well as the unstable, were in danger of wresting and misinterpreting. I can well understand, however, what is and has been the practical consequence of this notion. It is this very consequence indeed, that occasioned the preceding remarks, makes them pertinent to my present subject, and gives them a place in the train of argument requisite for its illustration. For what need of any after-recurrence to the sources of information concerning a religion, the whole contents of which can be thoroughly acquired at once and in a few hours? An occasional remembrancing may, perhaps, be expedient; but what object of study can a man propose to himself in a matter of which he knows all that can be known, all at least that it is of use to know? Like the first rules of arithmetic, its few plain and obvious truths may hourly serve the man's purposes, yet never once occupy his thoughts. But it is impossible that the affections should be kept constant to an object which gives no employment to the understanding. The energies of the intellect, increase of insight, and enlarging views, are necessary to keep alive the substantial faith in the heart. They are the appointed fuel to the sacred fire. . . . It is not probable that Christianity will have any direct influence on men who pay it no other compliment than that of calling by its name the previous dictates and decisions of their own mother-wit.

Religion and capitalism

But the more numerous class is of those who do not trouble themselves at all with religious matters, which they resign to the clergyman of the parish. But while not a few among these men consent to pray and hear by proxy, and while others, more attentive to the prudential advantages of a decorous character, yield the customary evidence of their church-membership, but, this performed, are at peace with themselves, and

> . . . think their Sunday's task
> As much as God or man can fairly ask;

Religion reduced to ethics, or prudential motives, consorts well with commercialism

there exists amongst the most respectable laity of our cities and great towns an active, powerful, and enlarging minority, whose industry, while it enriches their families, is at the same time a support to the revenue, and not seldom enlivens their whole neighbourhood: men whose lives are free from all desruptable infirmities, and of whose activity in the origination, patronage, and management both of charitable and of religious associations,—who must not have read or heard? and who that has, will dare deny to be most exemplary? After the custom of our forefathers, and their pure household religion,[1]

[1] And pure religion breathing household laws.—
WORDSWORTH

these, in so many respects estimable persons, are for the greater part in the habit of having family prayer and a portion of Scripture read every morning and evening. In this class, with such changes or substitutions as the peculiar tenets of the sect require, we must include the sensible, orderly, and beneficent Society of the Friends, more commonly called Quakers. Here then, if anywhere (that is, in any class of men, for the present argument is not concerned with individuals) we may expect to find Christianity tempering commercial avidity and sprinkling its holy damps on the passion of accumulation. This, I say, we might expect to find, if an undoubting belief in the threats and promises of Revelation, and a consequent regularity of personal, domestic, and social demeanour, sufficed to constitute that Christianity the power and privilege of which is so to renew and irradiate the whole intelligential and moral life of man, as to overcome the spirit of the world. (St John, Epistle I). If this, the appointed test, were found wanting, should we not be forced to apprehend, nay, are we not impelled to infer, that the spirit of prudential motive, however ennobled by the magnitude and awfulness of its objects, and though, as the termination of a lower, it may be the commencement (and not seldom the occasion) of an higher state, is not, even in respect of morality itself, that abiding and continuous principle of action which is either *one* with the faith spoken of by St Paul, or its immediate offspring. It cannot be that *spirit* of obedience to the commands of Christ, by which the soul dwelleth in Him, and He in it (I John iii. 4), and which our Saviour himself announces as a being born again. . . . To abstain from acts of wrong and violence, to be moreover industrious, useful, and of seemly bearing, are qualities presupposed in the Gospel code, as the preliminary conditions rather than the proper and peculiar effects of Christianity. But they are likewise qualities so palpably indispensable to the temporal interests of mankind that, if we except the brief frenzies of revolutionary riot, there never was a time in which the world did not profess to reverence them: nor can we state any period in which a more than ordinary character for assiduity, regularity, and charitableness did not secure the world's praise and favour, and were not calculated to advance the individual's own worldly interests: provided only, that his manners and professed tenets were those of some known and allowed body of men.

I ask, then, what is the fact? We are—and, till its good purposes, which are many, have been all achieved, and we can become something better, long may we continue such!—a busy, enterprising, and commercial nation. The habits attached to this character must, if there exist no adequate counterpoise, inevitably lead us under the specious names of utility, practical knowledge, and so forth, to look at all things through the medium of the market, and to estimate the worth of all pursuits and attainments by their marketable value. In this does the spirit of trade consist. Now would the general experience bear us out in the assertion that, amid the absence or declension of all other antagonist forces, there is found in the very circle of the trading and opulent themselves, in the increase, namely, of religious professors among them, a spring of resistance to the excess of the commercial impetus, from the impressive example of their unworldly feelings evidenced by their moderation in worldly pursuits? I fear that we may anticipate the answer, wherever the religious zeal of such professors does not likewise manifest itself, by the glad devotion of as large a portion of their time and industry as the duty of providing a fair competence for themselves and their families leaves at their own disposal, to the comprehension of those inspired writings and the evolution of those pregnant truths which are proposed for our earnest, sedulous research, in order that by occupying our understandings they may more and more assimilate our affections. I fear that the inquiring traveller would more often hear of zealous religionists who have read (and as a duty too and with all due acquiescence) the prophetic, 'Woe to them that join house to house and lay field to field, that they may be alone in the land!' and yet find no object deform the beauty of the prospect from their window or even from their castle turrets so annoyingly as a meadow not their own, or a field under ploughing with the beam-end of the plough in the hands of its humble owner! I fear that he must too often make report of men lawful in their dealings, scriptural in their language, alms-givers, and patrons of Sunday schools, who are yet resistless and overawing bidders at all land auctions in their neighbourhood, who live in the centre of farms without leases, and tenants without attachments! Or if his way should lie through our great towns and manufacturing districts, instances would grow cheap with him of wealthy religious practitioners, who never travel for orders without cards of edification in prose and verse, and small tracts of admonition and instruction, all 'plain and easy, and suited to the meanest capacities'; who pray daily, as the first act of the morning and as the last of the evening, Lead us not into temptation, but deliver us from evil: and employ all the interval with an edge of appetite keen as the scythe of death in the pursuit of yet more and yet more of a temptation so perilous, that (as they have full often read, and heard read, without the least questioning, or whisper of doubt) no power short of Omnipotence could make their deliverance from it credible or conceivable. Of all denominations of Christians, there is not one in existence or on record whose whole scheme of faith and worship was so expressly framed for the one purpose of spiritualizing the mind and of abstracting it from the vanities of the world, as the Society of Friends! not one, in which the church members are connected, and their professed principles enforced, by so effective and wonderful a form of discipline. But in the zeal of their founders and first proselytes for perfect spirituality they excluded from their system all ministers specially trained and educated for the ministry, with all professional theologians: and they omitted to provide for the raising up among themselves any other established class of learned men, as teachers and schoolmasters, for instance, in their stead. Even at this day, though the Quakers are in general remarkably shrewd and intelligent in all worldly concerns, yet learning, and more particularly theological learning, is more rare among them in proportion to their wealth and rank in life, and held in less value, than among any other known sect of Christians. What has been the result?

Quaker business-men

If the occasion permitted, I could dilate with pleasure on their decent manners and decorous morals, as individuals, and their exemplary and truly illustrious philanthropic efforts as a body. From all the gayer and tinsel vanities of the world their discipline has preserved them, and the English character owes to their example some part of its manly plainness in externals. But my argument is confined to the question, whether religion in its present state and under the present conceptions of its demands and purposes does, even among the most religious, exert any efficient force of control over the commercial spirit, the excess of which we have attributed, not to the extent and magnitude of the commerce itself, but to the absence or imperfection of its appointed checks and counter-agents. Now as the system of the Friends in its first intention is of all others most hostile to worldly-mindedness on the one hand, and as, on the other, the adherents of this system both in confession and practice confine Christianity to feelings and motives, they may be selected as representatives of the strict but unstudied and uninquiring religionists of every denomination. Their characteristic propensities will supply, therefore, no unfair test for the degree of resistance which our present Christianity is capable of opposing to the cupidity of a trading people—that species of Christianity I mean, which, as far as knowledge and and the faculties of thought are concerned—which, as far as the growth and grandeur of the intellectual man is in question—is to be learnt extempore! A Christianity poured in on the catechumen all and all at once, as from a shower-bath: and which, whatever it may be in the heart, yet for the understanding and reason is from boyhood onward a thing past and perfected! If the almost universal opinion be tolerably correct, the question is answered. But I by no means appropriate the remark to the wealthy Quakers, or even apply it to them in any particular or eminent sense, when I say that, often as the motley reflexes of my experience move in a long procession of manifold groups before me, the distinguished and world-honoured company of Christian mammonists appear to the eye of my imagination as a drove of camels heavily laden, yet all at full speed, and each in the confident expectation of passing through the eye of the needle, without stop or halt, both beast and baggage.

Not without an uneasy reluctance have I ventured to tell the truth on this subject, lest I should be charged with the indulgence of a satirical mood and an uncharitable spleen. But my conscience bears me witness, and I know myself too near the grave to trifle with its name, that I am solely actuated by a sense of the exceeding importance of the subject at the present moment. I feel it an awful duty to exercise the honest liberty of free utterance in so dear a concernment as that of preparing my country for a change in its external relations, which must come sooner or later; which I believe to have already commenced; and that it will depend on the presence or absence of a corresponding change in the mind of the nation, and above all in the aims and ruling opinions of our gentry and moneyed men, whether it is to cast down our strength and prosperity, or to fix them on a firmer and more august basis. 'Surely to every good and peaceable man it must in nature needs be a hateful thing to be the displeaser and molester of thousands; but when God commands to take the trumpet and blow a dolorous or a jarring blast, it lies not in man's will what he shall say and what he shall conceal.'

Summary Thus, then, of the three most approved antagonists to the spirit of barter, and the accompanying disposition to overvalue riches with all the means and tokens thereof—of the three fittest and most likely checks to this tendency, namely, the feeling of ancient birth and the respect paid to it by the community at large; a genuine intellectual philosophy, with an accredited, learned, and philosophic class; and, lastly, religion; we have found the first declining, the second not existing, and the third efficient, indeed, in many respects and to many excellent purposes, only not in this particular direction: the religion here spoken of having long since parted company with that inquisitive and bookish theology which tends to defraud the student of his worldy wisdom, inasmuch as it diverts his mind from the accumulation of wealth by pre-occupying his thoughts in the acquisition of knowledge. For the religion of best repute among us holds all the truths of Scripture and all the doctrines of Christianity so very transcendent, or so very easy, as to make study and research either vain or needless. It professes, therefore, to hunger and thirst after righteousness alone, and the rewards of the righteous; and thus habitually taking for granted all truths of spiritual import, leaves the understanding vacant and at leisure for a thorough insight into present and temporal interests, which doubtless, is the true reason why its followers are in general such shrewd, knowing, wary, well-informed, thrifty, and thriving men of business. But this is likewise the reason why it neither does nor can check or circumscribe the spirit of barter; and to the consequent monopoly which this commercial spirit possesses must its overbalance be attributed, not to the extent or magnitude of the commerce itself.

Historical growth of over-balance of the spirit of trade

Before I enter on the result assigned by me as the chief ultimate cause of the present state of the country, and as the main ground on which the immediate occasions of the general distress have worked, I must entreat my readers to reflect that the spirit of trade has been a thing of insensible growth; that whether it be enough, or more or less than enough, is a matter of relative rather than of positive determination; that it depends on the degree in which it is aided or resisted by all the other tendencies that co-exist with it; and that in the best of times this spirit may be said to live on a narrow isthmus between a sterile desert and a stormy sea, still threatened and encroached on either by the too much or the too little. As the argument does not depend on any precise accuracy in the dates, I shall assume it to have commenced, as an influencing part of the national character, with the institution of the funds in the reign of William the Third; and from the peace of Aix-la-Chapelle in 1748, to have been hurrying onward to its maximum, which it seems to have attained during the late war. The short interruptions may be well represented as a few steps backward, that it might leap forward with an additional momentum. The words, old and modern, then and now, are applied by me, the latter to the whole period since the Revolution, and the former to the interval between this epoch and the Reformation; the one from 1460 to 1680, the other from 1680 to the present time. [17]

Why are the antidotes less effective now than formerly?

Having premised this explanation, I can now return an intelligible answer to a question that will have arisen in the reader's mind during his perusal of the last three or four pages. How, it will be objected, does all this apply to the present times in particular? When was the industrious part of mankind not attached to the pursuits most likely to reward their industry? Was the wish to make a fortune, or, if you prefer an invidious phrase, the lust of lucre, less natural to our forefathers than to their descendants? If you say that, though a not less frequent or less powerful passion with them than with us, it yet met with a more frequent and more powerful check, a stronger and more advanced boundary-line, in the religion of old times, and in the faith, fashion, habits, and authority of the religious: in what did this difference consist? and in what way did these points of difference act? If, indeed, the antidote in question once possessed virtues which it no longer possesses, or not in the same degree, what is the ingredient, either added, omitted, or diminished since that time, which can have rendered it less efficacious now than then?

Well (I might reply), grant all this: and let both the profession and the professors of a spiritual principle, as a counterpoise to the worldly weights at the other end of the balance, be supposed much the same in the one period as in the other. Assume, for a moment, that I can establish neither the fact of its lesser efficiency, nor any points of difference capable of accounting for it. Yet it might still be a sufficient answer to this objection that, as the commerce of the country, and with it the spirit of commerce, has increased fifty-fold since the commencement of the latter period, it is not enough that the counter-weight should be as great as it was in the former period: to remain the same in its effect, it ought to have become very much greater. But though this be a consideration not less important than it is obvious, yet I do not purpose to rest in it.

I affirm that a difference may be shown, and of no trifling importance as to that one point, to which my present argument is confined. For let it be remembered that it is not to any extraordinary influences of the religious principle that I am referring, not to voluntary poverty, or sequestration from social and active life, or schemes of mortification. I speak of religion merely as I should of any worldly object, which as far as it employs and interests a man, leaves less room in his mind for other pursuits: except that this must be more especially the case in the instance of religion, because beyond all other interests it is calculated to occupy the whole mind, and employ successively all the faculties of man; and because the objects which it presents to the imagination as well as to the intellect cannot be actually contemplated, much less can they be the subject of frequent meditation, without dimming the lustre and blunting the rays of all rival attractions. It is well known, and has been observed of old, that poetry tends to render its devotees careless of money and outward appearances, while philosophy inspired a contempt of both as objects of desire or admiration. But religion is the poetry and philosophy of all mankind; unites in itself whatever is most excellent in either, and, while it at one and the same time calls into action and supplies with the noblest materials both the imaginative and the intellective faculties, superadds the interests of the most substantial and home-felt reality to both, to the poetic vision and the philosophic idea. [18] But in order to produce a similar effect it must act in a similar way: it must reign in the thoughts of a man, and in the powers akin to thought, as well as exercise an admitted influence over his hopes and fears and through these on his deliberate and individual acts.

Decline of intellectual weight of ecclesiastical writings and sermons

Now as my first presumptive proof of a difference (I might almost have said, of a contrast) between the religious character of the period since the Revolution, and that of the period from the accession of Edward the Sixth to the abdication of the second James, I refer to the sermons and to the theological works generally of the latter period. It is my full conviction, that in any half-dozen sermons of Dr Donne, or Jeremy

Taylor, there are more thoughts, more facts and images, more excitements to inquiry and intellectual effort, than are presented to the congregations of the present day in as many churches or meetings during twice as many months. Yet both these were the most popular preachers of their times, were heard with enthusiasm by crowded and promiscuous audiences, and the effect produced by their eloquence was held in reverential and affectionate remembrance by many attendants on their ministry, who, like the pious Isaac Walton, were not themselves men of learning or education. In addition to this fact, think likewise on the large and numerous editions of massy, closely printed folios: the impressions so large and the editions so numerous, that all the industry of destruction for the last hundred years has but of late sufficed to make them rare. From the long list select those works alone which we know to have been the most current and favourite works of their day: and of these again no more than may well be supposed to have had a place in the scantiest libraries, or perhaps, with the Bible and Common Prayer Book, to have formed the library of their owner. Yet on the single shelf so filled we should find almost every possible question that could interest or instruct a reader whose whole heart was in his religion, discussed with a command of intellect that seems to exhaust all the learning and logic, all the historical and moral relations, of each several subject. The very length of the discourses, with which these 'rich souls of wit and knowledge' fixed the eyes, ears, and hearts of their crowded congregations, are a source of wonder now-a-days, and (we may add) of self-congratulation, to many a sober Christian, who forgets with what delight he himself has listened to a two hours' harangue on a loan or tax, or at the trial of some remarkable cause or culprit. The transfer of the interest makes and explains the whole difference. For though much may be fairly charged on the Revolution in the mode of preaching as well as in the matter, since the fresh morning and fervent noon of the Reformation, when there was no need to visit the conventicles of fanaticism in order to

See God's ambassador in the pulpit stand,
Where they could take notes from his look and hand;
And from his speaking action bear away
More sermon than our preachers use to say;

yet this too must be referred to the same change in the habits of men's minds—a change that involves both the shepherd and the flock: though, like many other effects, it tends to reproduce and strengthen its own cause.

Decline of warmth and frequency of religious controversy

The last point to which I shall appeal is the warmth and frequency of the religious controversies during the former of the two periods; the deep interest excited by them among all but the lowest and most ignorant classes; the importance attached to them by the very highest; the number, and in many instances the transcendent merit, of the controversial publications—in short, the rank and value assigned to polemic divinity. The subjects of the controversies may or may not have been trifling; the warmth with which they were conducted may have been disproportionate and indecorous; and we may have reason to congratulate ourselves that the age in which we live is grown more indulgent and less captious. The fact is introduced not for its own sake, but as a symptom of the general state of men's feelings, as an evidence of the direction and main channel, in which the thoughts and interests of men were then flowing. We all know, that lovers are apt to take offence and wrangle with each other on occasions that perhaps are but trifles, and which assuredly would appear such to those who had never been under the influence of a similar passion. These quarrels may be no proofs of wisdom; but still in the imperfect state of our nature the entire absence of the same, and this too on far more serious provocations, would excite a strong suspicion of a comparative indifference in the feelings of the parties towards each other, who can love so coolly where they profess to love so well. I shall believe our present religious tolerancy to proceed from the abundance of our charity and good sense, when I can see proofs that we are equally cool and forbearing, as litigators and political partisans. And I must again entreat my reader to recollect, that the present argument is exclusively concerned with the requisite correctives of the commercial spirit, and with religion therefore no otherwise than as a countercharm to the sorcery of wealth: and my main position is, that neither by reasons drawn from the nature of the human mind, or by facts of actual experience, are we justified in expecting this from a religion which does not employ and actuate the understandings of men, and combine their affections with it as a system of truth gradually and progressively manifesting itself to the intellect; no less than as a system of motives and moral commands learnt as soon as heard, and containing nothing but what is plain and easy to the lowest capacities. Hence it is, that objects, the ostensible principle of which I have felt it my duty to oppose (*vide* the *Statesman's Manual*), and objects the which, and the measures for the attainment of which, possess my good wishes and have had the humble tribute of my public advocation and applause—I am here alluding to the British and Foreign Bible Society—may yet converge, as to the point now in question. They may, both alike, be symptoms of the same predominant disposition to that Coalition system in Christianity, [19] for the expression of which theologians have invented or appropriated the term *Syncretism*: although the former may be an ominous, the latter an auspicious symptom, though the one may be worse from bad, while the other is an instance of good educed from evil. Nay, I will dare confess, that I know not how to think otherwise, when I hear a Bishop of an established Church publicly exclaim (and not viewing it as a lesser inconvenience to be endured for the attainment of a far greater good, but as a thing desirable and to be preferred for its own sake), 'No notes! No comment! Distribute the Bible and the Bible only among the poor!'—a declaration, which from any lower quarter I should have been under the temptation of attributing either to a fanatical notion of immediate illumination superseding the necessity of human teaching, or to an ignorance of difficulties which (and what more worthy?) have successfully employed all the learning, sagacity, and unwearied labours of great and wise men and eminent servants of Christ during all

Defects of Undenominational religious instruction

the ages of Christianity, and will doubtless continue to yield new fruits of knowledge and insight to a long series of followers.

Revolutions of credit: the trade-cycle

Though an overbalance of the commercial spirit is involved in the deficiency of its counter-weights, yet the facts that exemplify the mode and extent of its operation will afford a more direct and satisfactory kind of proof. And first I am to speak of this over-balance as displayed in the commercial world itself. But as this is the first, so is it for my present purpose the least important point of view. A portion of the facts belonging to this division of the subject I have already noticed; and for the remainder let the following suffice as the substitute or representative. The moral of the tale I leave to the reader's own reflections. Within the last sixty years, or perhaps a somewhat larger period (for I do not pretend to any nicety of dates, and the documents are of easy access), there have occurred, at intervals of about twelve or thirteen years each, certain periodical revolutions of credit. [20] Yet revolution is not the precise word. To state the thing as it is, I ought to have said, certain gradual expansions of credit ending in sudden contractions, or, with equal propriety, ascensions to a certain utmost possible height, which has been different in each successive instance; but in every instance the attainment of this, its *ne plus ultra*, has been instantly announced by a rapid series of explosions (in mercantile language, a crash), and a consequent precipitation of the general system. For a short time this Icarian credit, or rather this illegitimate offspring of confidence, to which it stands in the same relation as Phaethon to his parent god in the old fable, seems to lie stunned by the fall; but soon recovering, again it strives upward, and having once more regained its mid-region,

> Thence many a league,
> As in a cloudy chair, ascending rides
> Audacious! PARADISE LOST

till at the destined zenith of its vaporous exaltation, 'all unawares, fluttering its pennons vain, plump down it drops!' Or that I may descend myself to the 'cool element of prose,' alarm and suspicion gradually diminish into a judicious circumspectness; but by little and little, circumspection gives way to the desire and emulous ambition of doing business; till impatience and incaution on one side, tempting and encouraging headlong adventure, want of principle, and confederacies of false credit on the other, the movements of trade become yearly gayer and giddier, and end at length in a vortex of hopes and hazards, of blinding passions and blind practices, which should have been left, where alone they ought ever to have been found, among the wicked lunacies of the gaming-table.

I am not ignorant that the power and circumstantial prosperity of the nation has been increasing during the same period, with an accelerated force unprecedented in any country, the population of which bore the same proportion to its productive soil: and partly, perhaps, even in consequence of this system. By facilitating the means of enterprise, it must have called into activity a multitude of enterprising individuals and a variety of talent that would otherwise have lain dormant: while by the same ready supply of excitements to labour, together with its materials and instruments, even an unsound credit has been able within a short time to substantiate itself. We shall, perhaps, be told too that the very evils of this system, even the periodical crash itself, are to be regarded but as so much superfluous steam ejected by the escape pipes and safety valves of a self-regulating machine: and lastly, that in a free and trading country all things find their level. . . .

The 'self-adjusting economic machine' a menace to human personality

Much I still concede to the arguments for the present scheme of things as adduced in the preceding paragraph: but I likewise see, and always have seen, much that needs winnowing. Thus, instead of the position that all things find, it would be less equivocal and far more descriptive of the fact to say that things are always finding their level: which might be taken as the paraphrase or ironical definition of a storm. . . . But persons are not things—but man does not find his level. Neither in body nor in soul does the man find his level! After a hard and calamitous season, during which the thousand wheels of some vast manufactory had remained silent as a frozen waterfall, be it that plenty has returned and that trade has once more become brisk and stirring: go, ask the overseer, and question the parish doctor, whether the workman's health and temperance with the staid and respectful manners best taught by the inward dignity of conscious self-support, have found their level again? Alas! I have more than once seen a group of children in Dorsetshire, during the heat of the dog-days, each with its little shoulders up to its ears, and its chest pinched inward—the very habit and fixtures, as it were, that had been impressed on their frames by the former ill-fed, ill-clothed, and unfuelled winters. But as with the body, so or still worse with the mind. Nor is the effect confined to the labouring classes, whom by an ominous but too appropriate a change in our phraseology we are now accustomed to call the labouring poor. I cannot persuade myself that the frequency of failures with all the disgraceful secrets of fraud and folly, of unprincipled vanity in expending and desperate speculation in retrieving, can be familiarized to the thoughts and experience of men, as matters of daily occurrence, without serious injury to the moral sense: more especially in times when bankruptcies spread like a fever, at once contagious and epidemic; swift too as the travel of an earthquake, that with one and the same chain of shocks opens the ruinous chasm in cities that have an ocean between them! —in times when the fate flies swifter than the fear, and yet the report that follows the flash has a ruin of its own, and arrives but to multiply the blow!—when princely capitals are often but the telegraphs of distant calamity: and still worse, when no man's treasure is safe who has adopted the ordinary means of safety, neither the high nor the humble; when the lord's rents and the farmer's store, entrusted perhaps but as yesterday, are asked after at closed doors!—but worst of all, in its moral influences as well as in the cruelty of suffering, when the old labourer's savings, the precious robberies of self-denial from every day's comfort; when the orphan's funds, the widow's livelihood, the fond confiding sister's humble fortune, are found among the victims to the remorseless mania of dishonest speculation, or to the desperate cowardice of embarrassment, and the drunken stupor of a usurious selfishness that for a few months' respite dares incur a debt of guilt and infamy, for which the grave itself can plead no statute of limitation. Name to me any revolution recorded in history that was not followed by a depravation of the national morals. The Roman character during the Triumvirate, and under Tiberius, the reign of Charles the Second, and Paris at the present moment, are obvious instances. What is the main cause? The sense of insecurity. On what ground, then, dare we hope that, with the same accompaniment, commercial revolutions should not produce the same effect in proportion to the extent of their sphere?

Increase of life, and of the means of life—for what?

But these blessings, with all the specific terms, into which this most comprehensive phrase is to be resolved? Dare we unpack the bales and cases so marked, and look at the articles, one by one? Increase of human life and increase of the means of life are, it is true, reciprocally cause and effect: and the genius of commerce and manufacture has been the cause of both to a degree that may well excite our wonder. But do the last results justify our exultation likewise? Human life, alas! is but the malleable metal, out of which the thievish picklock, the slave's collar, and the assassin's stiletto are formed, as well as the clearing axe, the feeding ploughshare, the defensive sword, and the mechanic tool. But the subject is a painful one: and fortunately the labours of others, with the communications of medical men concerning the state of the manufacturing poor, have rendered it unnecessary. I will rather (though in strict method it should perhaps be reserved for the following head) relate a speech made to me near Fort Augustus, as I was travelling on foot through the Highlands of Scotland. [21] The speaker was an elderly and respectable widow, who expressed herself with that simple eloquence which strong feeling seldom fails to call forth in humble life, but especially in women. She spoke English, as indeed most Highlanders do who speak it at all, with a propriety of phrase and a discrimination of tone and emphasis that more than compensated for the scantiness of her

A voice from the Highlands

vocabulary. After an affecting account of her own wrongs and ejectment (which however, she said, bore with comparative lightness on her, who had had saved up for her a wherewithal to live, and was blessed with a son well to do in the world), she made a movement with her hand in a circle, directing my eye meanwhile to various objects as marking its outline: and then observed, with a deep sigh and a suppressed and slow voice which she suddenly raised and quickened after the first drop or cadence—'Within this space—how short a time back! —there lived a hundred and seventy-three persons: and now there is only a shepherd, and an underling or two. Yes, sir! One hundred and seventy-three Christian souls, man, woman, boy, girl, and babe; and in almost every home an old man by the fire-side, who would tell you of the troubles, before our roads were made; and many a brave youth among them who loved the birthplace of his forefathers, yet would swing about his broad-sword and want but a word to march off to the battles over sea; aye, sir, and many a good lass, who had a respect for herself. Well, but they are gone, and with them the bristled bear,[1] and the pink haver,[2] and the potato plot that looked as gay as any flower-garden with its blossoms! I sometimes fancy that the very birds are gone—all but the crows and the gleads! Well, and what then? Instead of us all, there is one shepherd man, and it may be a pair of small lads—and a many, many sheep! And do you think, sir, that God allows of such proceedings?'

Some days before this conversation, and while I was on the shores of Loch Katrine,[3] I had heard of a sad counterpart to the widow's tale, and told with a far fiercer indignation, of a 'Laird who had raised a company from the country found about for the love that was borne to his name, and who gained high

[1] A species of barley. [2] A species of oats.

[3] The lake so widely celebrated since then by a poet, to whose writings a larger number of persons have owed a larger portion of innocent, refined, and heart-bettering amusement than perhaps to any favourite of the Muses recorded in English literature: while the most learned of his readers must feel grateful for the mass of interesting and highly instructive information scattered throughout his works, in which respect Southey is his only rival.

preferment in consequence: and that it was but a small part of those that he took away whom he brought back again. And what were the thanks which the folks had both for those that came back with him, some blind and more in danger of blindness, and for those that had perished in the hospitals, and for those that fell in battle, fighting before or beside him? Why, that their fathers were all turned out of their farms before the year was over, and sent to wander like so many gipsies, unless they would consent to shed their gray hairs, at tenpence a day, over the new canals. Had there been a price set upon his head, and his enemies had been coming upon him, he needed but have whistled, and a hundred brave lads would have made a wall of flame round about him with the flash of their broadswords! Now if the French should come among us, as (it is said) they will, let him whistle to his sheep and see if they will fight for him!' The frequency with which I heard, during my solitary walk from the end of Loch Lomond to Inverness, confident expectations of the kind expressed in his concluding words—nay, far too often eager hopes mingled with vindictive resolves—I spoke of with complaint and regret to an elderly man, whom by his dress and way of speaking I took to be a schoolmaster. Long shall I recollect his reply: 'O, sir, it kills a man's love for his country, the hardships of life coming by change and with injustice!' I was some time afterwards told by a very sensible person who had studied the mysteries of political economy, and was therefore entitled to be listened to, that more food was produced in consequence of this revolution, that the mutton must be eat somewhere, and what difference where? If three were fed at Manchester instead of two at Glencoe or the Trosachs, the balance of human enjoyment was in favour of the former. I have passed through many a manufacturing town since then, and have watched many a group of old and young, male and female, going to, or returning from, many a factory, but I could never yet persuade myself to be of his opinion. Men, I still think, ought to be weighed, not counted. Their worth ought to be the final estimate of their value.

Men should be weighed, not counted

Effects of economic changes on class structure

The universal practice of enhancing the sale price of every article on the presumption of bad debts . . . is mentioned here . . . as one of the appendages to the twin paramount causes, the paper currency and the national debt, and for the sake of the conjoint results. Would we learn what these results are? What they have been in the higher, and what in the most numerous, class of society? Alas! that some of the intermediate rounds in the social ladder have been broken and not replaced, is itself one of these results. Retrace the progress of things from 1792 to 1813, when the tide was at its height, and then, as far as its rapidity will permit, the ebb from its first turn to the dead low-water mark of the last quarter. Then see whether the remainder may not be generalized under the following heads. Fluctuation in the wages of labour, alternate privation and excess (not in all at the same time, but successively in each), consequent improvidence, and over all discontent and a system of factious confederacy—these form the history of the mechanics and lower ranks of our cities and towns. In the country, a peasantry sinking into pauperism, step for step with the rise of the farmer's profits and indulgences. On the side of the landlord and his compeers, we shall find the presence of the same causes attested by answerable effects. Great as 'their almost magical effects' on the increase of prices were in the necessaries of life, they were still greater, disproportionally greater, in all articles of show and luxury. With few exceptions, it soon became difficult, and at length impracticable, for the gentry of the land, for the possessors of fixed property to retain the rank of their ancestors, or their own former establishments, without joining in the general competition under the influence of the same trading spirit. Their dependents were of course either selected from, or driven into, the same eddy; while the temptation of obtaining more than the legal interest for their principal became more and more strong with all persons who, neither trading nor farming, had lived on the interest of their fortunes. It was in this latter class that the rash, and too frequently the unprincipled, projector found his readiest dupes. Had we but the secret history of the building speculations only in the

Extension of the spirit of trade to agriculture

vicinity of the metropolis, too many of its pages would supply an afflicting but instructive comment. That both here, and in all other departments, this increased momentum in the spirit of trade has been followed by results of the most desirable nature, I have myself exerted my best powers to evince, at a period when to present the fairest and most animating features of the system, and to prove their vast and charm-like influence on the power and resources of the nation, appeared a duty of patriotism. Nothing, however, was advanced incompatible with the position, which even then I did not conceal, and which from the same sense of duty I am now attempting to display; namely, that the extension of the commercial spirit into our agricultural system, added to the overbalance of the same spirit, even within its own sphere, aggravated by the operation of our revenue laws, and finally reflected in the habits and tendencies of the labouring classes, is the groundwork of our calamity, and the main predisposing cause, without which the late occasions would (some of them not have existed, and the remainder) not have produced the present distresses.

Peculiar character of landed property

That agriculture requires principles essentially different from those of trade,—that a gentleman ought not to regard his estate as a merchant his cargo, or a shopkeeper his stock,—admits of an easy proof from the different tenure of landed property, [22] and from the purposes of agriculture itself, which ultimately are the same as those of the State of which it is the offspring. (For we do not include in the name of agriculture the cultivation of a few vegetables by the women of the less savage hunter tribes.) If the continuance and independence of the State be its object, the final causes of the State must be its final causes. We suppose the negative ends of a State already attained, viz. its own safety by means of its own strength, and the protection of person and property for all its members, there will then remain its positive ends: 1. To make the means of subsistence more easy to each individual. 2. To secure to each of its members the hope of bettering his own condition or that of his children. 3. The development of those faculties which are essential to his

Positive ends of the State

humanity, i.e. to his rational and moral being. Under the last head we do not mean those degrees of intellectual cultivation which distinguish man from man in the same civilized society, but those only that raise the civilized man above the barbarian, the savage, and the animal. We require, however, on the part of the State, in behalf of all its members, not only the outward means of knowing their essential duties and dignities as men and free men, but likewise, and more especially, the discouragement of all such tenures and relations as must in the very nature of things render this knowledge inert, and cause the good seed to perish as it falls. Such at least is the appointed aim of a State: and at whatever distance from the ideal mark the existing circumstances of a nation may unhappily place the actual statesman, still every movement ought to be in this direction. But the negative merit of not fowarding—the exemption from the crime of necessitating—the debasement and virtual disfranchisement of any class of the community, may be demanded of every State under all circumstances: and the government that pleads difficulties in repulse or demur of this claim impeaches its own wisdom and fortitude. [23] But as the specific ends of agriculture are the maintenance, strength, and security of the State, so (we repeat) must its ultimate ends be the same as those of the State: even as the ultimate end of the spring and wheels of a watch must be the same as that of the watch. Yet least of all things dare we overlook or conceal that, morally and with respect to the character and conscience of the individuals, the blame of unfaithful stewardship is aggravated in proportion as the difficulties are less and the consequences lying within a narrower field of vision are more evident and affecting. An injurious system, the connivance at which we scarcely dare more than regret in the cabinet or senate of an empire, may justify an earnest reprobation in the management of private estates: provided always, that the system only be denounced, and the pleadings confined to the court of conscience. For from this court only can the redress be awarded. All reform or innovation, not won from the free agent by the presentation of juster views and nobler interests, and that does

Specific ends of agriculture are the ends of the State itself

Voluntary reform the best reform

not leave the merit of having effected it sacred to the individual proprietor, it were folly to propose, and worse than folly to attempt. Madmen only would dream of digging or blowing up the foundation of a house in order to employ the materials in repairing the walls. Nothing more dare be asked of the State, no other duty is imposed on it, than to withhold or retract all extrinsic and artificial aids to an injurious system; or at the utmost to invalidate in extreme cases such claims as have arisen indirectly from the letter or unforeseen operations of particular statutes: claims that, instead of being contained in the rights of its proprietary trustees, are incroachments on its own rights, and a destructive trespass on a part of its own inalienable and untransferable property—I mean the health, strength, honesty, and filial love of its children.

Grounds and limits of State intervention

Marketable produce of the land less important than a healthy rural population

It would border on an affront to the understandings of our landed interest, were I to explain in detail what the plan and conduct would be of a gentleman; if, as the result of his own free conviction, the marketable produce of his estates were made a subordinate consideration to the living and moral growth that is to remain on the land. I mean a healthful, callous-handed, but high and warm-hearted tenantry, twice the number of the present landless, parish-paid labourers, and ready to march off at the first call to their country with a son of the house at their head, because under no apprehension of being (forgive the lowness of the expression) marched off at the whisper of a land-taster! If the admitted rule, the paramount self-commandment, were comprised in the fixed resolve—I will improve my estate to the utmost; and my rent-roll I will raise as much as, but no more than, is compatible with the three great ends (before enumerated), which being those of my country must be mine inclusively! This, I repeat, it would be more than superfluous to particularize. It is a problem the solution of which may be safely entrusted to the common sense of every one who has the hardihood to ask himself the question. But how encouraging even the approximations to such a system, of what fair promise the few fragmentary samples are, may be seen in the Report of the Board of Agriculture for 1816,

[24] p.11, from the Earl of Winchelsea's communication, in every paragraph of which wisdom seems to address us in behalf of goodness.

'To buy in cheapest and sell in dearest market' a legitimate maxim of trade

But the plan of my argument requires the reverse of this picture. I am to ask what the results would be, on the supposition that agriculture is carried on in the spirit of trade; and if the necessary answer coincide with the known general practice, to show the connection of the consequences with the present state of distress and uneasiness. In trade, from its most innocent form to the abomination of the African commerce, nominally abolished after a hard-fought battle of twenty years, no distinction is or can be acknowledged between things and persons. If the latter are part of the concern, they come under the denomination of the former. Two objects only can be proposed in the management of an estate, considered as a stock in trade—first, that the returns should be the largest, quickest, and securest possible; and secondly, with the least out-goings in the providing, overlooking, and collecting the same—whether it be expenditure of money paid for other men's time and attention, or of the tradesman's own, which are to him money's worth, makes no difference in the argument. Am I disposing of a bale of goods? The man whom I most love and esteem must yield to the stranger that outbids him; or if it be sold on credit, the highest price, with equal security, must have the preference. I may fill up the deficiency of my friend's offer by a private gift or loan; but as a tradesman, I am bound to regard honesty and established character themselves as things, as securities, for which the known unprincipled dealer may offer an unexceptionable substitute. Add to this that, the security being equal, I shall prefer, even at a considerable abatement of price, the man who will take a thousand chests or bales at once, to twenty who can pledge themselves only for fifty each. For I do not seek trouble for its own sake; but among other advantages I seek wealth for the sake of freeing myself more and more from the necessity of taking trouble in order to attain it. The personal worth of those, whom I benefit in the course of the process, or whether the persons are really benefited or

Consequences of application of this maxim to agriculture

no, is no concern of mine. The market and the shop are open to all. To introduce any other principle in trade, but that of obtaining the highest price with adequate security for articles fairly described, would be tantamount to the position that trade ought not to exist. If this be admitted, then, what as a tradesman I cannot do it cannot be my duty, as a tradesman, to attempt: and the only remaining question in reason or morality is—what are the proper objects of trade? If my estate be such, my plan must be to make the most of it, as I would of any other mode of capital. As my rents will ultimately depend on the quantity and value of the produce raised and brought into the best market from my land, I will entrust the latter to those who, bidding the most, have the largest capital to employ on it: and this I cannot effect but by dividing it into the fewest tenures, as none but extensive farms will be an object to men of extensive capital and enterprising minds. I must prefer this system likewise for my own ease and security. The farmer is of course actuated by the same motives as the landlord: and, provided they are both faithful to their engagements, the objects of both will be: 1, the utmost produce that can be raised without injuring the estate; 2, with the least possible consumption of the produce on the estate itself; 3, at the lowest wages; and 4, with the substitution of machinery for human labour wherever the former will cost less and do the same work. What are the modest remedies proposed by the majority of correspondents in the last Report of the Board of Agriculture? Let measures be taken, that rents, taxes, and wages be lowered, and the markets raised! A great calamity has befallen us, from importation, the lessened purchases of government, and 'the evil of a superabundant harvest'—of which we deem ourselves the more entitled to complain, because, 'we had been long making 112 shillings per quarter of our corn', and of all other articles in proportion. As the best remedies for this calamity, we propose that we should pay less to our landlords, less to our labourers, nothing to our clergymen, and either nothing or very little to the maintenance of the government and of the poor; but that we should sell at our former prices to the

The poor laws

consumer!—In almost every page we find deprecations of the poor laws: and I hold it impossible to exaggerate their pernicious tendency and consequences. But let it not be forgotten, that in agricultural districts three-fourths of the poor rates are paid to healthy, robust, and (O sorrow and shame!) industrious hard-working paupers in lieu of wages [25] (for men cannot at once work and starve): and therefore if there are twenty housekeepers in the parish, who are not holders of land, their contributions are so much bounty money to the latter. But the poor laws form a subject, which I should not undertake without trembling, had I the space of a whole volume to allot to it. Suffice, that this enormous mischief is undeniably the offspring of the commercial system. In the only plausible work, that I have seen, in favour of our poor laws on the present plan, the defence is grounded, first, on the expediency of having labour cheap, and estates let out in the fewest possible portions—in other words, of large farms and low wages—each as indispensable to the other, and both conjointly as the only means of drawing capital to the land, by which alone the largest surplus is attainable for the State: that is, for the market, or in order that the smallest possible proportion of the largest possible produce may be consumed by the raisers and their families! secondly, on the impossibility of supplying, as we have supplied, all the countries of the civilized world (India perhaps and China excepted), and of underselling them even in their own markets, if our working manufacturers were not secured by the State against the worse consequences of those failures, stagnations, and transfers, to which the different branches of trade are exposed, in a greater or less degree, beyond all human prevention; or if the master manufacturers were compelled to give previous security for the maintenance of these whom they had, by the known law of human increase, virtually called into existence....

Spirit of commerce capable of being counteracted by the spirit of the State

I have already denied, and I now repeat the denial, that these are necessary consequences of our extended commerce. On the contrary, I feel assured that the spirit of commerce is itself capable of being at once counteracted and enlightened by the spirit of the State, to the advantage of both. But I do assert that they are necessary consequences of the commercial spirit uncounteracted and unenlightened, wherever trade has been carried to so vast an extent as it has been in England. I assert too, historically and as a matter of fact, that they have been the consequence of our commercial system. . . . But we have shewn that the same system has gradually taken possession of our agriculture. What have been the results? For him who is either unable or unwilling to deduce the whole truth from the portion of it revealed in . . . Lord Winchelsea's Report, whatever I could have added would have been equally in vain. His Lordship, speaking of the causes which oppose all attempts to better the labourer's condition, mentions, as one great cause, the dislike the generality of farmers have to seeing the labourers rent any land. . . . In confirmation of his Lordship's statement, I find in the Agricultural Reports, that the county . . . of nothing but farms of 1000, 1500, 2000 and 2500 acres, is likewise that in which the poor rates are most numerous, the distresses of the poor most grievous, and the prevalence of revolutionary principles the most alarming. But if we consider the subject on the largest scale and nationally, the consequences are, that the most important rounds in the social ladder are broken, and the hope, which above all other things distinguishes the free man from the slave, is extinguished. The peasantry therefore are eager to have their children add as early as possible to their wretched pittances, by letting them out to manufactories; while the youths take every opportunity of escaping to towns and cities. And if I were questioned as to my opinion respecting the ultimate cause . . . of a state of things so remote from the simplicity of nature, that we have almost deprived Heaven itself of the power of blessing us; a state in which, without absurdity, a superabundant harvest can be complained of as an evil, and the recurrence of the same a ruinous calamity —I should not hesitate to answer—the vast and disproportionate number of men who are to be fed from the produce of the fields on which they do not labour.

Flight from the land

The remedy is national and individual action as Christians

What then is the remedy? Who the physicians? The reply may be anticipated. An evil, which has come on gradually, and in the growth of which all men have more or less conspired, cannot be removed otherwise than gradually, and by the joint efforts of all. If we are a Christian nation, we must learn to act nationally, as well as individually, as Christians. We must remove half-truths, the most dangerous of errors (as those of the poor visionaries called Spenceans) [26] by the whole truth. The government is employed already in retrenchments; but he who expects immediate relief from these, or who does not even know that, if they do anything at all, they must for a time tend to aggravate the distress, cannot have studied the operation of public expenditure.

The evil of State lotteries

I am persuaded that more good would be done, not only ultimate and permanent, but immediate good, by the abolition of the lotteries, [27] accompanied with a public and parliamentary declaration of the moral and religious grounds that had determined the legislature to this act; of their humble confidence in the blessing of God on the measure; and of their hopes that this sacrifice to principle, as being more exemplary from the present pressure on the revenue of the State, would be the more effective in restoring confidence between man and man—I am deeply convinced, that more sterling and visible benefits would be derived from this one solemn proof and pledge of moral fortitude and national faith than from retrenchments to a tenfold greater amount. Still more, if our legislators should pledge themselves at the same time that they would hereafter take counsel for the gradual removal or counteraction of all similar encouragements and temptations to vice and folly, that had alas! been tolerated hitherto, as the easiest way of supplying the exchequer. And truly, the financial motives would be strong, indeed, if the revenue laws in question were but half as productive of money to the State as they are of guilt and wretchedness to the people.

State regulation of manufacture and return to the conception of land as a trust

Our manufacturers must consent to regulations; our gentry must concern themselves in the education as well as in the instructions of their natural clients and dependents—must regard their estates as secured indeed from all human interference by every principle of law and policy, but yet as offices of trust with duties to be performed, in the sight of God and their country. Let us become a better people, and the reform of all the public (real or supposed) grievances, which we use as pegs whereon to hang our own errors and defects, will follow of itself. In short, let every man measure his efforts by his power and his sphere of action, and do all he can do! Let him contribute money where he cannot act personally; but let him act personally and in detail [28] wherever it is practicable. Let us palliate where we cannot cure, comfort where we cannot relieve; and for the rest rely upon the promise of the King of kings by the mouth of His Prophet—'Blessed are ye that sow beside all waters.'

Limits of political reform

Concerning

THE RELATIONS
of
GREAT BRITAIN, SPAIN, AND PORTUGAL,

To each other, and to the common enemy,
at this crisis;

and specifically as affected by

THE CONVENTION OF CINTRA:

The whole brought to the test of those principles,
by which alone the Independence and Freedom
of Nations can be preserved or recovered.

Qui didicit patriae quid debeat;—
Quod sit conscripti, quod judicis officium; quae
Partes in bellum missi ducis.

BY WILLIAM WORDSWORTH

LONDON:
Printed for Longman, Hurst, Rees, and Orme,
PATERNOSTER ROW
1809

Lines composed while the Author was engaged in writing a Tract occasioned by the Convention of Cintra.

I dropped my pen; and listened to the wind
That sang of trees up-torn and vessels tost—
A midnight harmony; and wholly lost
To the general sense of men by chains confined
Of business, care, or pleasure; or resigned
To timely sleep. Thought I, the impassioned strain,
Which, without aid of numbers, I sustain,
Like acceptation from the world will find.
Yet some with apprehensive ear shall drink
A dirge devoutly breathed o'er sorrows past;
And to the attendant promise will give heed—
The prophecy,—like that of this wild blast,
Which, while it makes the heart with sadness shrink,
Tells also of bright calms that shall succeed.

Bitter and earnest writing must not hastily be condemned; for men cannot contend coldly, and without affection, about things which they hold dear and precious. A politic man may write from his brain, without touch and sense of his heart; as in a speculation that pertaineth not unto him; but a feeling Christian will express, in his words, a character of zeal or love.

Lord Bacon

SUMMARY OF CONTENTS

CONCERNING THE CONVENTION OF CINTRA

News of the Convention a shock to public sentiment

THE CONVENTION, recently concluded by the Generals at the head of the British army in Portugal, is one of the most important events of our time. It would be deemed so in France, if the Ruler of that country could dare to make it public with those merely of its known bearings and dependences with which the English people are acquainted; it has been deemed so in Spain and Portugal as far as the people of those countries have been permitted to gain, or have gained, a knowledge of it; and what this nation has felt and still feels upon the subjects is sufficiently manifest. Wherever the tidings were communicated, they carried agitation along with them—a conflict of sensations in which, though sorrow was predominant, yet, through force of scorn, impatience, hope, and indignation, and through the universal participation in passions so complex, and the sense of power which this necessarily included—the whole partook of the energy and activity of congratulation and joy. Not a street, not a public room, not a fire-side in the island which was not disturbed as by a local or private trouble; men of all estates, conditions, and tempers were affected apparently in equal degrees. Yet was the event by none received as an open and measurable affliction: it had indeed features bold and intelligible to every one; but there was an under-expression which was strange, dark and mysterious—and, accordingly as different notions prevailed, or the object was looked at in different points of view, we were astonished like men who are overwhelmed without forewarning—fearful like men who feel themselves to be helpless, and indignant and angry like men who are betrayed. In a word, it would not be too much to say that the tidings of this event did not spread with the commotion of a storm which sweeps visibly over our heads, but like an earthquake which rocks the ground under our feet.

National enthusiasm for the expedition to the Peninsula

How was it possible that it could be otherwise? For that army [1] had been sent upon a service which appealed so strongly to all that was human in the heart of this nation—that there was scarcely a gallant father of a family who had not his moments of regret that he was not a soldier by profession, which might have made it his duty to accompany it; every high-minded youth grieved that his first impulses, which would have sent him upon the same errand, were not to be yielded to, and that after-thought did not sanction and confirm the instantaneous dictates or the reiterated persuasions of an heroic spirit. The army took its departure with prayers and blessings which were as widely spread as they were fervent and intense. For it was not doubted that, on this occasion, every person of which it was composed, from the General to the private soldier, would carry both into his conflicts with the enemy in the field, and into his relations of peaceful intercourse with the inhabitants, not only the virtues which might be expected from him as a soldier, but the antipathies and sympathies, the loves and hatreds, of a citizen—of a human-being—acting, in a manner hitherto unprecedented under the obligation of his human and social nature. . . . The discipline of the army was well-known; and as a machine, or a vital organized body, the Nation was assured that it could not but be formidable; but thus to the standing excellence of mechanic or organic power seemed to be superadded, at this time, and for this service, the force of *inspiration*: could anything therefore be looked for, but a glorious result? The army proved its prowess in the field; and what has been the result is attested, and long will be attested, by the downcast looks—the silence—the passionate exclamations—the sighs and shame of every man who is worthy to breathe the air or to look upon the green-fields of Liberty in this blessed and highly-favoured Island which we inhabit. . . .

A just and necessary war, nationally supported

This just and necessary war, as we have been accustomed to hear it styled from the beginning of the contest in the year 1793, had, some time before the Treaty of Amiens, viz. after the subjugation of Switzerland, and not till then, begun to be regarded by the body of the people, as indeed both just and necessary; and this justice and necessity were by none more clearly perceived, or more feelingly bewailed, than by those who had most eagerly opposed the war in its commencement, and who continued most bitterly to regret that this nation had ever borne a part in it. [2] Their conduct was herein consistent: they proved that they kept their eyes steadily fixed upon principles; for, though there was a shifting or transfer of hostility in their minds as far as regarded persons, they only combated the same enemy opposed to them under a different shape; and that enemy was the spirit of selfish tyranny and lawless ambition. This spirit . . . when it became undeniably embodied in the French government, they wished, in spite of all dangers, should be opposed by war; because peace was not to be procured without submission, which could not but be followed by a communion, of which the word of greeting would be, on the one part, insult,—and, on the other, degradation. The people now wished for war, as their rulers had done before, because open war between nations is a defined and effectual partition, and the sword, in the hands of the good and the virtuous, is the most intelligible symbol of abhorrence. It was in order to be preserved from spirit-breaking submissions —from the guilt of seeming to approve that which they had not the power to prevent, and out of a consciousness of the danger that such guilt would otherwise actually steal upon them, and that thus, by evil communications and participations, would be weakened and finally destroyed, those moral sensibilities and energies, by virtue of which alone, their liberties, and even their lives, could be preserved,—that the people of Great Britain determined to encounter all perils which could follow in the train of open resistance.

The war as a painful necessity

There were some, and those deservedly of high character in the country, who exerted their utmost influence to counteract this resolution; nor did they give to it so gentle a name as want of prudence, but they boldly termed it blindness and obstinacy. Let them be judged with charity! But there are promptings of wisdom from the penetralia of human nature, which a people can hear, though the wisest of their practical Statesmen be deaf towards them. This authentic voice, the people of England had heard and obeyed: and, in opposition to French tyranny growing daily more insatiate and implacable, they ranged themselves zealously under their Government; though they neither forgot nor forgave its transgressions, in having first involved them in a war with a people then struggling for its own liberties under a two-fold infliction—confounded by inbred faction, and beleagured by a cruel and imperious external foe. But these remembrances did not vent themselves in reproaches, nor hinder us from being reconciled to our Rulers, when a change or rather a revolution in circumstances had imposed new duties: and, in defiance of local and personal clamour, it may be safely said, that the nation united heart and hand with the Government in its resolve to meet the worst, rather than stoop its head to receive that which, it was felt, would not be the garland but the yoke of peace. Yet it was an afflicting alternative; and it is not to be denied, that the effort, if it had the determination, wanted the cheerfulness of duty. Our condition savoured too much of a grinding constraint—too much of the vassalage of necessity;—it had too much of fear, and therefore of selfishness, not to be contemplated in the main with rueful emotion. We desponded though we did not despair. In fact a deliberate and preparatory fortitude—a sedate and stern melancholy, which had no sunshine and was exhilarated only by the lightnings of indignation—this was the highest and best state of moral feeling to which the most noble-minded among us could attain.

The risings of Spain and Portugal gave moral inspiration to the war

But, from the moment of the rising of the people of the Pyrenean peninsula, there was mighty change; we were instantaneously animated; and, from that moment, the contest assumed the dignity, which it is not in the power of anything but hope to bestow: and, if I may dare to transfer language, prompted by a revelation of the state of being that admits not of decay or change, to the concerns and interests of our transitory planet, from that moment 'this corruptible put on incorruption, and this mortal put on immortality'. This sudden elevation was on no account more welcome—was by nothing more endeared, than by the returning sense which accompanied it of inward liberty and choice, which gratified our moral yearnings, inasmuch as it would give henceforth to our actions as a people, an origination and direction unquestionably moral—as it was free—as it was manifestly in sympathy with the species—as it admitted therefore of fluctuations of generous feeling—of approbation and of complacency. We were intellectualized also in proportion; we looked backward upon the records of the human race with pride, and, instead of being afraid, we delighted to look forward into futurity. It was imagined that this new-born spirit of resistance, rising from the most sacred feelings of the human heart, would diffuse itself through many countries; and not merely for the distant future, but for the present, hopes were entertained as bold as they were disinterested and generous.

Anglo-Spanish brotherhood-in arms

Never, indeed, was the fellowship of our sentient nature more intimately felt—never was the irresistible power of justice more gloriously displayed than when the British and Spanish Nations, with an impulse like that of two ancient heroes throwing down their weapons and reconciled in the field, cast off at once their aversions and enmities, and mutually embraced each other—to solemnize this conversion of love, not by the festivities of peace, but by combating side by side through danger and under affliction in the devotedness of perfect brotherhood. This was a conjunction which excited hope as fervent as it was rational. On the one side was a nation which brought with it sanction and authority, inasmuch as it had tried and approved the blessings for which the other had risen to contend: the one was a people which, by the help of the surrounding ocean and its own virtues, had preserved to itself through ages its liberty, pure and inviolated by a foreign invader; the other a high-minded nation, which a tyrant, presuming on its decrepitude, had, through the real decrepitude of its Government, perfidiously enslaved. What could be more delightful than to think of an intercourse beginning in this manner? On the part of the Spaniards their love towards us was enthusiasm and adoration; the faults of our national character were hidden from them by a veil of splendour; they saw

A people old in freedom, and a people seeking to be free

nothing around us but glory and light; and, on our side, we estimated *their* character with partial and indulgent fondness; —thinking of their past greatness, not as the undermined foundation of a magnificent building, but as the root of a majestic tree recovered from a long disease, and beginning again to flourish with promise of wider branches and a deeper shade than it had boasted in the fulness of its strength. If in the sensations with which the Spaniards prostrated themselves before the religion of their country we did not keep pace with them—if even their loyalty was such as, from our mixed constitution of government and from other causes, we could not thoroughly sympathize with—and if, lastly, their devotion to the person of their Sovereign appeared to us to have too much of the alloy of delusion,—in all these things we judged them gently; and taught by the reverses of the French revolution, we looked upon these dispositions as more human—more social—and therefore as wiser, and of better omen, than if they had stood forth the zealots of abstract principles, drawn out of the laboratory of unfeeling philosophists. Finally, in this reverence for the past and present, we found an earnest that they were prepared to contend to the death for as much liberty as their habits and their knowledge enabled them to receive. To assist them and their neighbours the Portuguese in the attainment of this end, we sent to them in love and in friendship a powerful army to aid—to invigorate—and to chastise:— they landed; and the first proof they afforded of their being worthy to be sent on such a service—the first pledge of amity given by them was the victory of Vimiera; the second pledge (and this was from the hand of their Generals) was the Convention of Cintra. [3]

First-fruit of brotherhood—the victory of Vimiera

The second—the Convention of Cintra!

The reader will by this time have perceived, what thoughts were uppermost in my mind, when I began with asserting, that this Convention is among the most important events of our time:—an assertion, which was made deliberately, and after due allowance for that infirmity which inclines us to magnify things present and passing, at the expense of those which are past. It is my aim to prove, wherein the real importance of this event lies; and, as a necessary preparative for forming a right judgment upon it, I have already given a representation of the sentiments, with which the people of Great Britain and those of Spain looked upon each other. I have indeed spoken rather of the Spaniards than of the Portuguese; but what has been said, will be understood as applying in the main to the whole Peninsula. The wrongs of the two nations have been equal, and their cause is the same: they must stand or fall together. . . . Doubtless, there is not a man in these Islands, who is not convinced that the cause of Spain is the most righteous cause in which, since the opposition of the Greek Republics to the Persian Invader at Thermopylae and Marathon, sword ever was drawn! But this is not enough. We are actors in the struggle; and, in order that we may have steady PRINCIPLES to control and direct us, (without which we may do much harm and can do no good,) we ought to make it a duty to revive in the memory those words and facts, which first carried the conviction to our hearts: that, as far as it is possible, we may see as we then saw, and feel as we then felt. . . .

Defeat of the Spanish armies no cause for despair because—

It appears, then, that the Spanish armies have sustained great defeats, and have been compelled to abandon their positions, and that these reverses have been effected by an army greatly superior to the Spanish forces in number, and far excelling them in the art and practice of war. This is the sum of those tidings, which it was natural we should receive with sorrow, but which too many have received with dismay and despair, though surely no events could be more in the course of rational expectation. And what is the amount of the evil?—It is manifest that, though a great army may easily defeat or disperse another *army*, less or greater, yet it is not in a like degree formidable to a determined *people*, nor efficient in a like degree to subdue them, or to keep them in subjugation—much less if this people, like those of Spain in the present instance, be numerous, and, like them, inhabit a territory extensive and strong by nature. . . . Hence, if the Spanish armies have been defeated, or even dispersed, it not only argues a want of magnanimity, but of sense, to conclude that the cause *therefore* is lost. Supposing

(i) The war will now revert to a war of Partizans

that the spirit of the people is not crushed, the war is now brought back to that plan of conducting it, which was recommended by the Junta of Seville [4] in that inestimable paper entitled 'PRECAUTIONS'. . . . In this paper it is said, 'let the first object be to avoid all general actions, and to convince ourselves of the very great hazards without any advantage or the hope of it, to which they would expose us'. The paper then gives directions, how the war ought to be conducted as a war of partizans, and shows the peculiar fitness of the country for it. . . . To this mode of warfare, then, after experience of calamity from not having trusted in it; to this, and to the people in whom the contest originated, and who are its proper depository, that contest is now referred.

Spain peculiarly suited to partizan warfare

(ii) The Spaniards have a genius for spontaneous effort

Secondly, if the spirits of the Spaniards be not broken by defeat . . . then are there mighty resources in the country which have not yet been called forth. For all has hitherto been done by the spontaneous efforts of the people, acting under little or no compulsion of the Government, but with its advice and exhortation. It is an error to suppose, that, in proportion as a people are strong, and act largely for themselves, the Government must therefore be weak. This is not a necessary consequence even in the heat of Revolution, but only when the people are lawless from want of a steady and noble object among themselves for their love, or in the presence of a foreign enemy for their hatred. In the early part of the French Revolution, indeed as long as it was evident that the end was the common safety, the National Assembly had the power to turn the people into any course, to constrain them to any task, while their voluntary efforts, as far as these could be exercised, were not abated in consequence. That which the National Assembly did for France, the Spanish Sovereign's authority acting through those whom the people themselves have deputed to represent him, would, in their present enthusiasm of loyalty, and condition of their general feelings, render practicable and easy for Spain. . . .

The course which ought to be pursued is plain. Either the

cause has lost the people's love, or it has not. If it has, let the struggle be abandoned. If it has not, let the Government, in whatever shape it may exist, and however great may be the calamities under which it may labour, act up to the full stretch of its rights, nor doubt that the people will support it to the full extent of their power. If, therefore, the chiefs of the Spanish Nation be men of wise and strong minds, they will bring both the forces, those of the Government and of the people, into their utmost action; tempering them in such a manner that neither shall impair or obstruct the other, but rather that they shall strengthen and direct each other for all salutary purposes.

(iii) The Spanish people are the army of Spain

Thirdly, it was never dreamt by any thinking man, that the Spaniards were to succeed by their army; if by their *army* be meant any thing but the people. The whole people is their army, and their true army is the people, and nothing else. . . . The whole Spanish nation ought to be encouraged to deem themselves an army, embodied under the authority of their country and of human nature. A military spirit should be there, and a military action, not confined like an ordinary river in one channel, but spreading like the Nile over the whole face of the land. Is this possible? I believe it is: if there be minds among them worthy to lead, and if those leading minds cherish a *civic* spirit by all warrantable aids and appliances, and, above all other means, by combining a reverential memory of their elder ancestors with distinct hopes of solid advantage, from the privileges of freedom, for themselves and their posterity—to which the history and the past state of Spain furnish such enviable facilities; and if they provide for the sustenance of this spirit, by organizing it in its primary sources, not timidly jealous of a people, whose toils and sacrifices have proved them worthy of all love and confidence, and whose failing of excess, if such there exist, is assuredly on the side of loyalty to their Sovereign, [5] and predilection for all established institutions. We affirm, then, that a universal military spirit may be produced; and not only this, but that a much more rare and more admirable phenomenon may be realized—the civic and military spirit united in one people, and in enduring harmony with each other. The people of Spain, with arms in their hands, are already in an elevated mood, to which they have been raised by the indignant passions, and the keen sense of insupportable wrong and insult by the enemy, and its infamous instruments.—But they must be taught, not to trust too exclusively to the violent passions, which have already done much of their peculiar task and service. They must seek additional aid from affections, which less imperiously exclude all individual interests, while at the same time they consecrate them to the public good. But the enemy is in the heart of their Land! We have not forgotten this. We would encourage their military zeal, and all qualities especially military, by all rewards of honourable ambition, and by rank and dignity conferred on the truly worthy, whatever may be their birth or condition, the elevating influence of which would extend from the individual possessor to the class from which he may have sprung. For the necessity of thus raising and upholding the military spirit, we plead: but yet the *professional* excellencies of the soldier must be contemplated according to their due place and relation. Nothing is done, or worse than nothing, unless something higher be taught, *as* higher, something more fundamental, *as* more fundamental. In the moral virtues and qualities of passion which belong to a people, must the ultimate salvation of a people be sought for.

The place of the professional soldier

The salvation of Spain to be sought primarily in the moral virtues and passions of the people

Moral qualities of a high order, and vehement passions, and virtuous as vehement, the Spaniards have already displayed; nor is it to be anticipated, that the conduct of their enemies will suffer the heat and glow to remit and languish. These may be trusted to themselves, and to the provocations of the merciless Invader. They must now be taught, that their strength *chiefly* lies in moral qualities, more silent in their operation, more permanent in their nature; in the virtues of perseverance, constancy, fortitude, and watchfulness, in a long memory and a quick feeling, to rise upon a favourable summons, a texture of life which, though cut through (as hath been feigned of the bodies of the Angels) unites again—these are the virtues and qualities on which the Spanish People must be taught *mainly* to depend. These it is not in the powei of their Chiefs to create; but they may preserve and procure to them opportunities of unfolding themselves, by guarding the Nation against an intemperate reliance on other qualities and other modes of exertion, to which it could never have resorted in the degree in which it appears to have resorted to them without having been in contradiction to itself, paying at the same time an indirect homage to its enemy. Yet, in hazarding this conditional censure, we are still inclined to believe that in spite of our deductions on the score of exaggeration, we have still given too easy credit to the accounts furnished by the enemy, of the rashness with which the Spaniards engaged in pitched battles, and of their dismay after defeat. For the Spaniards have repeatedly proclaimed, and they have inwardly felt, that their strength was from their cause—of course, that it was moral. Why then should they abandon this, and endeavour to prevail by means in which their opponents are confessedly so much superior? Moral strength is theirs; but physical power for the purposes of immediate or rapid destruction is on the side of their enemies. This is to them no disgrace, but, as soon as they understand themselves, they will see that they are disgraced by mistrusting their appropriate stay, and throwing themselves upon a power which for them must be weak. Nor will it then appear to them a sufficient excuse that they were seduced into this by the splendid qualities of courage and enthusiasm, which, being the frequent companions, and, in given circumstances, the necessary agents of virtue, are too often themselves hailed as virtues by their own title. But courage and enthusiasm have equally characterized the best and the worst beings, a Satan, equally with an ABDIEL—a BONAPARTE equally with a LEONIDAS. They are indeed indispensable to the Spanish soldiery, in order that, man to man, they may not be inferior to their enemies in the field of battle. But inferior they are and long must be in warlike skill and coolness; inferior in assembled numbers, and in blind mobility to the preconceived purposes of their leader.

Mere courage and enthusiasm not enough

Superior strength of the French arises from their presumption and their sense of inevitable success

If, therefore, the Spaniards are not superior in some superior quality, their fall may be predicted with the certainty of a mathematical calculation. Nay, it is right to acknowledge, however depressing to false hope the thought may be, that from a people prone and disposed to war, as the French are, through the very absence of those excellencies which give a contra-distinguishing dignity to the Spanish character; that, from an army of men presumptuous by nature, to whose presumption the experience of constant success has given the confidence and stubborn strength of reason, and who balance against the devotion of patriotism the superstition so naturally attached by the sensual and disordinate to the strange fortunes and continual felicity of their Emperor; that, from the armies of such a people a more manageable enthusiasm, a courage less under the influence of accidents, may be expected in the confusion of immediate conflict, than from forces like the Spaniards, united indeed by devotion to a common cause, but not equally united by an equal confidence in each other, resulting from long fellowship and brotherhood in all conceivable incidents of war and battle. Therefore, I do not hesitate to affirm, that even the occasional flight of the Spanish levies, from sudden panic under untried circumstances, would not be so injurious to the Spanish cause; no, nor so dishonourable to the Spanish character, nor so ominous of ultimate failure, as a paramount reliance on superior valour, instead of a principled reposal on superior constancy and immutable resolve. Rather let them have fled once and again, than direct their prime admiration to the blaze and explosion of animal courage, in slight of the vital and sustaining warmth of fortitude; in slight of that moral contempt of death and privation, which does not need the stir and shout of battle to call it forth or support it, which can smile in patience over the stiff and cold wound, as well as rush forward regardless, because half senseless of the fresh and bleeding one.

A principled reposal on superior constancy and immutable resolve is better than the mere blaze and explosion of animal courage

A nation which by its virtues deserves freedom cannot lack the qualities necessary to win it

Why did we give our hearts to the present cause of Spain with a fervour and elevation unknown to us in the commencement of the late Austrian or Prussian resistance to France? Because we attributed to the former an heroic temperament which would render their transfer to such domination an evil to human nature itself, and an affrightening perplexity in the dispensations of Providence. But if in oblivion of the prophetic wisdom of their own first leaders in the cause, they are surprised beyond the power of rallying, utterly cast down and manacled by fearful thoughts from the first thunderstorm of defeat in the field, wherein do they differ from the Prussians and Austrians? Wherein are they a PEOPLE, and not a mere army or set of armies? If this be indeed so, what have we to mourn over but our own honourable impetuosity, in hoping where no ground of hope existed? A nation, without the virtues necessary for the attainment of independence, have failed to attain it. This is all. For little has that man understood the majesty of true national freedom, who believes that a population, like that of Spain, in a country like that of Spain, may want the qualities needful to fight out their independence, and yet possess the excellencies which render men susceptible of true liberty. The Dutch, the Americans, did possess the former; but it is, I fear, more than doubtful whether the one ever did, or the other ever will, evince the nobler morality indispensable to the latter. . . . [6]

[*After some description of the 'bloody-mindedness' and 'merciless ferocity' of the French in Spain:*]

The wrongs of Spain are not only material, but wrongs against the reason and conscience of man

Such tyranny is, in the strictest sense, intolerable; not because it aims at the extinction of life, but of every thing which gives life its value—of virtue, of reason, of repose in God, or in truth. . . . Many passages might be adduced to prove that carnage and devastation spread over their land have not afflicted this noble people so deeply as this more searching warfare against the conscience and the reason. . . . Accordingly, labouring under these violations done to their moral nature, they describe themselves, in the anguish of their souls, treated as a people at once dastardly and *insensible*. In the same spirit they make it even matter of complaint, as comparatively a far greater evil, that they have not fallen by the brute violence of open war, but by deceit and perfidy, by a subtle undermining or contemptuous overthrow of those principles of good faith, through prevalence of which, in some degree, or under some modification or other, families, communities, a people, or any frame of human society, even destroying armies themselves can exist.

Moral response of Spain to national chastisement

But enough of their wrongs; let us now see what were their consolations, their resolves, and their hopes. First, they neither murmur nor repine; but with genuine religion and philosophy they recognize in these dreadful visitations the ways of a benign Providence, [7] and find in them cause for thankfulness. The Council of Castile exhort the people of Madrid 'to cast off their lethargy, and purify their manners, and to acknowledge the calamities which the kingdom and that great capital had endured as a punishment necessary to their correction'. . . . With this general confidence, that the highest good may be brought out of the worst calamities, they have combined a solace, which is vouchsafed only to such nations as can recall to memory the illustrious deeds of their ancestors. The names of Pelayo and The Cid are the watch-words of the address to the people of Leon; and they are told that to these two deliverers of their country, and to the sentiments of enthusiasm which they excited in every breast, Spain owes the glory and happiness which she has *so long* enjoyed. . . . And surely to a people thus united in their minds with the heroism of years which have been long departed, and living under such obligation of gratitude to their ancestors, it is not difficult, nay it is natural, to take upon themselves the highest obligations of duty to their posterity; to enjoy in the holiness of imagination the happiness of unborn ages to which they shall have eminently contributed; and that each man, fortified by these thoughts, should welcome despair for himself, because it is the assured mother of hope for his country. . . .

Spain contends for the future of mankind—and of France itself

But let us now hear them, as becomes men with such feelings, express more cheering and bolder hopes rising from a confidence in the supremacy of justice—hopes, which, however the Tyrant from the iron fortresses of his policy may scoff at them and at those who entertained them, will render their memory dear to all good men, when his name will be pronounced with universal abhorrence. . . . 'Yes—Spain with the energies of Liberty has to contend with France debilitated by slavery. If she remain firm and constant, Spain will triumph. A whole people is more powerful than disciplined armies. Those, who unite to maintain the independence of their country, must triumph over tyranny. Spain will inevitably conquer, in a cause the most just that has ever raised the deadly weapon of war; for she fights, not for the concerns of a day, but for the security and happiness of ages; not for an insulated privilege, but for the rights of human nature; not for temporal blessings, but for eternal happiness; not for the benefit of one nation, but for all mankind, and even for France herself.'

Summary

I will now beg of my reader to pause for a moment, and to view in his own mind the whole of what has been laid before him. He has seen of what kind, and how great have been the injuries endured by these two nations; what they have suffered, and what they have to fear; he has seen that they have felt with that unanimity which nothing but the light of truth spread over the inmost concerns of human nature can create; with that simultaneousness which has led Philosophers upon like occasions to assert, that the voice of the people is the voice of God. He has seen that they have submitted as far as human nature could bear; and that at last these millions of suffering people have risen almost like one man, with one hope; for whether they look to triumph or defeat, to victory or death, they are full of hope—despair comes not near them—they will die, they say—each individual knows the danger, and, strong in the magnitude of it, grasps eagerly at the thought that he himself is to perish; and more eagerly, and with higher confidence, does he lay to his heart the faith that the nation will survive and be victorious;—or, at the worst, let the contest terminate how it may as to superiority of outward strength, that the fortitude and the martyrdom, the justice and the blessing, are theirs and cannot be relinquished.

Domestic reform of Spain is also an issue of the struggle

And not only are they moved by these exalted sentiments of universal morality, and of direct and universal concern to mankind, which have impelled them to resist evil and to endeavour to punish the evil-doer, but also they descend (for even this, great as in itself it is, may be here considered as a descent) to express a rational hope of reforming domestic abuses, and of re-constructing, out of the materials of their ancient institutions, customs and laws, a better frame of civil government, the same in the great outlines of its architecture, but exhibiting the knowledge, and genius, and the needs of the present race, harmoniously blended with those of their forefathers. Woe, then, to the unworthy who intrude with their help to maintain this most sacred cause! It calls aloud for the aid of intellect, knowledge, and love, and rejects every other. It is in vain to send forth armies if these do not inspire and direct them. The stream is as pure as it is mighty, fed by ten thousand springs in the bounty of untainted nature; any augmentation from the kennels and sewers of guilt and baseness may clog, but cannot strengthen it. . . . If then we do not forget that the Spanish and Portuguese Nations stand upon the loftiest ground of principle and passion, and do not suffer on our part those sympathies to languish which a few months since were so strong, and do not negligently or timidly descend from those heights of magnanimity to which as a Nation we were raised, when they first represented to us their wrongs and entreated our assistance, and we devoted ourselves sincerely and earnestly to their service, making with them a common cause under a common hope; if we are true in all this to them and to ourselves, we shall not be at a loss to conceive what actions are entitled to our commendation as being in the spirit of a friendship so nobly begun, and tending assuredly to promote the common welfare; and what are abject, treacherous, and pernicious, and therefore to be condemned and abhorred.

Is the signing of the Convention evidence of our moral unfitness for association in so high a cause?

Is then, I may now ask, the Convention of Cintra an act of this latter kind? Have the Generals, who signed and ratified that agreement, thereby proved themselves unworthy associates in such a cause? And has the Ministry, by whose appointment these men were enabled to act in this manner, and which sanctioned the Convention by permitting them to carry it into execution, thereby taken to itself a weight of guilt, in which the

Nation must feel that it participates, until the transaction shall be solemnly reprobated by the Government, and the remote and immediate authors of it brought to merited punishment? An answer to each of these questions will be implied in the proof which will be given that the condemnation which the People did with one voice pronounce upon this Convention when it first became known, was just; that the nature of the offence of those who signed it was such, and established by evidence of such a kind, making so imperious an exception to the ordinary course of action, that there was no need to wait here for the decision of a Court of Judicature, but that the People were compelled by a necessity involved in the very constitution of man as a moral Being to pass sentence upon them. And this I shall prove by trying this act of theirs by principles of justice which are of universal obligation, and by a reference to those moral sentiments which rise out of that retrospect of things which has been given.

The news of the Convention arrives in England

I shall now proceed to facts. The dispatches of Sir Arthur Wellesley, containing an account of his having defeated the enemy in two several engagements, spread joy throughout the Nation. . . . Sir Arthur Wellesley's dispatches had appeared in the Gazette on the 2nd of September, and on the 16th of the same month suspense was put an end to by the publication of Sir Hew Dalrymple's [8] letter, accompanied with the Armistice and Convention. The night before, by order of the ministers, an attempt had been made at rejoicing, and the Park and Tower guns had been fired in sign of good news.—Heaven grant that the ears of that great city may be preserved from such another outrage! As soon as the truth was known, never was there such a burst of rage and indignation—such an overwhelming of stupefaction and sorrow. . . . As soon as men had recovered from the shock and could bear to look somewhat steadily at these documents, it was found that the gross body of the transaction, considered as a military transaction, was this; that the Russian fleet of nine sail of the line, which had been so long watched, and could not have escaped, was to be delivered up to us; the ships to be detained till six months after

National stupefaction

the end of the war, and the sailors sent home by us, and to be by us protected in their voyage through the Swedish fleet, and to be at liberty to fight immediately against our ally, the King of Sweden. Secondly, that a French army of more than twenty thousand men, already beaten, and no longer able to appear in the field, cut off from all possibility of receiving reinforcements or supplies, and in the midst of a hostile country loathing and abhorring it, was to be transported with its arms, ammunition and plunder, at the expence of Great Britain, in British vessels, and landed within a few days' march of the Spanish frontier, —there to be at liberty to commence hostilities immediately! [9]

Military folly of the Convention

Omitting every characteristic which distinguishes the present contest from others, and looking at this issue merely as an affair between two armies, what stupidity of mind to provoke the accusation of not merely shrinking from future toils and dangers, but of basely shifting the burthen to the shoulders of an ally, already overpressed!—What infatuation to convey the imprisoned foe to the very spot, whither, if he had had wings, he would have flown! This last was an absurdity as glaring as if, the French having landed on our own island, we had taken them from Yorkshire to be set on shore in Sussex; but ten thousand times worse! from a place where without our interference they had been virtually blockaded, where they were cut off, hopeless, useless, and disgraced, to become an efficient part of a mighty host, carrying the strength of their numbers, and alas! the strength of their glory (not to mention the sight of their plunder), to animate that host; while the British army, more numerous in the proportion of three to two, with all the population and resources of the peninsula to aid it, within ten days' sail of its own country, and the sea covered with friendly shipping at its back, was to make a long march to encounter this same enemy . . . in a new condition of strength and pride. . . . The motive assigned for all this, was the great importance of gaining time; fear of an open beach and of equinoctial gales for the shipping; fear that reinforcements could not be landed; fear of famine;—fear of every thing but dishonour. . . .

Want of intellectual courage of our generals

Let me not be misunderstood. While I am thus forced to repeat things, which were uttered or thought of these men in reference to their military conduct, as heads of that army, it is needless to add, that their personal courage is in no wise implicated in the charge brought against them. But, in the name of my countrymen, I do repeat these accusations, and tax them with an utter want of *intellectual* courage—of that higher quality, which is never found without one or other of the three accompaniments, talents, genius, or principle;—talents matured by experience, without which it cannot exist at all; or the rapid insight of peculiar genius, by which the fitness of an act may be instantly determined, and which will supply higher motives than mere talents [10] can furnish for encountering difficulty and danger, and will suggest better resources for diminishing or overcoming them. Thus, through the power of genius, this quality of intellectual courage may exist in an eminent degree, though the moral character be greatly perverted; as in those personages, who are so conspicuous in history, conquerors and usurpers, the Alexanders, the Caesars, and Cromwells; and in that other class still more perverted, remorseless and energetic minds, the Catalines and Borgias, whom poets have denominated 'bold, bad men'. But, though a course of depravity will neither preclude nor destroy this quality, nay, in certain circumstances will give it a peculiar promptness and hardihood of decision, it is not on this account the less true, that, to *consummate* this species of courage, and to render it equal to all occasions (especially when a man is not acting for himself, but has an additional claim on his resolution from the circumstance of responsibility to a superior) *Principle* is indispensably requisite. I mean that fixed and habitual principle, which implies the absence of all selfish anticipations, whether of hope or fear, and the inward disapproval of any tribunal higher and more dreaded than the mind's own judgment upon its own act. [11]

Nature of intellectual courage

Intellectual courage a possible possession of bold, bad men

Consummate intellectual courage requires habitual reference to principle

The existence of such principle cannot but elevate the most commanding genius, add rapidity to the quickest glance, a wider range to the most ample comprehension; but, without this principle, the man of ordinary powers must, in the trying hour, be found utterly wanting. Neither, without it, can the man of excelling powers be trust-worthy, or have at all times a calm and confident repose in himself. But he, in whom talents, genius, and principle are united, will have a firm mind in whatever embarrassments he may be placed; will look steadily at the most undefined shapes of difficulty and danger, of possible mistake or mischance; nor will they appear to him more formidable than they really are. For HIS attention is not distracted—he has but one business, and that is with the object before him. Neither in general conduct nor in particular emergencies, are HIS plans subservient to considerations of rewards, estate, or title: these are not to have precedence in his thoughts, to govern his actions, but to follow in the train of his duty. Such men, in ancient times, were Phocion, Epaminondas, and Philopoemen; and such a man was Sir Philip Sidney, of whom it has been said, that he first taught this country *the majesty of honest dealing*. With these may be named, the honour of our own age, Washington, the deliverer of the American Continent; with these, though in many things unlike, Lord Nelson, whom we have lately lost. Lord Peterborough, who fought in Spain a hundred years ago, had the same excellence; with a sense of exalted honour, and a tinge of romantic enthusiasm, well suited to the country which was the scene of his exploits. Would that we had a man, like Peterborough or Nelson, at the head of our army in Spain at this moment! I utter this wish with more earnestness, because it is rumoured, that some of those, who have already called forth such severe reprehension from their countrymen, are to resume a command, [12] which must entrust to them a portion of those sacred hopes in which, not only we, and the people of Spain and Portugal, but the whole human race are so deeply interested.

The greatest men combine talents, genius and principle

Epaminondas

Sidney

Washington

Nelson

I maintain then that, merely from want of this intellectual courage, of courage as generals or chiefs, (for I will not speak at present of the want of other qualities equally needful upon this service,) grievous errors were committed by Sir Hew Dalrymple and his colleagues in estimating the relative strength of the two armies. A precious moment, it is most probable, had been lost after the battle of Vimiera; yet still the inferiority of the enemy had been proved; they themselves had admitted it—not merely by withdrawing from the field, but by proposing terms:—monstrous terms! and how ought they to have been received? Repelled undoubtedly with scorn, as an insult. If our Generals had been men capable of taking the measure of their real strength, either as existing in their own army, or in those principles of liberty and justice which they were commissioned to defend, they must of necessity have acted in this manner;—if they had been men of common sagacity for business, they must have acted in this manner;—nay, if they had been upon a level with an ordinary bargain-maker in a Fair or a market, they could not have acted otherwise.—Strange that they should so far forget the nature of their calling! They were soldiers, and their business was to fight. Sir Arthur Wellesley had fought, and gallantly; it was not becoming his high situation, or that of his successors, to treat, that is, to beat down, to chaffer, or on their part to propose: it does not become any general at the head of a victorious army so to do. They were to *accept*, and, if the terms offered were flagrantly presumptuous, our commanders ought to have rejected them with dignified scorn, and to have referred the proposer to the sword for a lesson of decorum and humility. This is the general rule of all high-minded men upon such occasions; and meaner minds copy them, doing in prudence what they do from principle. . . .

An ordinary bargain-maker at a fair would not have made such a bargain

The tender feelings, however, are pleaded against this determination; and, it is said, that one of the motives for the cessation of hostilities was to prevent the further effusion of human blood.—When, or how? The enemy was delivered over to us; it was not to be hoped that, cut off from all assistance as they were, these, or an equal number of men, could ever be reduced to such straits as would ensure their destruction as an enemy, with so small a sacrifice of life on their part, or on ours. What then was to be gained by this tenderness? The shedding of a few drops of blood is not to

The argument of 'prevention of further effusion of blood'

be risked in Portugal today, and streams of blood must shortly flow from the same veins in the fields of Spain! And, even if this had not been the assured consequence, let not the consideration, though it be one which no humane man can ever lose sight of, have more than its due weight. For national independence and liberty, and *that* honour by which these and other blessings are to be preserved, honour—which is no other than the most elevated and pure conception of justice which can be formed, these are more precious than life: else why have we already lost so many brave men in this struggle? —Why not submit at once, and let the tyrant mount upon his throne of universal dominion, while the world lies prostrate at his feet in indifference and apathy, which he will proclaim to it is peace and happiness? But peace and happiness can only exist by knowledge and virtue; slavery has no enduring connection with tranquillity or security—she cannot frame a league with anything which is desirable—she has no charter even for her own ignoble ease and darling sloth. Yet to this abject condition, mankind, betrayed by an ill-judging tenderness, would surely be led; and in the face of an inevitable contradiction! For neither in this state of things would the shedding of blood be prevented, nor would warfare cease. The only difference would be, that, instead of wars like those which prevail at this moment, presenting a spectacle of such character that, upon one side at least, a superior Being might look down with favour and blessing, there would follow endless commotions and quarrels without the presence of justice anywhere, —in which the alternations of success would not excite a wish or regret; in which a prayer could not be uttered for a decision either this way or that;—wars from no impulse in either of the combatants, but rival instigations of demoniacal passion.

National independence and liberty are more precious than life

Mere economy of life will not diminish wars, but merely render all wars equally unjust

If, therefore, by the faculty of reason we can prophecy concerning the shapes which the future may put on,—if we are under any bond of duty to succeeding generations, there is high cause to guard against a specious sensibility, which may encourage the hoarding up of life for its own sake, seducing us from those considerations by which we might learn when it

The hoarding up of life for its own sake

ought to be resigned. Moreover, disregarding future ages, and confining ourselves to the present state of mankind, it may be safely affirmed that he who is the most watchful of the honour of his country, most determined to preserve her fair name at all hazards, will be found, in any view of things which looks beyond the passing hour, the best steward of the *lives* of his countrymen. For, by proving that she is of a firm temper, that she will only submit or yield to a point of her own fixing, and that all beyond is immutable resolution, he will save her from being wantonly attacked; and, if attacked, will awe the aggressor into a speedier abandonment of an unjust and hopeless attempt. Thus will he preserve not only that which gives life its value, but life itself; and not for his own country merely, but for that of his enemies, to whom he will have offered an example of magnanimity, the reaction of which will be felt by his own countrymen, and will prevent them from becoming assailants unjustly or rashly. Nations will thus be taught to respect each other, and mutually to abstain from injuries. [13] And hence, by a benign ordinance of our nature, genuine honour is the handmaid of humanity; the attendant and sustainer—both of the sterner qualities which constitute the appropriate excellence of the male character, and of the gentle and tender virtues which belong more especially to motherliness and womanhood. These general laws, by which mankind is purified and exalted, and by which Nations are preserved, suggest likewise the best rules for the preservation of individual armies, and for the accomplishment of all equitable service upon which they can be sent. [14]

Readiness to fight for national honour is the best guarantee of peace

Genuine honour is the hand-maid of humanity

Not therefore rashly and unfeelingly, but from the dictates of thoughtful humanity, did I say that it was the business of our Generals to fight, and to persevere in fighting; and that they did not bear this duty sufficiently in mind; this, almost the sole duty which professional soldiers, till our time, (happily for mankind) used to think of. But the victories of the French have been attended everywhere by the subvertion of Governments; and their generals have accordingly united *political* with military functions; and with what success this has been done by them, the present state of Europe affords melancholy proof.

Our generals aped the French fashion of combining political with military functions

But have they, on this account ever neglected to calculate upon the advantages which might fairly be anticipated from future warfare? Or, in a treaty of today, have they ever forgotten a victory of yesterday? Eager to grasp at the double honour of captain and negociator, have they ever sacrificed the one to the other; or, in the blind effort, lost both? Above all, in their readiness to flourish with the pen, have they ever overlooked the sword, the symbol of their power, and the appropriate instrument of their success and glory? I notice this assumption of a double character on the part of the French, not to lament over it and its consequences, but to render somewhat more intelligible the conduct of our own Generals; and to explain how far men, whom we have no reason to believe other than brave, have, through the influence of such example, lost sight of their primary duties, apeing instead of imitating, and following only to be misled.

It is indeed deplorable that our Generals, from this infirmity, or from any other cause, did not assume that lofty deportment which the character and relative strength of the two armies authorized them, and the nature of the service upon which they were sent, enjoined them to assume;—that they were in such haste to treat—that, with such an enemy (let me say at once) and in such circumstances, they should have treated at all. Is it possible that they could ever have asked themselves who that enemy was, how he came into that country, and what he had done there? . . . Setting aside all natural sympathy with the Portuguese and Spanish nations, and all prudential considerations of regard or respect for *their feelings* towards these men, and for *their expectations* concerning the manner in which they ought to be dealt with, it is plain that the French had forfeited by their crimes all right to those privileges, or to those modes of intercourse, which one army may demand from another according to the laws of war. They were not soldiers in anything but the power of soldiers, and the outward frame of an army. During their occupation of Portugal, the laws and customs of war had never been referred to by them, but as a plea for some enormity, to the aggravated oppression of that unhappy

The French, by their crimes have put themselves outside the laws of war

country! Pillage, sacrilege and murder—sweeping murder and individual assassination, had been proved against them by voices from every quarter. They had outlawed themselves by their offences from membership in the community of war, and from every species of community acknowledged by reason. But even, should anyone be so insensible as to question this, he will not at all events deny, that the French ought to have been dealt with as having put on a double character. For surely they never considered themselves merely as an army. They had dissolved the established authorities of Portugal, and had usurped the civil power of the government; and it was in this compound capacity, under this two-fold monstrous shape, that they had exercised, over the religion and property of the country, the most grievous oppressions. What then remained to protect them but their power? Right they had none,—and power! it is a mortifying consideration, but I will ask if Bonaparte (nor in the question do I mean to imply anything to his honour) had been in the place of Sir Hew Dalrymple, what would he have thought of their power?—Yet before this shadow the solid substance of *justice* melted away.

They never considered themselves merely an army

And this leads me from the contemplation of their errors in the estimate and application of means, to the contemplation of their heavier errors and worse blindness in regard to ends. The British Generals acted as if they had no purpose but that the enemy should be removed from the country in which they were, upon *any* terms. Now the evacuation of Portugal was not the prime object, [15] but the manner in which the event was to be brought about; this ought to have been deemed first both in order and importance:—the French were to be subdued, their ferocious warfare and heinous policy to be confounded; and in this way, and no other, was the deliverance of that country to be accomplished. It was not for the soil, or for the cities and forts, that Portugal was valued, but for the human feeling that was there; for the rights of human nature which might be there conspicuously asserted; for a triumph over injustice and oppression there to be achieved, which could neither be concealed nor disguised, and which should penetrate the darkest

Means and ends. Our prime object was not the evacuation of Portugal, but to vindicate the rights of outraged human nature

We fight for victory in the empire of reason, for strongholds in the imagination

corner of the dark Continent of Europe by its splendour. We combated for victory in the empire of reason, for strongholds in the imagination. Lisbon and Portugal, as city and soil, were chiefly prized by us as a *language*; but our Generals mistook the counters of the game for the stake played for. The nation required that the French should surrender at discretion;—grant that the victory of Vimiera had excited some unreasonable impatience—we were not so overweening as to demand that the enemy should surrender within a given time, but that they should surrender. Everything, short of this, was felt to be below the duties of the occasion; not only no service, but a grievous injury. Only as far as there was a prospect of forcing the enemy to an unconditional submission, did the British Nation deem that they had a right to interfere;—if that prospect failed, they expected that their army would know that it became it to retire, and take care of itself.

Unconditional surrender

Spain and Portugal needed honourable, not merely strong, allies

But our Generals have told us that the Convention would not have been admitted if they had not judged it right to effect, even upon these terms, the evacuation of Portugal—as ministerial to their future services in Spain. If this had been a common war between two established governments measuring with each other their regular resources, there might have been some appearance of force in this plea. But who does not cry out at once, that the affections and opinions, that is, the souls of the people of Spain and Portugal, must be the inspiration and the power, if this labour is to brought to a happy end? Therefore it was worse than folly to think of supporting Spain by physical strength at the expence of moral. Besides, she was strong in men; she never earnestly solicited troops from us; some of the Provinces had even refused them when offered—and all had been lukewarm in the acceptance of them. The Spaniards could not *ultimately* be benefitted but by allies acting under the same impulses of honour, roused by a sense of their wrongs, and sharing their loves and hatreds—above all, their *passion* for justice. . . .

If there ever was a case which could not in any rational sense of the word be prejudged, this is one. As to the fact—it appears, and sheds from its own body, like the sun in heaven, the light by which it is seen; as to the person—each has written down with his own hand, *I am the man.* Condemnation of actions and men like these is not, in the minds of a people, (thanks to the divine Being and to human nature!) a matter of choice; it is like a physical necessity, as the hand must be burned which is thrust into the furnace—the body chilled which stands naked in the freezing north-wind. I am entitled to make this assertion here, when the *moral* depravity of the Convention, of which I shall have to speak hereafter, has not even been touched upon. Nor let it be blamed in any man, though his station be in private life, that upon this occasion he speaks publicly, and gives a decisive opinion concerning that part of this public event, and those measures, which are more especially military. All have a right to speak, and to make their voices heard, as far as they have power. For these are times in which the conduct of military men concerns us, perhaps, more intimately than that of any other class; when the business of arms comes unhappily too near to the fire-side; when the character and duties of a soldier ought to be understood by every one who values his liberty, and bears in mind how soon he may have to fight for it. Men will and ought to speak upon things in which they are so deeply interested; how else are right notions to spread, or is error to be destroyed?

The Convention condemned by the mind and conscience of the people

Modern wars are everybody's business

These are times also in which . . . the heads of the army, more than at any other period, stand in need of being taught wisdom by the voice of the people. It is their own interest, both as men and soldiers, that the people should speak fervently and fearlessly of their actions;—from no other quarter can they be so powerfully reminded of the duties which they owe to themselves, to their country, and to human nature. Let any one read the evidence given before [the Board of Inquiry] and he will there see how much the intellectual and moral constitution of many of our military officers has suffered by a profession, which, if not countered by admonitions willingly listened to, and by habits of meditation, does, more than any other, denaturalize—and therefore degrade the human being;

Times when the voice of the people can, and must, teach the soldiers wisdom

—he will note with sorrow how faint are their sympathies with the best feelings, and how dim their apprehension of some of the most awful truths relating to the happiness and dignity of man in society. But on this I do not mean to insist at present; it is too weighty a subject to be treated incidentally: and my purpose is—not to invalidate the authority of military men, *positively* considered, upon a military question, but *comparatively*;—to maintain that there are military transactions upon which the people have a right to be heard, and upon which their authority is entitled to far more respect than any man or number of men can lay claim to, who speak merely with the ordinary professional views of soldiership;—that there are such military transactions;—and that *this* is one of them.

Terms of the Convention examined

I will now proceed to another division of the subject, on which I feel a still more earnest wish to speak; because, though in itself of the highest importance, it has been comparatively neglected;—I mean the political injustice and moral depravity which are stamped upon the front of this agreement and pervade every regulation which it contains. I shall show that our Generals (and with them our Ministers, as far as they might have either given directions to this effect, or have countenanced what has been done)—when it was their paramount duty to maintain at all hazards the noblest principles in unsuspected integrity; because, upon the summons of these, and in defence of them, their Allies had risen, and by these alone could stand —not only did not perform this duty, but descended as far below the level of ordinary principles as they ought to have mounted above it;—imitating not the majesty of the oak with which it lifts its branches towards the heavens, but the vigour with which, in the language of the poet, it strikes its roots downwards towards hell:—

Radice in Tartara tendit.

[Here follows an examination of the Articles of the Armistice, which was the basis of the Convention. Objection is raised most strongly to the use of the title 'His Imperial and Royal

Majesty, Napoleon I', while the name of the legitimate Sovereign of Portugal is unmentioned. This conduct, it is pointed out, 'acknowledges, by implication, that principle which, by his actions, the enemy has for a long time covertly maintained, and now openly and insolently avows in his words—that power is the measure of right. . . .' Equally insulting to Portugal, it is objected, are the provisions by which recaptured ships and forts are to be occupied by British forces, under the British flag, without a word of 'their being to be holden in trust for the prince regent, or his government, to whom they belonged!' The severest condemnation, however, is reserved for Art. V, under which the French forces were permitted to carry away not only their equipment, but 'to dispose of their private property of every description'—in other words, their loot. 'And these wages of guilt . . . are to be guaranteed to him by a British *army*!' The discussion continues:]

I have animadverted, heretofore, upon the unprofessional eagerness of our Generals to appear in the character of negociators when the sword would have done them more service than the pen. But, if they had confined themselves to mere military regulations, they might indeed have been grievously censured as injudicious commanders, whose notion of the honour of armies was of a low pitch, and who had no conception of the peculiar nature of the service in which they were engaged: but the censure must have stopped here. Whereas, by these provisions, they have shown that they have never reflected upon the nature of military authority as contra-distinguished from civil. French example had so far dazzled and blinded them, that the French army is suffered to denominate itself '*the French government*'; and, from the whole tenour of these instruments, (from the preamble, and these articles especially), it should seem that our Generals fancied themselves and their army to be *the British government*. For these regulations, emanating from a mere military authority, are purely civil; but of such a kind, that no power on earth could confer a right to establish them. [16] And this trampling upon the most sacred rights—this sacrifice of the consciousness of a self-preserving principle,

French example: our generals assumed civil functions

without which neither societies nor governments can exist, is not made by our Generals in relation to subjects of their own sovereign, but to an independent nation, our ally, into whose territories we could not have entered but from its confidence in our friendship and good faith. Surely the persons, who (under the countenance of too high authority) have talked so loudly of prejudging this question, entirely overlooked or utterly forgot this part of it. What have these monstrous provisions to do with the relative strength of the two armies, or with any point admitting a doubt? What need here of a Court of Judicature to settle who were the persons (their names are subscribed by their own hands), and to determine the quality of the thing? Actions and agents like these, exhibited in this connection with each other, must of necessity be condemned the moment they are known: and to assert the contrary is to maintain that man is a being without understanding, and that morality is an empty dream.

The right of the people to condemn the Convention follows from the constitution of human nature

And if this condemnation must after this manner follow, to utter it is less a duty than a further inevitable consequence from the constitution of human nature. They who hold that the formal sanction of a Court of Judicature is in this case required before a people has a right to pass sentence, know not to what degree they are enemies to that people and to mankind; to what degree selfishness, whether arising from their peculiar situation or from other causes, has in them prevailed over those faculties which are our common inheritance, and cut them off from fellowship with the species. Most deplorable would be the result, if it were possible that the injunctions of these men could be obeyed, or their remonstrances acknowledged to be just. For (not to mention that, if it were not for such prompt decisions of the public voice, misdemeanours of men high in office would rarely be accounted for at all), we must bear in mind, at this crisis, that the adversary of all good is hourly and daily extending his ravages; and, according to such notions of fitness, our indignation, our sorrow, our shame, our sense of right and wrong, and all those moral affections, and powers of the understanding, by which alone he can be effectually opposed, are to enter upon a long vacation; their motion is to be suspended—a thing impossible; if it could, it would be destroyed. . . .

Our reputation in Europe as a free people

We have, throughout Europe, the character of a sage and meditative people. Our history has been read by the degraded Nations of the Continent with admiration, and some portions of it with awe; with a recognition of superiority and distance, which was honourable to us—salutary for those to whose hearts, in their depressed state, it could find entrance—and promising for the future condition of the human race. We have been looked up to as a people who have acted nobly; whom their constitution of government has enabled to speak and write freely, and who therefore have thought comprehensively; as a people among whom philosophers and poets, by their surpassing genius—their wisdom—and knowledge of human nature, have circulated—and made familiar—divinely-tempered sentiments and the purest notions concerning the duties and true dignity of individual and social man in all situations and under all trials. By so readily acceding to the prayers with which the Spaniards and Portuguese entreated our assistance, we have proved to them that we were not wanting in fellow-feeling. Therefore might we be admitted to be judges between them and their enemies—unexceptionable judges—more competent even than a dispassionate posterity, which, from the very want comparatively of interest and passion, might be in its examination remiss and negligent, and therefore in its decision erroneous. We, their contemporaries, were drawn towards them as suffering beings; but still their sufferings were not ours, nor could be; and we seemed to stand at that due point of difference from which right and wrong might be fairly looked at and seen in their just proportions. Everything conspired to prepossess the Spaniards and the Portuguese in our favour, and to give the judgment of the British Nation authority in their eyes. Strange, then, would be their first sensations, when, upon further trial, instead of a growing sympathy, they met with demonstrations of a state of sentiment and opinion abhorrent from their own. . . .

Our special claims to speak for liberty and independence

Again: independence and liberty were the blessings for which the people of the Peninsula were contending—immediate independence, which was not to be gained but by modes of exertion from which liberty must ensue. Now, liberty—healthy, matured, time-honoured liberty—this is the growth and peculiar boast of Britain; and Nature herself, by encircling with the ocean the country which we inhabit, has proclaimed that this mighty Nation is for ever to be her own ruler, and that the land is set apart for the home of immortal independence. Judging then from these first fruits of British friendship, what bewildering and depressing and hollow thoughts must the Spaniards and Portuguese have entertained concerning the real value of these blessings, if the people who have possessed them longest, and who ought to understand them best, could send forth an army capable of enacting the oppressions and baseness of the Convention of Cintra; if the government of that people could sanction this treaty; and if, lastly, this distinguished and favoured people themselves could suffer it to be held forth to the eyes of men as expressing the sense of their hearts—as in an image of their understandings.

Hope that the government would disavow the Convention

But it did not speak their sense—it was not endured—it was not submitted to in their hearts. Bitter was the sorrow of the people of Great Britain when the tidings first came to their ears, when they first fixed their eyes upon this covenant—overwhelming was their astonishment, tormenting their shame; their indignation was tumultuous; and the burthen of the past would have been insupportable, if it had not involved in its very nature a sustaining hope for the future. Among many alleviations, there was one, which (not wisely, but overcome by circumstances) all were willing to admit;—that the event was so strange and uncouth, exhibiting such discordant characteristics of innocent fatuity and enormous guilt, that it could not without violence be thought of as indicative of a general constitution of things, either in the country or the government; but that it was a kind of *lusus naturae* in the moral world—a solitary straggler out of the circumference of Nature's law—a monster which could not propagate, and had no birth-right in futurity. Accordingly, the first expectation was that the government would deem itself under the necessity of disannulling the Convention; a necessity which, though in itself a great evil, appeared small in the eyes of judicious men, compared with the consequences of admitting that such a contract could be binding. For they who had signed and ratified it, had not only glaringly exceeded all power which could be supposed to be vested in them as holding a military office; but, in the exercise of political functions, they had framed ordinances which neither the government, nor the Nation, nor any Power on earth, could confer upon them a right to frame: therefore the contract was self-destroying from the beginning. [16] It is a wretched oversight, or a wilful abuse of terms still more wretched, to speak of the good faith of a Nation as being pledged to an act which was not a shattering of the edifice of justice, but a subversion of its foundations. One man cannot sign away the faculty of reason in another; much less can one or two individuals do this for a whole people. Therefore the contract was void, both from its injustice and its absurdity; [16] and the party with whom it was made must have known it to be so. It could not then but be expected by many that the government would reject it.

Moreover, extraordinary outrages against reason and virtue demand that extraordinary sacrifices of atonement should be made upon their altars; and some were encouraged to think that a government might upon this impulse rise above itself, and turn an exceeding disgrace into true glory, by a public profession of shame and repentance for having appointed such unworthy instruments; that, this being acknowledged, it would clear itself from all imputation of having any further connection with what had been done, and would provide that the Nation should as speedily as possible be purified from all suspicion of looking upon it with other feelings than those of abhorrence. . . .

The government shown to be infected by the spirit of the Convention

These thoughts, if not welcomed without scruple and relied upon without fear, were at least encouraged; till it was recollected that the persons at the head of government had ordered that the event should be communicated to the inhabitants of the metropolis with signs of national rejoicing. No wonder if, when these rejoicings were called to mind, it was impossible to entertain the faith which would have been most consolatory. The evil appeared no longer as the forlorn monster which I have described. It put on another shape and was endued with a more formidable life—with power to generate and transmit after its kind. A new and alarming import was added to the event by this open testimony of gladness and approbation; which intimated—which declared—that the spirit which swayed the individuals who were the ostensible and immediate authors of the Convention was not confined to them; but that it was widely prevalent: else it could not have been found in the very council-seat; there, where if wisdom and virtue have not some influence, what is to become of the Nation in these times of peril? rather say, into what an abyss is it already fallen!

His Majesty's ministers, by this mode of communicating the tidings, indiscreet as it was unfeeling, had committed themselves. Yet still they might have recovered from the lapse, have awakened after a little time. And accordingly, notwithstanding an annunciation so ominous, it was matter of surprise and sorrow to many, that the ministry appeared to deem the Convention binding, and that its terms were to be fulfilled. There had indeed been only a choice of evils: but, of the two the worse—ten thousand times the worse—was fixed upon. The ministers, having thus officially applauded the treaty,—and, by suffering it to be carried into execution, made themselves a party to the transaction,—drew upon themselves those suspicions which will ever pursue the steps of public men who abandon the direct road which leads to the welfare of their country. It was suspected that they had taken this part against the dictates of conscience, and from selfishness and cowardice . . . that the ministry took upon itself a final responsibility, with a vain hope that, by so doing and incorporating its own credit with the transaction, it might bear down the censures of the people, and overrule their judgment to the superinducing of a belief that the treaty was not so unjust and inexpedient: and thus would be included—in one sweeping exculpation—the misdeeds of the servant and the master.

City of London petitions for an inquiry: it is reproved as 'pronouncing judgment before investigation'

But—whether these suspicions were reasonable or not, whatever motives produced a determination that the Convention should be acted upon,—there can be no doubt of the manner in which the ministry wished that the people should appreciate it; when the same persons, who had ordered that it should at first be received with rejoicing, availed themselves of his Majesty's high authority to give a harsh reproof to the City of London for having prayed 'that an enquiry might be instituted into this dishonourable and unprecedented transaction'. In their petition they styled it also 'an afflicting event—humiliating and degrading to the country, and injurious to his Majesty's Allies'. [17] And for this, to the astonishment and grief of all sound minds, the petitioners were severely reprimanded; and told, among other admonitions, 'that it was inconsistent with the principles of British jurisprudence to pronounce judgment without previous investigation'. . . .

If the persons who signed this petition acted inconsistently with the principles of British jurisprudence; the offence must have been committed by giving an answer before adequate and lawful evidence had entitled them so to do, to one or other of these questions:—'What is the act? and who is the agent?'—or to both conjointly. Now the petition gives no opinion upon the agent; it pronounces only upon the act, and that some one must be guilty; but *who*—it does not take upon itself to say. It condemns the act; and calls for punishment upon the authors, whoever they may be found to be; and does no more. After the analysis which has been made of the Convention, I may ask if there be anything in this which deserves reproof; and reproof from an authority which ought to be most enlightened and most dispassionate,—as it is, next to the legislative, the most solemn authority in the Land.

Petition of complaint a constitutional safeguard of liberty

It is known to every one that the privilege of complaint, in cases where the Nation feels itself aggrieved, *itself* being the judge (and who else ought to be, or can be?)—a privilege, the exercise of which implies condemnation of something complained of, followed by a prayer for its removal or correction—not only is established by the most grave and authentic charters of Englishmen, who have been taught by their wisest statesmen and legislators to be jealous over its preservation, and to call it into practice upon every reasonable occasion; but also that this privilege is an indispensable condition of all civil liberty. . . . To enter upon this argument is indeed both astounding and humiliating: for the adversary in the present case is bound to contend that we cannot pronounce upon evil or good, either in the actions of our own or in past time, unless the decision of a Court of Judicature has empowered us so to do. Why then have historians written? and why do we yield to the impulses of our nature, hating, or loving—approving or condemning according to the appearances which their records present to our eyes? But the doctrine is as nefarious as it is absurd. For those public events in which men are most interested, namely, the crimes of rulers and of persons in high authority, for the most part are such as either have never been brought before tribunals at all, or before unjust ones. . . . Therefore to make a verdict of a Court of Judicature a necessary condition for enabling men to determine the quality of an act, when the 'head and front'—the life and soul of the offence may have been, that it eludes or rises above the reach of all judicature, is a contradiction which would be too gross to merit notice, were it not that men willingly suffer their understandings to stagnate. And hence this rotten bog, rotten and unstable as the crude consistence of Milton's chaos, 'smitten . . . by the petrific mace—and bound with Gorgonian rigour by the look'—of despotism, is transmuted; and becomes a high-way of adamant for the sorrowful steps of generation after generation. . . .

To sum up the matter—the right of petition (which, we have shown as a general proposition, supposes a right to condemn, and is in itself an act of qualified condemnation) may in too many instances take the ground of absolute condemnation, both with respect to the crime and the criminal. It was confined, in this case, to the crime; but, if the City of London had proceeded further, they would have been justifiable; because the delinquents had set their hands to their own delinquency. The petitioners, then, are not only clear of all blame; but are entitled to high praise: and we have seen whither the doctrines lead, upon which they were condemned. . . .

Vox populi. . . .

Never surely was there a public event more fitted to reduce men, in all ranks of society, under the supremacy of their common nature; to impress upon them one belief; to infuse into them one spirit. . . . Every human being in these islands was unsettled; the most slavish broke loose as from fetters; and there was not an individual—it need not be said of heroic virtue, but of ingenuous life and sound discretion—who, if his father, his son, or his brother, or if the flower of his house had been in that army, would not rather that they had perished, and the whole body of their countrymen, their companions in arms, had perished to a man, than that a treaty should have been submitted to upon such conditions. This was the feeling of the people; an awful feeling: and it is from these oracles that rulers are to learn wisdom. For, when the people speaks loudly, it is from being strongly possessed either by the Godhead or the Demon; and he, who cannot discover the true spirit from the false, hath no ear for profitable communion. But in all that regarded the destinies of Spain, and her own as connected with them, the voice of Britain had the unquestionable sound of inspiration. If the gentle passions of pity, love, and gratitude, be porches of the temple; if the sentiments of admiration and rivalry be pillars upon which the structure is sustained; if, lastly, hatred, and anger, and vengeance, be steps which, by a mystery of nature, lead to the House of Sanctity; —then was it manifest to what power the edifice was consecrated; and that the voice within was of Holiness and Truth. [18]

Safety and deliverance are the proximate, regeneration and liberty the ultimate, ends of the war

Spain had risen not merely to be delivered and saved;—deliverance and safety were but intermediate objects;—regeneration and liberty were the end, and the means by which this end was to be attained. . . . She had risen—not merely to be free; but, in the act and process of acquiring that freedom, to recompense herself, as it were in a moment, for all which she had suffered through ages. . . . They [the Spaniards] did not wander madly about the world—like the Tamerlanes, or the Chengiz Khans, or the present barbarian Ravager of Europe —under a mock title of Delegates of the Almighty, acting upon self-assumed authority. Their commission had been thrust upon them. They had been trampled upon, tormented, wronged—bitterly, wantonly wronged, if ever a people on the earth was wronged. And this it was which legitimately incorporated their law with the supreme conscience, and gave to them the deep faith which they have expressed—that their power was favoured and assisted by the Almighty. . . . Riddance, mere riddance—safety, mere safety—are objects far too defined, too inert and passive in their own nature, to have ability either to rouze or to sustain. They win not the mind by any attraction of grandeur or sublime delight, either in effort or in endurance: for the mind gains consciousness of its strength to undergo only by exercise among materials which admit the impression of its power,—which grow under it, which bend under it,—which resist,—which change under its influence,—which alter either through its might or in its presence, by it or before it. These, during times of tranquillity, are the objects with which, in the studious walks of sequestered life, Genius most loves to hold intercourse; by which it is reared and supported;—these are the qualities in action and in object, in image, in thought, and in feeling, from communion with which proceeds originally all that is creative in art and science, and all that is magnanimous in virtue.—Despair thinks of *safety*, and hath no purpose; fear thinks of safety; despondency looks the same way:—but these passions are far too selfish, and therefore too blind, to reach the thing at which they aim; even when there is in them sufficient dignity to have an aim.—All courage is a projection from ourselves; however short-lived, it is a motion of hope. But these thoughts bind too closely to something inward,—to the present and to the past,—that is, to the self which is or has been. Whereas the vigour of the human soul is from without and from futurity,—in breaking down limit, and losing and

In times of trial the mind finds its strength in objects which are the normal concerns of genius and the inspiration of creative art

Courage

forgetting herself in the sensation and image of Country and of the human race; and, when she returns and is most restricted and confined, her dignity consists in the contemplation of a better and more exalted being, which, though proceeding from herself, she loves and is devoted to as to another.

Body and soul, mechanic power and vital power, are not commensurate

In following the stream of these thoughts, I have not wandered from my course: I have drawn out to open day the truth from its recesses in the minds of my countrymen.—Something more perhaps may have been done: a shape hath perhaps been given to that which was before a stirring spirit. I have shown in what manner it was their wish that the struggle with the adversary of all that is good should be maintained—by pure passions and high actions. They forbid that their noble aim should be frustrated by measuring against each other things which are incommensurate—mechanic against moral power—body against soul. They will not suffer, without expressing their sorrow, that purblind calculation should wither the purest hopes in the face of all-seeing justice. These are times of strong appeal—of deep-searching visitation; when the best abstractions of the prudential understanding give way, and are included and absorbed in a supreme comprehensiveness of intellect and passion; which is the perfection and the very being of humanity.

Not considerations of policy, but only moral passion, can sustain a people in great endeavour

How base! how puny! how inefficient for all good purposes, are the tools and implements of policy, compared with these mighty engines of Nature!—There is no middle course: two masters cannot be served:—Justice must either be enthroned above might, and the moral law take place of the edicts of selfish passion; or the heart of the people, which alone can sustain the efforts of the people, [19] will languish: their desires will not spread beyond the plough and the loom, the field and the fire-side: the sword will appear to them an emblem of no promise; and instrument of no hope; an object of indifference, of disgust, or fear. Was there ever—since the earliest actions of men which have been transmitted by affectionate tradition or recorded by faithful history, or sung to the impassioned harp of poetry—was there ever a people who presented themselves to the reason and the imagination, as under more holy influences than the dwellers upon the Southern Peninsula; as rouzed more instantaneously from a deadly sleep to a more hopeful wakefulness; as a mass fluctuating with one motion under the breath of a mightier wind; [20] as breaking themselves up, and settling into several bodies, in more harmonious order; as reunited and embattled under a standard which was reared to the sun with more authentic assurance of final victory?

Spanish religion and the cause

The superstition (I do not dread the word) which prevailed in these nations, may have checked many of my countrymen who would otherwise have exultingly accompanied me in a challenge which, under the shape of a question, I have been confidently uttering; as I know that this stain (so the same persons termed it) did, from the beginning, discourage their hopes for the cause. Short-sighted despondency! Whatever mixture of superstition there might be in the religious faith or devotional practices of the Spaniards; this must have necessarily been transmuted by that triumphant power, wherever that power was felt, which grows out of intense moral suffering—from the moment in which it coalesces with fervent hope. The chains of bigotry, which enthralled the mind, must have been turned into armour to defend and weapons to annoy. Wherever the heaving and effort of freedom was spread, purification must have followed it. And the types and ancient instruments of error, where emancipated men shewed their foreheads to the day, must have become a language and a ceremony of imagination; expressing, consecrating, and invigorating, the most pure deductions of Reason and the holiest feelings of universal Nature. . . . Even the very faith in miraculous interposition, which is so dire a weakness and cause of weakness in tranquil times when the listless Being turns to it as a cheap and ready substitute upon every occasion, where the man sleeps, and the Saint, or the image of the Saint, is to perform his work, and to give effect to his wishes;—even this infirm faith . . . is subjugated in order to be exalted; and—instead of operating as a temptation to relax or to be remiss, as an encouragement to indolence or cowardice . . . passes into a habit of obscure and infinite confidence of the mind in its own energies, in the cause from its own sanctity, and in the ever-present invisible aid or momentary conspicuous approbation of the supreme Disposer of things. [21]

The power of emancipated imagination

Let the fire, which is never wholly to be extinguished, break out afresh; let but the human creature be rouzed; whether he have lain heedless and torpid in religious or civil slavery—have languished under a thraldom, domestic or foreign, or under both these alternately—or have drifted about a helpless member of a clan of disjointed and feeble barbarians; let him rise and act;—and his domineering imagination, by which from childhood he has been betrayed, and the debasing affections which it has imposed upon him, will from that moment participate the dignity of the newly ennobled being whom they will now acknowledge for their master; and will further him in his progıess, whatever be the object at which he aims. Still more inevitable and momentous are the results when the individual knows that the fire which is reanimated in him is not less lively in the breasts of his associates. . . . Hence those marvellous achievements which were performed by the first enthusiastic followers of Mohammed; and by other conquerors, who with their armies have swept large portions of the earth like a transitory wind, or have founded new religions or empires. —But if the object contended for be worthy and truly great (as, in the instance of the Spaniards, we have seen that it is); if cruelties have been committed upon an ancient and venerable people, which 'shake the human frame with horror'; if not alone the life which is sustained by the bread of the mouth, but that—without which there is no life—the life in the soul, has been directly and mortally warred against; if reason has had abominations to endure in her inmost sanctuary;—then does intense passion, consecrated by a sudden revelation of justice, give birth to those higher and better wonders which I have described; and exhibit true miracles to the eyes of men, and the noblest which can be seen.

It may be added that,—as this union brings back to the right road the faculty of imagination, where it is prone to err, and has gone furthest astray; as it corrects those qualities which . . . are more immediately dependent upon the imagination, and which may have received from it a thorough taint of dishonour;—so the domestic loves and sanctities which are in their nature less liable to be stained,—so these, wherever they have flowed with a pure and placid stream, do instantly, under the same influence, put forth their strength as in a flood; and without being sullied or polluted, pursue—exultingly and with song—a course which leads the contemplative reason to the ocean of eternal love.

The purifying power of justice and moral passion

I feel that I have been speaking in a strain which it is difficult to harmonize with the petty irritations, the doubts and fears, and the familiar (and therefore frequently undignified) exterior of present and passing events. But the theme is justice; and my voice is raised for mankind; for us who are alive, and for all posterity:—justice and passion; clear-sighted and aspiring justice, and passion sacred as vehement. These, like twin-born Deities delighting in each other's presence, have wrought marvels in the inward mind through the whole region of the Pyrenean Peninsula. I have shown by what process these united powers sublimated the objects of outward sense in such rites—practices—and ordinances of Religion—as deviate from simplicity and wholesome piety; how they converted them to instruments of nobler use; and raised them to a conformity with things truly divine. The same reasoning might have been carried into the customs of civil life and their accompanying imagery, wherever these also were inconsistent with the dignity of man; and like effects of exaltation and purification have been shewn. . . .

Seville . . . Andalusia . . . Saragossa! . . . The multitudes of men who were arrayed in the fields of Baylen, and upon the mountains of the North; the peasants of Asturias, and the students of Salamanca; and many a solitary and untold-of hand, which, quitting for a moment the plough or the spade, has discharged a more pressing debt to the country by levelling with the dust at least one insolent and murderous Invader;—these have attested the efficacy of the passions which we have been contemplating—that the will of good men is not a vain impulse, heroic desires a delusive prop;—have proved that the condition of human affairs is not so forlorn and desperate, but that there are golden opportunities when the dictates of justice may be unrelentingly enforced, and the beauty of the inner mind substantiated in the outward act;—for a visible standard to look back upon; for a point of realized excellence at which to aspire; a monument to record;—for a charter to fasten down; and, as far as it is possible to preserve.

Promise of the internal regeneration of Spain

Yes! there was an annunciation which the good received with gladness; a bright appearance which emboldened the wise to say—We trust that Regeneration is at hand. . . . The government which had been exercised under the name of the old Monarchy of Spain—this government, imbecile even to dotage, whose very selfishness was destitute of vigour, had been removed; taken laboriously and foolishly by the plotting Corsican to his own bosom; in order that the world might see, more triumphantly set forth than since the beginning of things had ever been seen before, to what degree a man of bad principles is despicable—though of great power—working blindly against his own purposes. . . . The work of liberation was virtually accomplished—we might almost say established. The interests of the people were taken from a government whose sole aim it had been to prop up the last remains of its own decrepitude by betraying those whom it was its duty to protect;—withdrawn from such hands, to be committed to those of the people; at a time when the double affliction which Spain had endured, and the return of affliction with which she was threatened, made it impossible that the emancipated Nation could abuse its new-born strength to any substantial injury to itself. . . . Then it was,—when the people of Spain were thus rouzed; after this manner released from the natal burthen of that government which had bowed them to the ground; in the free use of their understandings, and in the play and 'noble rage' of their passions; while yet the new authorities, which they had generated, were truly living members of their body and . . . organs of their life; when that numerous people were

The Convention a betrayal in the very hour of liberation and regeneration

in a stage of their journey which could not be accomplished without the spirit which was then prevalent in them, and which (as might be feared) would too soon abate of itself;—then it was that we—not we, but the heads of the British army and Nation . . . stepped in with their forms, their impediments, their rotten customs and precedents, their narrow desires, their busy and purblind fears; and called out to these aspiring travellers to halt . . . confounded them . . . spell-bound them. . . . We had power to give a brotherly aid to our Allies in supporting the mighty world which their shoulders had undertaken to uphold; and, while they were expecting from us this aid, we undermined—without forewarning them—the ground upon which they stood. The evil is incalculable; and the stain will cleave to the British name as long as the story of this island shall endure. . . .

Sources of our failings:

If then (to return to ourselves) there be such strong obstacles in the way of our drawing benefit either from the maxims of policy or the principles of justice; what hope remains that the British Nation should repair, by its future conduct, the injury which has been done?—We cannot advance a step towards a rational answer to this question—without previously adverting to the original source of our miscarriages; which are these: —First, a want, in the minds of the members of government and public functionaries, of knowledge indispensable for this service; and, secondly a want of power, in the same persons acting in their corporate capacities, to give effect to the knowledge which individually they possess.—Of the latter source of weakness,—this inability as caused by decay in the machine of government, and by illegitimate forces which are checking and controlling its constitutional motions,—I have not spoken, nor shall I now speak: for I have judged it best to suspend my task for a while: and this subject, being in its nature delicate, ought not to be lightly or transiently touched. Besides, no *immediate* effect can be expected from the soundest and most unexceptionable doctrines which might be laid down for the correcting of this evil. The former source of weakness,—

(i) Want of requisite knowledge on the part of our governors

(ii) Want of power to give their knowledge effect

Constitutional reform no immediate remedy

namely, the want of appropriate and indispensable knowledge, —has in the past investigation, been reached, and shall be further laid open; not without a hope of some result of *immediate* good by a direct application to the mind; and in full confidence that the best and surest way to render operative that knowledge which is already possessed—is to increase the stock of knowledge. . . .

After the view of things which has been taken,—we may confidently affirm that nothing but a knowledge of human nature directing the operations of our government, can give it a right to an intimate association with a cause which is that of human nature. . . . It is plain *a priori* that the minds of Statesmen and Courtiers are unfavourable to the growth of this knowledge. For they are in a situation exclusive and artificial; which has the further disadvantage, that it does not separate men from men by collateral partitions which leave, along with difference, a sense of equality—that they, who are divided, are yet upon the same level; but by a degree of superiority which can scarcely fail to be accompanied with more or less of pride. This situation therefore must be eminently unfavourable for the reception and establishment of that knowledge which is founded not upon things but upon sensations;—sensations which are general, and under general influences. . . . Passing by the kindred and usually accompanying influence of birth in a certain rank [22]—and, where education has been pre-defined from childhood for the express purpose of future political power, the tendency of such education to warp (and therefore weaken) the intellect; [23]—we may join at once, with the privation which I have been noticing, a delusion equally common. It is this: that practical Statesmen assume too much credit to themselves for their ability to see into the motives and manage the selfish passions of their immediate agents and dependents; and for the skill with which they baffle or resist the aims of their opponents. A promptness in looking through the most superficial part of the characters of those men . . . is mistaken for a knowledge of human kind. Hence, where higher knowledge is a prime requisite, they not only are unfurnished,

Minds of statesmen generally unfavourable to attainment of knowledge of human nature

Lack of the common touch

Early education for political power warps the intellect

Practical statesmen too often confuse insight into the minds of their agents with insight into average human nature

but, being unconscious that they are so, they look down contemptuously upon those who endeavour to supply (in some degree) their want.

The routine statesman, in his concern with the formal machine of administration, is blind to the forces which constitute the vital life of society

The instincts of natural and social man; the deeper emotions; the simpler feelings; the spacious range of the disinterested imagination; the pride in country for country's sake, when to serve has not been a formal profession—and the mind is therefore left in a sate of dignity only to be surpassed by having served nobly and generously; the instantaneous accomplishment in which they start up who, upon a searching call, stir for the Land which they love—not from personal motives, but for a reward which is undefined and cannot be missed; the solemn fraternity which a great Nation composes—gathered together, in a stormy season, under the shade of ancestral feeling; the delicacy of moral honour which pervades the minds of a people when despair has been suddenly thrown off and expectations are lofty; . . . the power of injustice and inordinate calamity to transmute, to invigorate, and to govern . . .; these arrangements and resources of nature, these ways and means of a society, have so little connection with those others upon which a ruling minister of a long-established government is accustomed to depend; these—elements as it were of a universe, functions of a living body—are so opposite, in their mode of action, to the formal machine which it has been his pride to manage;—that he has but a faint perception of their immediate efficacy; knows not the facility with which they assimiliate with other powers; nor the property by which such of them—as, from necessity of nature, must change or pass away—will, under wise and fearless management, surely generate lawful successors to fill their place when their appropriate work is performed. . . . [24]

Such knowledge is not necessary in ordinary times

That specific knowledge,—the paramount importance of which, in the present condition of Europe, I am insisting upon, —they, who usually fill places of high trust in old governments, neither do—nor, for the most part, can—possess: nor is it necessary, for the administration of affairs in ordinary circumstances that they should.—The progress of their own country, and of the other nations of the world, in civilization, in true refinement, in science, in religion, in morals, and in all the real wealth of humanity, might indeed be quicker, and might correspond more happily with the wishes of the benevolent,—if Governors better understood the rudiments of nature as studied in the walks of common life; if they were men who had themselves felt every strong emotion 'inspired by nature and by fortune taught'; and could calculate upon the force of the grander passions. Yet, at the same time, there is temptation in this. To know may seduce; and to have been agitated may compel. Arduous cares are attractive for their own sakes. Great talents are naturally driven towards hazard and difficulty; as it is there that they are most sure to find their exercise, and their evidence, and joy in anticipated triumph—the liveliest of all sensations. Moreover; magnificent desires when least under the bias of personal feeling, dispose the mind—more than itself is conscious of—to regard commotion with complacency, and to watch the aggravation of distress with welcoming; from an immoderate confidence that, when the appointed day shall come, it will be in the power of intellect to relieve. There is danger in being a zealot in any cause—not excepting that of humanity. Nor is it to be forgotten that the incapacity and ignorance of the regular agents of long-established governments do not prevent some progress in the dearest concerns of men; and that society may owe to these very deficiencies, and to the tame and unenterprizing course which they necessitate, much security and tranquil enjoyment.

Dangers of such knowledge

Great talents are tempted to welcome commotion and distress as a challenge

Nor, on the other hand . . . is it so desirable as might at first sight be imagined, much less is it desirable as an absolute good, that men of comprehensive sensibility and tutored genius—either for the interests of mankind or for their own—should, in ordinary times, have vested in them political power. [25] The Empire which they hold is more independent: its constituent parts are sustained by a stricter connection: the dominion is purer and of higher origin; as mind is more excellent than body—the search of truth an employment more inherently dignified than the application of force—the determinations of

Undesirability of power being vested in men of comprehensive sensibility and tutored genius in ordinary times

nature more venerable than the accidents of human institution. Chance and disorder, vexation and disappointment, malignity and perverseness within or without the mind, are a sad exchange for the steady and genial processes of reason. Moreover; worldly distinctions and offices of command do not lie in the path—nor are they any part of the appropriate retinue—of Philosophy and Virtue. Nothing but a strong spirit of love can counteract the consciousness of pre-eminence which ever attends pre-eminent intellectual power with correspondent attainments: and this spirit of love is best encouraged by humility and simplicity in mind, manners, and conduct of life; virtues to which wisdom leads.

Undesirable for the men themselves

All power corrupts. . . .

But,—though these be virtues in a Man, a Citizen, or a Sage,—they cannot be recommended to the especial culture of the Political or Military Functionary; and still less of the Civil Magistrate. Him, in the exercise of his functions, it will often become to carry himself highly and with state; in order that evil may be suppressed, and authority respected by those who have not understanding. The power also of office, whether the duties be discharged well or ill, will ensure a never-failing supply of flattery and praise; and of these—a man (becoming at once double-dealer and dupe) may, without impeachment of his modesty, receive as much as his weakness inclines him to; under the shew that the homage is not offered up to himself, but to that portion of the public dignity which is lodged in his person. But, whatever may be the cause, the fact is certain—that there is an unconquerable tendency in all power, save that of knowledge acting by and through knowledge, to injure the mind of him who exercises that power; so much so, that best natures cannot escape the evil of such alliance. . . .

But these are not ordinary times

To prevent misconception; and to silence (at least to throw discredit upon) the clamours of ignorance;—I have thought proper thus, in some sort, to strike a balance between the claims of men of routine—and men of original and accomplished minds—to the management of State affairs in ordinary circumstances. But ours is not an age of this character: and, after having seen such a long series of misconduct . . . it is reasonable that we should endeavour to ascertain to what cause these evils are to be ascribed. I have directed the attention of the Reader to one primary cause: and can he doubt of its existence, and of the operation which I have attributed to it?

Insensibility to the principles of human nature shown in two wars against liberty, and now in a war for liberty

In the course of the last thirty years we have seen two wars waged against Liberty—the American war, and the war against the French people in the early stages of their Revolution. In the latter instance, the Emigrants and the Continental Powers and the British did, in all their expectations and in every movement of their efforts, manifest a common ignorance—originating in the same source. And, for what more especially belongs to ourselves at this time, we may affirm—that the same presumptuous irreverence of the principles of justice, and blank insensibility to the affections of human nature, which determined the conduct of our government in those two wars *against* liberty, have continued to accompany its exertions in the present struggle *for* liberty,—and have rendered them fruitless. The British government deems (no doubt) on its own part, that its intentions are good. It must not deceive itself: nor must we deceive ourselves. Intentions—thoroughly good—could not mingle with the unblessed actions which we have witnessed. A disinterested and pure intention is a light that guides as well as cheers, and renders desperate lapses impossible.

Our duty is,—our aim ought to be,—to employ the true means of liberty and virtue for the ends of liberty and virtue. In such policy, thoroughly understood, there is fitness and concord and rational subordination; it deserves a higher name—organization, health, and grandeur. Contrast, in a single instance, the two processes; and the qualifications which they require. The ministers of that period found it any easy task to hire a band of Hessians, and to send it across the Atlantic, that they might assist *in bringing the Americans* (according to the phrase then prevalent) *to reason*. The force with which those troops would attack was gross—tangible—and might be calculated; but the spirit of resistance which their presence would create was subtle—ethereal—mighty—and incalculable. Accordingly, from the moment when these foreigners landed

The war of American Independence

—men who had no interest, no business, in the quarrel, but what the wages of their master bound him to, and he imposed upon his miserable slaves;—nay, from the first rumour of their destination, the success of the British was (as hath since been affirmed by judicious Americans) impossible. The British government of the present day have been seduced, as we have seen, by the same common-place facilities on the one side; and have been equally blind on the other. A physical auxiliar force of thirty-five thousand men is to be added to the army of Spain: but the moral energy . . . is overlooked or slighted; the material being too fine for their calculation. . . .

Let our rulers look to the state of their own minds

It surely then behoves those who are in authority—to look to the state of their own minds. There is indeed an inherent impossibility that they should be equal to the arduous duties which have devolved upon them; but it is not unreasonable to hope that something higher might be aimed at; and that the People might see, upon great occasions,—in the practice of its Rulers—a more adequate reflection of its own wisdom and virtue. . . .

Immediate policy in the Peninsula:

Either supply *Spain with overwhelming numbers—*

Or support Spain *in* things *rather than men*

Deeming it then not to be doubted that the British government will continue its endeavours to support its Allies; one or other of two maxims of policy follow obviously from the painful truths which we have been considering:—Either, first, that we should put forth to the utmost of our strength as a military power—strain it to the very last point, and prepare (no erect mind will start at the proposition) to pour into the Peninsula a force of two hundred thousand men or more,—and make ourselves for a time, upon Spanish ground, principals in the contest; or, secondly, that we should direct our attention to giving support rather in *Things* than in Men.

How formidable is the enemy?

The former plan, though requiring a great effort and many sacrifices, is (I have no doubt) practicable: its difficulties would yield to a bold and energetic Ministry, in despite of the present constitution of Parliament. . . . A further encouragement for adopting this plan he will find, who perceives that the military power of our Enemy is not in substance so formidable, by many—many degrees of terror, as outwardly it appears to be. The last campaign has not been wholly without advantage: since it has proved that the French troops are indebted, for their victories, to the imbecility of their opponents far more than to their own discipline and courage—or even to the skill and talents of their Generals. . . .

His power rests on: (i) despotic government in France, and (ii) the character of the Emperor

All—which is comparatively inherent, or can lay claim to any degree of permanence, in the tyranny which the French Nation maintains over Europe—rests upon two foundations: —First; Upon the despotic rule which has been established in France over a powerful People who have lately passed from a state of revolution, in which they supported a struggle begun for domestic liberty and national independence:—and, secondly, upon the personal character of the Man by whom that rule is exercised.

(i) Despotism: its general weakness as a form of government

As to the former; everyone knows that Despotism, in a general sense, is but another word for weakness. Let one generation disappear; and a whole people over whom such rule has been extended, if it have not virtue to free itself, is condemned to embarrassment in the operations of its government, and to perpetual languor; with no better hope than that which may spring from the diseased activity of some particular Prince on whom the authority may happen to devolve. . . . The feebleness of despotic power we have had before our eyes in the late condition of Spain and Prussia; and in that of France before the Revolution; and in the present condition of Austria and Russia. But, in a *new-born* arbitrary and military Government (especially if, like that of France, it have been immediately preceded by a popular Constitution) not only this weakness is not found; but it possesses, for the purposes of external annoyance, a preternatural vigour. Many causes contribute to this: we need mention only that fitness—real or supposed—being necessarily the chief (and almost sole) recommendation to offices of trust, it is clear that such offices will in general be ably filled; and their duties, comparatively, well executed: and that, from the conjunction of absolute civil and military authority in a single Person, there naturally follows promptness

Why it is not weak in France

The career open to talent

The conjunction of absolute civil and military power in a single person

of decision; concentration of effort; rapidity of motion; and confidence that the movements made will be regularly supported. This is all which need now be said upon the subject of this first basis of French Tyranny.

(ii) Character of the Emperor

For the second—namely, the personal character of the Chief; I shall at present content myself with noting (to prevent misconception) that this basis is not laid in any superiority of talents in him, but in his utter rejection of the restraints of morality—in wickedness which acknowledges no limit but the extent of its own power. Let anyone reflect a moment; and he will feel that a new world of forces is opened to a Being who has made this desperate leap. [26] It is a tremendous principle to be adopted, and steadily adhered to, by a man in the station which Buonaparte occupies; and he has taken the full benefit of it. . . . [It] is a duty which we owe to the present moment to proclaim—in vindication of the dignity of human nature, and for an admonition to men of prostrate spirit—that the dominion, which this Enemy of mankind holds, has neither been acquired nor is sustained by endowments of intellect which are rarely bestowed, or by uncommon accumulations of knowledge; but that it has risen from circumstances over which he had no influence; circumstances which, with the power they conferred, have stimulated passions whose natural food hath been and is ignorance; from the barbarian impotence and insolence of a mind—originally of ordinary constitution—lagging, in moral sentiment and knowledge, three hundred years behind the age in which it acts. In such manner did the power originate; and, by the forces which I have described, it is maintained. This should be declared: and it should be added—that the crimes of Buonaparte are more to be abhorred than those of other denaturalized creatures whose actions are painted in History; because the Author of those crimes is guilty with less temptation, and sins in the presence of a clearer light. [27]

Advantages of a ruler who rejects restraints of morality

Bonaparte's dominion due less to his superior endowments than to circumstances and his barbarian moral backwardness

The loss of two pitched battles by Bonaparte would raise the subjugated nations of his empire in revolt

No doubt in the command of almost the whole military force of Europe . . . he has, *at this moment*, a third source of power which may be added to these two. . . . But the enormity of this power has in it nothing *inherent* or *permanent*. Two signal overthrows in pitched battles would, I believe, go far to destroy it. . . . In a word; the vastness of Buonaparte's military power is formidable—not because it is impossible to break it; but because it has not yet been penetrated. . . . A hundred thousand men, such as fought at Vimiera and Corunna, would accomplish three such victories as I have been anticipating. . . . The oppressed Continental Powers . . . seeing such unquestionable proof that Great Britain was sincere and earnest, would lift their heads again; and, by so doing, would lighten the burthen of war which might remain for the Spaniards.

In treating of this plan—I have presumed that a General might be placed at the head of this great military power who would not sign a treaty like that of the Convention of Cintra . . . a General and a Ministry whose policy would be comprehensive enough to perceive that the true welfare of Britain is best promoted by the independence, freedom, and honour of other nations; and that it is only by the diffusion and prevalence of these virtues that French Tyranny can be ultimately reduced; or the influence of France over the rest of Europe brought within its natural and reasonable limits.

Advantages to be gained by our supplying both men and things

If this attempt be 'above the strain and temper' of the country, there remains only a plan laid down upon the other principles; namely, service (as far as is required) in *things* rather than in men; that is, men being secondary to things. . . .

Folly of any middle course

But from a middle course—an association sufficiently intimate and wide to scatter everywhere unkindly passions, and yet unable to attain the salutary point of decisive power—no good is to be expected. Great would be the evil, at this momentous period, if the hatred of the Spaniards should look two ways. Let it be as steadily fixed upon the French, as the Pilot's eye upon his mark. Military stores and arms should be furnished with unfailing liberality: let Troops also be supplied; but let these act separately,—taking strong positions upon the coast, if such can be found, to employ twice their numbers of the enemy; and above all, let there be floating Armies—keeping the Enemy in constant uncertainty where he is to be attacked. The peninsular frame of Spain and Portugal lays that region

Combined operations

open to the full shock of British warfare. Our Fleet and Army should act, wherever it is possible, as parts of one body—a right hand and a left; and the Enemy ought to be made to feel the force of both. . . .

Failure of a parliamentary vote of censure on the Convention

The Debates in Parliament, and measures of Government, every day furnish new proofs of the truths which I have been attempting to establish—of the utter want of general principles; —new and lamentable proofs! This moment . . . I learn, from the newspaper reports, that the House of Commons has refused to declare that the Convention of Cintra *disappointed the hopes and expectations of the Nation.* [28] The motion, according to the letter of it, was ill-framed; for the Convention might have been a very good one, and still have disappointed the hopes and expectations of the Nation—as those might have been unwise: at all events, the words ought to have stood—the *just* and *reasonable* hopes of the Nation. But the hacknied phrase of '*disappointed hopes and expectations*'—should not have been used at all: it is a centre round which much delusion has gathered. The Convention not only did not satisfy the Nation's hopes of good; but sunk it into a pitfall of unimagined and unimaginable evil. . . The question was—whether principles affecting the very existence of society had not been violated. . . . If the People would constitutionally and resolutely assert their rights, their Representatives would be taught another lesson; and for their own profit. Their understandings would be enriched accordingly: for it is there,—there where least suspected—that the want from which this country suffers, chiefly lies.

Its improper phrasing

Not venality and corruption, but the non-existence of wide-ranging intellect, is the master-evil of the day

They err who suppose that venality and corruption (though now spreading more and more) are the master-evils of this day: neither these nor immoderate craving for power are so much to be deprecated, as the non-existence of a widely-ranging intellect; [29] of an intellect which, if not efficacious to infuse truth as a vital fluid into the heart, might at least make it a powerful tool in the hand. Outward profession,—which for practical purposes, is an act of most desirable submission,—would then wait upon those objects to which inward reverence, though not felt, was known to be due. Schemes of ample reach and true benefit would also promise best to insure the rewards coveted by personal ambition: and men of baser passions, finding it their interest, would naturally combine to perform useful service under the direction of strong minds: while men of good intentions would have their own pure satisfaction; and would exert themselves with more upright—I mean, more hopeful—cheerfulness, and more successfully. It is not, therefore, inordinate desire for wealth or power which is so injurious—as the means which are and must be employed, in the present intellectual condition of the Legislature, to sustain and secure that power: these are at once an effect of barrenness, and a cause; acting and mutually reacting incessantly. An enlightened Friend [30] has, in conversation, observed to the Author of these pages—that formerly the principles of men were better than they who held them; but that now (a far worse evil!) men are better than their principles. I believe it:—of the deplorable quality and state of principles, the public proceedings in our Country furnish daily new proof.

Men and principles

The events of the last year, gloriously destroying many frail fears, have placed—in the rank of serene and immortal truths—a proposition which, as an object of belief, hath in all ages been fondly cherished; namely,—that a numerous Nation, determined to be free, may effect its purpose in despite of the mightiest power which a foreign Invader can bring against it. These events also have pointed out how, in the ways of Nature and under the guidance of Society, this happy end is to be attained: in other words they have shown that the cause of the People . . . is safe while it remains not only in the bosom but in the hands of the People; or (what amounts to the same thing) in those of a government which, being truly *from* the People, is faithfully *for* them. . . .

A numerous nation determined to be free can defeat any army

Talk not of the perishable nature of enthusiasm; [31] and rise above a craving for perpetual manifestation of things. He is to be pitied whose eye can only be pierced by the light of a meridian sun, whose frame can only be warmed by the heat of midsummer. Let us hear no more of the little dependence to

Enthusiasm

be had in war upon voluntary service. The things with which we are primarily and mainly concerned are inward passions and not outward arrangements. These latter may be given at any time when the parts, to be put together, are in readiness. Hatred and love, and each in its intensity, and pride (passions which, existing in the heart of a Nation, are inseparable from hope)—these elements being in constant preparation—enthusiasm will break out from them, or coalesce with them, upon the summons of a moment. And these passions are scarcely less than inextinguishable. . . . He then is a sorry Statist who desponds or despairs (nor is he less so who is too much elevated) from any considerations connected with the quality of enthusiasm. Nothing is so easy as to sustain it by partial and gradual changes of its object; and by placing it in the way of receiving new interpositions according to the need. The difficulty lies—not in kindling, feeding, or fanning the flame; but in continuing so to regulate the relations of things—that the fanning breeze and the feeding fuel shall come from no unworthy quarter, and shall neither of them be wanting in appropriate consecration. The Spaniards have as great helps towards ensuring this as ever were vouchsafed to a People.

The three aims of Spain

Of the ultimate independence of the Spanish Nation there is no reason to doubt: and for the immediate furtherance of the good cause, and a throwing-off of the yoke upon the first favourable opportunity by the different tracts of the country upon which it has been re-imposed, nothing is wanting but sincerity on the part of the government towards the provinces which are yet free. The first end to be secured by Spain is riddance of the enemy: the second, permanent independence: and the third, a free constitution of government; which will give their main (though far from sole) value to the other two: and without which little more than a formal independence, and perhaps scarcely that, can be secured. . . .

Slavery bred at home and slavery imposed from abroad

It is a common saying among those who profess to be lovers of civil liberty, and give themselves some credit for understanding it,—that if a Nation be not free, it is mere dust in the balance whether the slavery be bred at home, or comes from abroad; be of their own suffering, or of a stranger's imposing. They see little of the underground part of the tree of liberty, and know less of the nature of man, who can think thus. Where indeed there is an indisputable and immeasurable superiority in one nation over another; to be conquered may, in the course of time, be a benefit to the inferior nation; and, upon this principle, some of the conquests of the Greeks and Romans may be justified. But in what of really useful or honourable are the French superior to their neighbours? Never far advanced, and, now barbarizing apace, they may carry—amongst the sober and dignified Nations which surround them—much to be avoided, but little to be imitated.

When loss of national independence may be a benefit

There is yet another case in which a People may be benefitted by resignation or forfeiture of their rights as a separate independent State; I mean, where—of two contiguous or neighbouring countries, both included by nature under one conspicuously defined limit—the weaker is united with, or absorbed into, the more powerful; and one and the same government is extended over both. This, with due patience and foresight, may (for the most part) be amicably effected, without the intervention of conquest; but—even should a violent course have been resorted to, and have proved successful—the result will be matter of congratulation rather than of regret, if the countries have been incorporated with an equitable participation of natural advantages and civil privileges. . . . [32] The several independent Sovereignties of Italy . . . have yet this good to aim at; and it will be a happy day for Europe, when the natives of Italy and the natives of Germany . . . shall each dissolve the pernicious barriers which divide them, and form themselves into a mighty People. [33] But Spain, excepting a free union with Portugal, has no benefit of this kind to look for: she has long since attained it. The Pyrenees on the one side, and the Sea on every other; the vast extent and great resources of the territory; a population numerous enough to defend itself against the whole world, and capable of great increase; language; and long duration of independence;—point out and command that the two nations of the Peninsula should be united in friendship

The cases of Italy and Germany

Why Spain should be a free and independent nation

and strict alliance; and, as soon as it may be effected without injustice, form one independent and indissoluble sovereignty. The Peninsula cannot be protected but by itself: it is too large a tree to be framed by nature for a station among underwoods; it must have power to toss its branches in the wind and lift a bold forehead to the sun.

Would the Spaniards be 'better off' under French rule?

Allowing that the *regni novitas* should either compel or tempt the Usurper to do away some ancient abuses, and to accord certain insignificant privileges to the People upon the purlieus of the forest of Freedom (for assuredly he will never suffer them to enter the body of it); allowing this, and much more; that the mass of the population would be placed in a condition outwardly more thriving—would be *better off* (as the phrase in conversation is); it is still true that—in the act and consciousness of submission to an imposed lord and master, to a will not growing out of themselves, to the edicts of another People their triumphant enemy—there would be the loss of a sensation within for which nothing external, even though it should come close to the garden and the field—to the door and the fire-side, can make amends. The Artisan and the Merchant (men of classes perhaps least attached to their native soil) would not be insensible to this loss; and the Mariner, in his thoughtful mood, would sadden under it upon the wide ocean. . . .

Means and ends: experimental philosophy and the technical advances of the modern world have been accompanied by the fading of imagination and sensibility

There are multitudes by whom, I know, these sentiments will not be languidly received at this day; and sure I am—that, a hundred and fifty years ago, they would have been ardently welcomed by all. But in many parts of Europe (and especially in our own country) men have been pressing forward, for some time, in a path which has betrayed by its fruitfulness; furnishing them with constant employment for picking up things about their feet, when thoughts were perishing in their minds. While Mechanic Arts, Manufactures, Agriculture, Commerce, and all those products of knowledge which are confined to gross—definite—and tangible objects, have, with the aid of Experimental Philosophy, been every day putting on more brilliant colours; the splendour of the Imagination has been fading; Sensibility, which was formerly a nursling of rude

'Good sense' replaces sensibility

Nature, has been chased from its ancient range in the wide domain of patriotism and religion with the weapons of derision by a shadow calling itself Good Sense; calculations of presumptuous Expediency—groping its way among partial and temporary consequences—have been substituted for the dictates of paramount and infallible Conscience, the supreme embracer of consequences: lifeless and circumspect Decencies have banished the graceful negligence and unsuspicious dignity of Virtue.

The progress of these arts also, by furnishing such attractive stores of outward accommodation, has misled the higher orders of society in their more disinterested exertions for the service of the lower. Animal comforts have been rejoiced over, as if they were the end of being. A neater and more fertile garden; a greener field; implements and utensils more apt; a dwelling more commodious and better furnished;—let these be attained, say the actively benevolent, and we are sure not only of being in the right road, but of having successfully terminated our journey. Now a country may advance for some time in this course with apparent profit: these accommodations, by zealous encouragement, may be attained: and still the Peasant or Artisan, their master, be a slave in mind; [34] a slave rendered even more abject by the very tenure under which these possessions are held: and—if they veil from us this fact, or reconcile us to it—they are worse than worthless. The springs of emotion may be relaxed or destroyed within him; he may have little thought of the past, and less interest in the future. The great end and difficulty of life for men of all classes, and especially difficult for those who live by manual labour, is a union of peace with innocent and laudable animation. [35] Not by bread alone is the life of Man sustained; not by raiment alone is he warmed;—but by the genial and vernal inmate of the breast, which at once pushes forth and cherishes; by self-support and self-sufficing endeavours; by anticipations, apprehensions, and active remembrances; by elasticity under insult, and firm resistance to injury; by joy, and by love; by pride which his imagination gathers in from afar; by patience, because life wants not promises; by admiration; by gratitude which—debasing him not when his fellow-being is its object—habitually expands itself, for his elevation, in complacency towards his Creator.

National independence and self-government are the prime conditions of rational life

Now, to the existence of these blessings, national independence is indispensable; and many of them it will itself produce and maintain. For it is some consolation to those who look back upon the history of the world to know—that, even without civil liberty, society may possess—diffused through its inner recesses in the minds even of its humblest members—something of dignified enjoyment. But, without national independence, this is impossible. The difference between inbred oppression and that which is from without, is *essential*; inasmuch as the former does not exclude from the minds of a people the feeling of being self-governed; does not imply (as the latter does, when patiently submitted to) an abandonment of the first duty imposed by the faculty of reason. In reality: where this feeling has no place, a people are not a society, but a herd; man being indeed distinguished among them from the brute; but only to his disgrace. I am aware that there are too many who think that, to the bulk of the community this independence is of no value; that it is a refinement with which they feel that they have no concern; inasmuch as under the best frame of government there is an inevitable dependence of the poor upon the rich—of the many upon the few—so unrelenting and imperious as to reduce this other, by comparison, into a force which has small influence and is entitled to no regard. Superadd civil liberty to national independence, and this position is overthrown at once; for there is no more certain mark of a sound frame of polity than this: that, in all individual instances (and it is upon these generalized that this position is laid down), the dependence is in reality far more strict on the side of the wealthy, and the labouring man leans less upon others than any man in the community.—But the case before us is of a country not internally free, yet supposed capable of repelling an external enemy who attempts its subjugation. If a country have put on chains of its own forging; in the name of virtue, let it be conscious that to itself it is accountable: let it not have

The fallacy of the complaint that 'the poor have no country' and are indifferent to national independence

Chains of our own forging are to be preferred

cause to look beyond its own limits for reproof: and, in the name of humanity,—if it be self-depressed, let it have its pride and some hope within itself. . . .

Why the peasant is the best patriot

The poorest Peasant, in an unsubdued land, feels this pride. . . . In fact, the Peasant, and he who lives by the fair reward of his manual labour, has ordinarily a larger proportion of his gratifications dependent upon these thoughts than—for the most part—men in other classes have. For he is in his person attached, by stronger roots, to the soil of which he is the growth: [36] his intellectual notices are generally confined within narrower bounds: in him no partial or unpatriotic interests counteract the force of those nobler sympathies and antipathies which he has in right of his Country; and lastly, the belt or girdle of his mind has never been stretched to utter relaxation by false philosophy, under a conceit of making it sit more easily and gracefully. These sensations are a social inheritance to him: more important, as he is precluded from luxurious—and those which are usually called refined—enjoyments. . . .

The present appeal is addressed not to the poor but to our worldlings

In the conduct of this argument I am not speaking *to* the humbler ranks of society: it is unnecessary: [37] *they* trust in nature and are safe. . . . It is to the worldlings of our own country, and to those who think without carrying their thoughts far enough, that I address myself. Let them know, there is no true wisdom without imagination; no genuine sense;—that the man who, in this age, feels no regret for the ruined honour of other Nations, must be poor in sympathy for the honour of his own Country; and that, if he be wanting here towards that which circumscribes the whole, he neither has—nor can have—a social regard for the lesser communities which Country includes. Contract the circle, and bring him to his family; such a man cannot protect *that* with dignified loves. Reduce his thoughts to his own person; he may defend himself—what *he* deems his honour; but it is the *action* of a brave man from the impulse of the brute or the motive of a coward.

French rule no real benefit to Spain

But it is time to recollect that this vindication of human feeling began from an *hypothesis*,—that the *outward state* of the mass of the Spanish people would be improved by the French usurpation. To this I now give an unqualified denial. Let me also observe to those men for whose infirmity this hypothesis was tolerated,—that the true point of comparison does not lie between what the Spaniards have been under a government of their own, and what they may become under French domination; but between what the Spaniards may do (and in all likelihood will do) for themselves, and what Frenchmen would do for them. . . . Strange that there are men who can be so besotted as to see in the decrees of the Usurper concerning feudal tenures and a worn-out Inquisition, any other evidence than that of insidiousness and of a constrained acknowledgment of the strength which he felt he had to overcome. What avail the lessons of history if men can be duped thus? . . . The fate of subjugated Spain may be expressed in these words,—pillage—depression—and helotism —for the supposed aggrandizement of the imaginary freeman, its master. There would indeed be attempts at encouragement, that there might be a supply of something to pillage: studied depression there would be, that there might arise no power of resistance: and lastly helotism. . . .

France herself not indebted to despotism for her prosperity

What good can the present arbitrary power confer upon France itself? Let that point be first settled by those who are inclined to look further. The earlier proceedings of the French Revolution no doubt infused health into the country; something of which survives to this day; [38] but let not the now-existing Tyranny have the credit of it. . . . Let us attend to the springs of action and we shall not be deceived. The works of peace cannot flourish in a country governed by an intoxicated Despot. . . . '*I have bestowed; I have created; I have regenerated; I have been pleased to organize;*'—this is the language perpetually upon his lips, when his ill-fated activities turn that way. Now commerce, manufactures, agriculture, and all the peaceful arts, are of the nature of virtues or intellectual powers; they cannot be given; they cannot be stuck in here and there; they must spring up; they must grow of themselves; they may be encouraged; they may thrive better with encouragement, and delight in it; but the obligation must have bounds nicely defined; for they are delicate, proud and independent. But a Tyrant has no joy in anything which is endued with such excellence: he sickens at the sight of it: he turns away from it as an insult to his own attributes. . . .

The benevolent economy of nature may finally, but does not directly, bring good out of evil

It is immutably ordained that power, taken and exercised in contempt of right, never can bring forth good. Wicked actions indeed have oftentimes happy issues: the benevolent economy of nature counterworking and diverting evil; and educing finally benefits from injuries, and turning curses to blessings. But I am speaking of good in a direct course. All good in this order—all moral good—begins and ends in reverence of right. The whole Spanish people are to be treated not as a mighty multitude with feeling, will, and judgment; not as rational creatures;—but as objects without reason; in the language of human law insuperably laid down not as Persons but as Things. [39] Can good come from this beginning; which, in matter of civil government, is the fountain-head and the main feeder of all the pure evil upon earth?

Persons and things

Spain immune against the spread of Jacobinism

Why should the People of Spain be dreaded by their leaders? . . . Spain has nothing to dread from Jacobinism. [40] Manufactures and commerce have there, in far less degree than elsewhere—by unnaturally clustering the people together—enfeebled their bodies, inflamed their passions by intemperance, vitiated from childhood their moral affections, and destroyed their imaginations. Madrid is no enormous city, like Paris, over-grown and disproportionate, sickening and bowing down, by its corrupt humours, the frame of the body politic. Nor has the pestilential philosophism of France made any progress in Spain. No flight of infidel harpies has alighted on their ground. A Spanish understanding is a hold too strong to give way to the meagre tactics of the 'Systeme de la Nature': or to the pellets of logic which Condillac [41] has cast in the foundry of national vanity. . . . The Spaniards are a people with imagination: and the paradoxical reveries of Rousseau, and the flippancies of Voltaire, are plants which will not naturalize in the country of Calderon and Cervantes. Though bigotry among the Spaniards leaves much to be lamented, I have proved that the religious habits of the nation must, in a contest of this kind, be of inestimable service. . . .

Frightful spectacle of the French: a barbarized people armed by modern science

And this once again leads us directly to that immense military force which the Spaniards have to combat; and which, many think, more than counterbalances every internal advantage. It is indeed formidable, as revolutionary appetites and energies must needs be, when, among a people as numerous as the people of France, they have ceased to spend themselves in conflicting factions within the country for objects perpetually changing shape, and are carried out of it under the strong controul of an absolute despotism, as opportunity invites, for a definite object—plunder and conquest. It is, I allow, a frightful spectacle—to see the prime of a vast nation propelled out of their territory with the rapid sweep of a horde of Tartars; moving from the impulse of like savage instincts; and furnished, at the same time, with those implements of physical destruction which have been produced by science and civilization. Such are the motions of the French armies; unchecked by any thought which philosophy and the spirit of society, progressively humanizing, have called forth—to determine or regulate the application of the murderous and desolating apparatus with which by philosophy and science they have been provided. With a like perversion of things, and the same mischievous reconcilement of forces in their nature adverse, these revolutionary impulses and these appetites of barbarous (nay, what is far worse, of barbarized) men are embodied in a new frame of polity; which possesses the consistency of an ancient Government without its embarrassments and weaknesses. And at the head of all is the mind of one man who acts avowedly upon the principle that every thing which can be done by the supreme power of a State may be done; and who has at his command the greatest part of the Continent of Europe—to fulfil what yet remains unaccomplished of his nefarious purposes.

Science makes modern despotism more frightful than ancient

Possibility of internal collapse of France

Now it must be obvious to a reflecting mind that everything which is desperately immoral, being in its constitution monstrous, is of itself perishable: decay it cannot escape; and, further, it is liable to sudden dissolution: time would evince this in the instance before us, though not perhaps until infinite and irreparable harm had been done. But even at present each of the sources of this preternatural strength (as far as it is formidable to Europe) has its corresponding seat of weakness; which, were it fairly touched, would manifest itself immediately. —The power is indeed a Colossus; but, if the trunk be of molten brass, the members are of clay, and would fall to pieces upon a shock which need not be violent. . . . For present annoyance his power is no doubt mighty; but liberty—in which it originated, and of which it is a depravation,—is far mightier; and the good in human nature is stronger than the evil. The events of our age indeed have brought this truth into doubts with some persons: and scrupulous observers have been astonished and have repined at the sight of enthusiasm, courage, perseverance, and fidelity, put forth seemingly to their height —and all engaged in the furtherance of wrong. But the minds of men are not always devoted to this bad service as strenuously as they appear to be. . . . If the tide of success were, by any effort, fairly turned;—not only a general desertion, as we have the best reason to believe, would follow among the troops of the enslaved nations, but a moral change would also take place in the minds of the native French soldiery. . . . As long as guilty actions thrive, guilt is strong. . . . But there is no independent spring at the heart of the machine which can be relied upon for a support of these motions in a change of circumstances. Disaster opens the eyes of conscience; and, in the minds of men who have been employed in bad actions, defeat and a feeling of punishment are inseparable.

Superior strength of morally free men

On the other hand, the power of an unblemished heart and a brave spirit is shewn, in the events of war, not only among unpractised citizens and peasants, but among troops in the most perfect discipline. Large bodies of the British army have been several times broken—that is, technically vanquished—in Egypt and elsewhere. Yet they who were conquered as formal soldiers, stood their ground and became conquerors as men.

This paramount efficacy of moral causes is not willingly admitted by persons high in the profession of arms; because it seems to diminish their value in society by taking from the importance of their art: but the truth is indisputable: and those Generals are as blind to their own interests as to the interests of their country, who, by submitting to inglorious treaties or by other misconduct, hazard the breaking down of those personal virtues in the men under their command—to which they themselves, as leaders, are mainly indebted for the fame which they acquire. . . .

The best field of battle for a people fighting for their freedom

Most gloriously have the Citizens of Saragossa proved that the true army of Spain, in a contest of this nature, is the whole people. The same city has also exemplified a melancholy—yea, a dismal truth; yet consolatory, and full of joy; that—when a people are called suddenly to fight for their liberty, and are sorely pressed upon,—their best field of battles is the floors upon which their children have played; the chambers where the family of each man has slept (his own and his neighbours'); upon or under the roofs by which they have been sheltered; in the gardens of their recreation; in the street, or in the market-place; before the Altars of the Temples; and among their congregated dwellings—blazing or up-rooted. The Government of Spain must never forget Saragossa for a moment. Nothing is wanting, to produce the same effects everywhere. but a leading mind such as that city was blessed with. . . . Beginning from these invincible feelings, and the principles of justice which are involved in them; let nothing be neglected, which policy and prudence dictate, for rendering subservient to the same end those qualities in human nature which are indifferent or even morally bad, and for making the selfish propensities contribute to the support of wise arrangements, civil and military.

The morale of the Ironsides

Perhaps there never appeared in the field more steady soldiers—troops which it would have been more difficult to conquer with such knowledge of the art of war as then existed —than those commanded by Fairfax and Cromwell: let us see from what root these armies grew. 'Cromwell', says Sir Philip

Warwick, [42] 'made use of the zeal and credulity of these persons' (that is—such of the people as had, in the author's language, the fanatic humour); 'teaching them (as they too readily taught themselves) that they engaged for God, when he led them against his vicegerent the King. And, where this opinion met with a natural courage, it made them bolder—and too often crueller; and, where natural courage wanted, zeal supplied its place. And at first they chose rather to die than flee; and custom removed fear of danger: and afterwards—finding the sweet of good pay, and of opulent plunder, and of preferment suitable to activity and merit—the lucrative part made gain seem to them a natural member of godliness. And I cannot here omit' (continues the author) 'a character of this army which General Fairfax gave unto myself; when, complimenting him with the regularity and temperance of his army, he told me, The best common soldiers he had—came out of our army and from the garrisons he had taken in. So (says he) I found you had made them good soldiers; and I have made them good men. But, upon this whole matter, it may appear' (concludes the author) 'that the spirit of discipline of warr may beget that spirit of discipline which even Solomon describes as the spirit of wisdom and obedience.' Apply this process to the growth and maturity of an armed force in Spain. In making a comparison of the two cases; to the sense of the insults and injuries which, as Spaniards, and as human beings, they have received and have to dread,—and to the sanctity which an honourable resistance has already conferred upon their misfortunes,—add the devotion of that people to their religion as Catholics; [43]—and it will not be doubted that the superiority of the radical feelings is, on their side, immeasurable. . . .

Good men are the best soldiers

It is a belief propagated in books, and which passes currently among talking men as part of their familiar wisdom, that the hearts of the many *are* constitutionally weak; that they *do* languish; and are slow to answer to the requisitions of things. I entreat those who are in this delusion, to look behind them and about them for the evidence of experience. Now this, rightly understood, not only gives no support to any such

The hearts of the many do not fail

belief, but proves that the truth is in direct opposition to it. The history of all ages; tumults after tumults; wars, foreign or civil, with short or with no breathing-spaces, from generation to generation; wars—Why and wherefore? yet with courage, with perseverance, with self-sacrifice, with enthusiasm—with cruelty driving forward the cruel man from its own terrible nakedness, and attracting the more benign by the accompaniment of some shadow which seems to sanctify it; the senseless weaving and interweaving of factions—vanishing and reviving and piercing each other like the Northern Lights; public commotions, and those in the bosom of the individual; the long calenture to which the Lover is subject; the blast, like the blast of the desart, which sweeps perenially through a frightful solitude of its own making in the mind of the Gamester; the slowly quickening but ever quickening descent of appetite down which the Miser is propelled; the agony and cleaving oppression of grief; the ghost-like hauntings of shame; the incubus of revenge; the life-distemper of ambition;—these outward existences, and the visible and familiar occurences of daily life in every town and village; the patient curiosity and contagious acclamations of the multitude in the streets of the city and within the walls of the theatre; a procession or a rural dance; a hunting, or a horse-race; a flood, or a fire; rejoicing and ringing of bells for an unexpected gift of good fortune, or the coming of a foolish heir to his estate;—these demonstrate incontestably that the passions of men (I mean, the soul of sensibility in the heart of man)—in all quarrels, in all contests, in all quests, in all delights, in all employments which are either sought by men or thrust upon them—do immeasurably transcend their objects. The true sorrow of humanity consists in this;—not that the mind of man fails; but that the course and demands of action and of life so rarely correspond with the dignity and intensity of human desires; and hence that, which is slow to languish, is too easily turned aside and abused. But—with the remembrance of what has been done, and in the face of the interminable evils which are threatened—a Spaniard can never have cause to complain of

Human energy is endless, but easily misdirected

this, while a follower of the tyrant remains in arms upon the Peninsula.

The spiritual community of generations

Here then they, with whom I *hope*, take their stand. There is a spiritual community binding together the living and the dead; the good, the brave, and the wise, of all ages. [44] We would not be rejected from this community; and therefore do we hope. We look forward with erect mind, thinking, and feeling: it is an obligation of duty: take away the sense of it, and the moral being would die within us. . . .

Man's higher and lower faculties are not enemies but allies

The outermost and all-embracing circle of benevolence has inward concentric circles which, like those of the spider's web, are bound together by links, and rest upon each other; making one frame, and capable of one tremor; circles narrower and narrower, closer and closer, as they lie more near to the centre of self from which they proceeded, and which sustains the whole. The order of life does not require that the sublime and disinterested feelings should have to trust long to their own unassisted power. Nor would the attempt consist either with their dignity or their humility. They condescend, and they adopt: they know the time of their repose, and the qualities which are worthy of being admitted into their service—of being their inmates, their companions, or their substitutes. . . .

Wisdom and prudence

These principles and movements of wisdom—so far from towering above the support of prudence, or rejecting the rules of experience, for the better conduct of those multifarious actions which are alike necessary to the attainment of ends good or bad—do instinctively prompt the sole prudence which cannot fail. The higher mode of being does not exclude, but necessarily includes, the lower; the intellectual does not exclude, but necessarily includes, the sentient; the sentient, the animal; and the animal, the vital—to its lowest degrees. Wisdom is the hidden root which thrusts forth the stalk of prudence; and these uniting feed and uphold 'the bright consummate flower'—National Happiness—the end, the conspicuous crown, and ornament of the whole. [45]

The spiritual community of mankind.

Man's higher and lower functions are not exclusive, but allied.

A DEFENCE OF POETRY

BY

PERCY BYSSHE SHELLEY

1821

SUMMARY OF CONTENTS

A DEFENCE OF POETRY

Reason and imagination

ACCORDING TO one mode of regarding those two classes of mental action which are called reason and imagination, [1] the former may be considered as mind contemplating the relations borne by one thought to another, however produced; and the latter as mind acting upon those thoughts so as to colour them with its own light, and composing from them, as from elements, other thoughts, each containing within itself the principle of its own integrity. The one is the τὸ ποιεῖν, or the principle of synthesis, and has for its objects those forms which are common to universal nature and existence itself; the other is the τὸ λογίζειν or principle of analysis, and its action regards the relations of things, simply as relations; considering thoughts, not in their integral unity, but as the algebraical representations which conduct to certain general results. Reason is the enumeration of quantities already known; imagination is the perception of the value of those quantities, both separately, and as a whole. Reason respects the differences, and imagination the similitudes of things. Reason is to the imagination as the instrument to the agent, as the body to the spirit, as the shadow to the substance.

The creative principle in man

Poetry, in a general sense, may be defined to be 'the expression of the imagination': and poetry is connate with the origin of man. Man is an instrument over which a series of external and internal impressions are driven, like the alternations of an ever-changing wind over an Aeolian lyre, which move it by their motion to ever-changing melody. But there is a principle within the human being, [2] and perhaps within all sentient beings, which acts otherwise than in the lyre, and produces not melody alone, but harmony, by an internal adjustment of the sounds or motions thus excited to the impressions which excite them. It is as if the lyre could accommodate its chords to the motions of that which strikes them, in a determined proportion of sound; even as a musician can accommodate his voice to the sound of the lyre. . . .

All authors were poets in the infancy of society

In the infancy of society every author is necessarily a poet, because language itself is poetry; and to be a poet is to apprehend the true and the beautiful, in a word, the good which exists in the relation, subsisting, first between existence and perception, and secondly between perception and expression. Every original language near to its source is in itself the chaos of a cyclic poem: the copiousness of lexicography and the distinctions of grammar are the works of a later age, and are merely the catalogue and the form of the creations of poetry.

Poets are legislators and prophets

But poets, or those who imagine and express this indestructible order, [3] are not only the authors of language and of music, of the dance, and architecture, and statuary, and painting; they are the institutors of laws, and the founders of civil society, and the inventors of the arts of life, and the teachers who draw into a certain propinquity with the beautiful and the true, that partial apprehension of the agencies of the invisible world which is called religion. . . . Poets, according to the circumstances of the age and nation in which they appeared, were called, in the earlier epochs of the world, legislators or prophets: a poet essentially comprises and unites both these characters. For he not only beholds intensely the present as it is, but he beholds the future in the present, [4] and his thoughts are the germs of the flower and the fruit of latest time. Not that I assert poets to be prophets in the gross sense of the word, or that they can foretell the form as surely as they foreknow the spirit of events: such is the pretence of superstition, which would make poetry an attribute of prophecy, rather than prophecy an attribute of poetry. A poet participates in the eternal, the infinite, and the one; as far as relates to his conceptions, time and place and number are not. . . .

All great philosophers are poets

The distinction between philosophers and poets has been anticipated. Plato was essentially a poet—the truth and splendour of his imagery, and the melody of his language, are the most intense that it is possible to conceive. . . . Lord Bacon was a poet. His language has a sweet and majestic rythm, which satisfies the sense, no less than the almost superhuman wisdom of his philosophy satisfies the intellect; it is a strain which distends, and then bursts, the circumference of the reader's mind, and pours itself forth together with it into the universal element with which it has perpetual sympathy. All the authors of revolution in opinion are not only necessarily poets as they are inventors, nor even as their words unveil the permanent analogy of things by images which participate in the life of truth; [5] but as their periods are harmonious and rythmical, and contain in themselves the elements of verse; being the echo of the eternal music. Nor are those supreme poets, who have employed traditional forms of rhythm on account of the form and action of their subjects, less capable of receiving and teaching the truth of things, than those who have omitted that form. Shakespeare, Dante, and Milton (to confine ourselves to modern writers) are philosophers of the very loftiest power. [6]

A poem is the very image of life expressed in its eternal truth. . . . [5]

Having determined what poetry is, and who are poets, let us proceed to estimate its effects upon society. . . .

The poet and society

A poet is a nightingale, who sits in darkness and sings to cheer its own solitude with sweet sounds; his auditors are as men entranced by the melody of an unseen musician, who feel that they are moved and softened, yet know not whence or why. The poems of Homer and his contemporaries were the delight of infant Greece; they were the elements of that social system which is the column upon which all succeeding civilization has reposed. Homer embodied the ideal perfection of his age in human character; nor can we doubt that those who read his verses were awakened to an ambition of becoming like to Achilles, Hector, and Ulysses: the truth and beauty of friendship, patriotism, and persevering devotion to an object, were unveiled to the depths in these immortal creations: the sentiments of the auditors must have been refined and enlarged by a sympathy with such great and lovely impersonations, until from admiring they imitated, and from imitation they identified themselves with the objects of their admiration. Nor let it be objected that these characters are remote from moral perfection, and that they can by no means be considered as edifying patterns for general imitation. Every epoch, under names more or less specious, has deified its peculiar errors. . . . But a poet considers the vices of his contemporaries as a temporary dress in which his creations must be arrayed, and which cover without concealing the eternal proportions of their beauty. . . .

How poetry affects society

The whole objection, however, of the immorality of poetry rests upon a misconception of the manner in which poetry acts to produce the moral improvement of man. Ethical science arranges the elements which poetry has created, and propounds schemes and proposes examples of civil and domestic life: nor is it for want of admirable doctrines that men hate, and despise, and censure, and deceive, and subjugate one another. But poetry acts in another and diviner manner. It awakens and enlarges the mind itself by rendering it the receptacle of a thousand unapprehended combinations of thought. Poetry lifts the veil from the hidden beauty of the world, and makes familiar objects be as if they were not familiar; it reproduces all that it represents, and the impersonations clothed in its Elysian light stand thenceforward in the minds of those who have once contemplated them, as memorials of that gentle and exalted content which extends itself over all thoughts and actions with which it co-exists.

Not by preachment, but by its exercise of the imagination

The great secret of morals is love; or a going out of our own nature, and an identification of ourselves with the beautiful which exists in thought, action, or person, not our own. A man, to be greatly good, must imagine intensely and comprehensively; he must put himself in the place of another and of many others; the pains and pleasures of his species must become his own. The great instrument of moral good is the imagination; and poetry administers to the effect by acting upon the cause. Poetry enlarges the circumference of the imagination by replenishing it with thoughts of ever new delight, which have the power of attracting and assimilating to their own nature all other thoughts, and which form new intervals and interstices whose void for ever craves fresh food. Poetry strengthens the faculty which is the organ of the moral nature of man, in the same manner as exercise strengthens a limb. A poet therefore would do ill to embody his own conceptions of right and wrong, which are usually those of his place and time, in his poetical creations, which participate in neither. [7] By this assumption of the inferior office of interpreting the effect, in which perhaps after all he might acquit himself but imperfectly, he would resign a glory in a participation in the cause. There was little danger that Homer, or any of the eternal poets, should have so far misunderstood themselves as to have abdicated this throne of their widest dominion. Those in whom the poetical faculty, though great, is less intense, as Euripides, Lucan, Tasso, Spenser, have frequently affected a moral aim, and the effect of their poetry is diminished in exact proportion to the degree in which they compel us to advert to this purpose. . . .

The two kinds of utility

But poets have been challenged to resign the civic crown to reasoners and mechanists. . . . It is admitted that the exercise of the imagination is most delightful, but it is alleged that that of reason is more useful. [8] Let us examine as the grounds of this distinction, what is here meant by utility. Pleasure or good, in a general sense, is that which the consciousness of a sensitive and intelligent being seeks, and in which, when found, it acquiesces. There are two kinds of pleasure, one durable, universal and permanent; the other transitory and particular. Utility may either express the means of producing the former or the latter. In the former sense, whatever strengthens and purifies the affections, enlarges the imagination, and adds spirit to sense, is useful. But a narrower meaning may be assigned to the word utility, confining it to express that which banishes the importunity of the wants of our animal nature, the surrounding men with the security of life, the dispersing the grosser delusions of superstition, and the conciliating such a degree of mutual forbearance among men as may consist with the motives of personal advantage.

Overgrowth of the calculating faculty in modern times

Undoubtedly the promoters of utility, in this limited sense, have their appointed office in society. They follow the footsteps of poets, and copy the sketches of their creations into the book of common life. They make space, and give time. Their exertions are of the highest value, so long as they confine their administration of the concerns of the inferior powers of our nature within the limits due to the superior ones. But whilst the sceptic destroys gross superstitions, let him spare to deface, as some of the French writers have defaced, [9] the eternal truths charactered upon the imaginations of men. Whilst the mechanist abridges, and the political economist combines labour, let them beware that their speculations, for want of correspondence with those first principles which belong to the imagination, [10] do not tend, as they have in modern England, to exasperate at once the extremes of luxury and want. [11] They have exemplified the saying, 'To him that hath, more shall be given; and from him that hath not, the little that he hath shall be taken away.' The rich have become richer, and the poor have become poorer; and the vessel of the state is driven between Scylla and Charybdis of anarchy and despotism. Such are the effects which must ever flow from an unmitigated exercise of the calculating faculty. . . .

The production and assurance of pleasure in this highest sense is true utility. Those who produce and preserve this pleasure are poets or poetical philosophers.

Superior utility, in the higher sense, of the poets

The exertions of Locke, Hume, Gibbon, Voltaire, Rousseau, and their disciples, in favour of oppressed and deluded humanity, are entitled to the gratitude of mankind. Yet it is easy to calculate the degree of moral and intellectual improvement which the world would have exhibited, had they never lived. A little more nonsense would have been talked for a century or two; and perhaps a few more men, women, and children, burnt as heretics. We might not at this moment have been congratulating each other on the abolition of the Inquisition in Spain. But it exceeds all imagination to conceive what would have been the moral condition of the world if neither Dante, Petrarch, Boccaccio, Chaucer, Shakespeare, Calderon, Lord Bacon, nor Milton, had ever existed; if Raphael and Michael Angelo had never been born; if Hebrew poetry had never been translated; if a revival of the study of Greek literature had never taken place; if no monuments of ancient sculpture had been handed down to us; and if the poetry of the religion of the ancient world had been extinguished together with its belief. The human mind could never, except by the intervention of these excitements, have been awakened to the invention of the grosser sciences, and that application of analytical reasoning to the aberrations of society, which it is now attempted to exalt over the direct expression of the inventive and creative faculty itself.

Social consequences of the overgrowth of the calculating faculty at the expense of imagination

We have more moral, political, and historical wisdom, than we know how to reduce into practice; we have more scientific and economical knowledge than can be accommodated to the just distribution of the produce which it multiplies. The poetry in these systems of thought, is concealed by the accumulation of facts and calculating processes. There is no want of knowledge respecting what is wisest and best in morals, government, and political economy, or at least what is wiser and better than what men now practice and endure. But we let '*I dare not* wait upon *I would*, like the poor cat in the adage'. We want the creative faculty to imagine that which we know; we want the generous impulse to act that which we imagine; we want the poetry of life: our calculations have outrun conception; we have eaten more than we can digest. The cultivation of those sciences which have enlarged the limits of the empire of man over the external world, has, for want of the poetical faculty, proportionally circumscribed those of the internal world; and man, having enslaved the elements, remains himself a slave. [12] To what but a cultivation of the mechanical arts in a degree disproportioned to the presence of the creative faculty, which is the basis of all knowledge, [13] is to be attributed the abuse of all invention for abridging and combining labour, to the exasperation of the inequality of mankind? From what other cause has it arisen that the discoveries which should have lightened, have added a weight to the curse imposed on Adam? Poetry, and the principle of Self, of which money is the visible incarnation, are the God and Mammon of the world. . . . The cultivation of poetry is never more to be desired than at periods

Social need of poetry in an age of excessive calculation

when, from an excess of the selfish and calculating principle, the accumulation of the materials of external life exceed the quantity of the power of assimilating them to the internal laws of human nature. . . .

Social renaissance heralded by present renaissance of poetry

The literature of England, an energetic development of which has ever preceded or accompanied a great and free development of the national will, has arisen as it were from a new birth. In spite of the low-thoughted envy which would undervalue contemporary merit, our own will be a memorable age in intellectual achievements, and we live among such philosophers and poets as surpass beyond comparison any who have appeared since the last great struggle for civil and religious liberty. [14] The most unfailing herald, companion, and follower of the awakening of a great people to work a beneficial change in opinion or institution, is poetry. At such periods there is an accumulation of the power of communicating and receiving intense and impassioned conceptions respecting man and nature. The persons in whom this power resides may often, as far as regards many portions of their nature, have little apparent correspondence with that spirit of good of which they are the ministers. But even whilst they deny and abjure, they are yet compelled to serve, the power which is seated on the throne of their own soul. It is impossible to read the compositions of the most celebrated writers of the present day without being startled with the electric life which burns within their words. They measure the circumference and sound the depths of human nature with a comprehensive and all-penetrating spirit, and they are themselves perhaps the most sincerely astonished at its manifestations: for it is less their spirit than the spirit of the age. Poets are the hierophants of an unapprehended inspiration; the mirrors of the gigantic shadows which futurity casts upon the present; the words which express what they understand not; the trumpets which sing to battle, and feel not what they inspire; the influence which is moved not, but moves. Poets are the unacknowledged legislators of the world.

A PHILOSOPHICAL VIEW OF REFORM

BY

PERCY BYSSHE SHELLEY

(1819-20)

A PHILOSOPHICAL VIEW OF REFORM

A PHILOSOPHICAL VIEW OF REFORM

1ST. SENTIMENT OF THE NECESSITY OF CHANGE
2ND. PRACTICABILITY AND UTILITY OF SUCH CHANGE
3RD. STATE OF PARTIES AS REGARDS IT
4TH. PROBABLE MODE—DESIRABLE MODE

Let us believe not only that it is necessary because it is just and ought to be, but necessary because it is inevitable and must be. [1]

Chapter I

INTRODUCTION

Necessity of change demonstrated from the History of Europe as a history of progress

THOSE WHO imagine that their personal interest is directly or indirectly concerned in maintaining the power in which they are clothed by the existing institutions of English Government do not acknowledge the necessity of a material change in those institutions. With this exception, there is no inhabitant of the British Empire of mature age and perfect understanding not fully persuaded of the necessity of Reform.

[2] From the dissolution of the Roman Empire, that vast and successful scheme for the enslaving of the most civilised portion of mankind, to the epoch of the French Revolution, have succeeded a series of schemes, on a smaller scale, operating to the same effect. Names borrowed from the life and opinions of Jesus Christ were employed as symbols of domination and imposture; and a system of liberty and equality—for such was the system planted by that great Reformer—was perverted to support oppression. Not his doctrines, for they are too simple and direct to be susceptible of such perversion, but the mere names. Such was the origin of the Catholic Church, which,

together with the several dynasties then beginning to consolidate themselves in Europe, means, being interpreted, a plan according to which the cunning and selfish few have employed the fears and hopes of the ignorant many to the establishment of their own power and the destruction of the real interests of all.

Renaissance in Italy, and emergence of modern literatures

The Republics and municipal Governments of Italy opposed for some time a systematic and effectual resistance to the all-surrounding tyranny. The Lombard League defeated the armies of the despot in open field, and until Florence was betrayed to those polished tyrants, the Medici, Freedom had one citadel wherein it could find refuge from a world which was its enemy. Florence, long balanced, divided and weakened the strength of the Empire and the Popedom. To this cause, if to anything, was due the undisputed superiority of Italy in literature and the arts over all its contemporary nations, that union of energy and of beauty which distinguishes from all other poets the writings of Dante, that restlessness of fervid power which expressed itself in painting and sculpture, and in daring architectural forms, and from which, and conjointly from the creations of Athens, its predecessor and its image, Raphael and Michael Angelo drew the inspiration which created those forms and colours now the astonishment of the world. The father of our own literature, Chaucer, wrought from the simple and powerful language of a nursling of this Republic the basis of our own literature. And thus we owe, among other causes, the exact condition belonging to intellectual existence to the generous disdain of submission which burned in the bosoms of men who filled a distant generation and inhabited other lands.

Reformation and emergence of constitutional government in England

When this resistance was overpowered, as what resistance to fraud and tyranny has not been overpowered? another was even then maturing. The progress of philosophy and civilization which ended in that imperfect emancipation of mankind from the yoke of priests and kings called the Reformation, had already commenced. Exasperated by their long sufferings, inflamed by the sparks of that superstition from the flames of which they were emerging, the poor rose against their natural enemies, the rich, and repaid with bloody interest the tyranny of ages. One of the signs of the times was that the oppressed peasantry rose like the negro slaves of West Indian plantations, and murdered their tyrants when they were unaware. So dear is power that the tyrants themselves neither then, nor now, nor ever, left or leave a path to freedom but through their own blood. The contest then waged under the names of religion which have seldom been any more than popular and visible symbols which express power in some shape or other, asserted by one party and disclaimed by the other, ended; and the result, though partial and imperfect, is perhaps the most animating that the philanthropist can contemplate in the history of man. The Republic of Holland, which has been so long an armoury of the arrows of learning by which superstition has been wounded even to death, was established by this contest. What though the name of Republic—and by whom but by conscience-stricken tyrants would it be extinguished—is no more? [3] The Republics of Switzerland derived from this event their consolidation and their union.

From England then first began to pass away the stain of conquest. The exposure of a certain portion of religious imposture drew with it an enquiry into political imposture, and was attended with an extraordinary exertion of the energies of intellectual power. Shakespeare and Lord Bacon and the great writers of the age of Elizabeth and James I were at once the effects of the new spirit in men's minds, and the causes of its more complete development. By rapid gradations the nation was conducted to the temporary abolition of aristocracy and episcopacy, and to the mighty example which, 'in teaching nations how to live', England afforded to the world—of bringing to public justice one of those chiefs of a conspiracy of privileged murderers and robbers whose impunity had been the consecration of crime.

After the selfish passions and temporizing interest of men had enlisted themselves to produce and establish the Restoration of Charles II the unequal combat was renewed under the reign of his successor, and that compromise between the unextinguishable spirit of Liberty, and the ever watchful spirit of fraud and tyranny, called the Revolution had place. On this occasion monarchy and aristocracy and episcopacy were at once established and limited by law. Unfortunately they lost no more in extent of power than they gained in security of possession. Meanwhile those by whom they were established acknowledged and declared that the Will of the People was the source from which those powers, in this instance, derived the right to subsist. [4] A man has not right to be a King or a Lord or a Bishop but so long as it is for the benefit of the People and so long as the People judge that it is for their benefit that he should impersonate that character. The solemn establishment of this maxim as the basis of our constitutional law, more than any beneficial and energetic application of it to the circumstances of the era of its promulgation, was the fruit of that vaunted event. Correlative with this series of events in England was the commencement of a new epoch in the history of the progress of civilization and society.

That superstition which has disguised itself under the name of the system of Jesus subsisted under all its forms, even where it had been separated from those things especially considered as abuses by the multitude, in the shape of an intolerant and oppressive hierarchy. Catholics massacred Protestants and Protestants proscribed Catholics, and extermination was the sanction of each faith within the limits of the power of its professors. The New Testament is in everyone's hand, and the few who ever read it with the simple sincerity of an unbiased judgement may perceive how distinct from the opinions of any of those professing themselves orthodox were the doctrines and the actions of Jesus Christ. At the period of the Reformation this test was applied, this judgement formed of the then existing hierarchy, and the same compromise was then made between the spirit of truth and the spirit of imposture after the struggle which ploughed up the area of the human mind, as was made in the particular instance of England between the spirit of freedom and the spirit of tyranny at that event called the Revolution. In both instances the maxims so solemnly recorded remain as trophies of our difficult and incomplete victory, planted on the enemies' soil. *The will of the People to change their government is an acknowledged right in the Constitution of England.* [5] The protesting against religious dogmas which present themselves to his mind as false is the inalienable prerogative of every human being.

Scientific revolution of the Seventeenth Century

The new epoch was marked by the commencement of deeper enquiries into the point of human nature than are compatible with an unreserved belief in any of those popular mistakes upon which popular systems of faith with respect to the cause and agencies of the universe, with all their superstructure of political and religious tyranny, [6] are built. Lord Bacon, Spinoza, Hobbes, Boyle, Montaigne, regulated the reasoning powers, criticized the history, exposed the past errors by illustrating their causes and their connexion, and anatomized the inmost nature of social man. Then, with a less interval of time than of genius, followed Locke and the philosophers of his exact and intelligible but superficial school. [7] Their illustrations of some of the minor consequences of the doctrines established by the sublime genius of their predecessors were correct, popular, simple and energetic. Above all, they indicated inferences the most incompatible with the popular religions and the established governments of Europe. (Philosophy went now into the enchanted forest of the demons of worldly power, as the pioneer of the overgrowth of ages.) Berkeley and Hume, and Hartley at a later age, following the traces of these inductions, have clearly established the certainty of our ignorance with respect to those obscure questions which under the name of religious truths have been the watchwords of contention and symbols of unjust power ever since they were distorted by the narrow passions of the immediate followers of Jesus from that meaning to which philosophers are even now restoring them. A crowd of writers in France seized upon the most popular topics of these doctrines, and developing those particular portions of the new philosophy which conducted to inferences at war with the dreadful oppressions under which

The 'Enlightenment'

that country groaned, made familiar to mankind the falsehood of the mediaeval pretences of their religious and political oppressors. Considered as philosophers their error seems to have consisted chiefly in a limitation of view; they told the truth, but not the whole truth. This might have arisen from the terrible sufferings of their countrymen inviting them rather to apply a portion of what had already been discovered to their immediate relief, than to pursue one interest, the abstractions of thought, as the great philosophers who preceded them had done, for the sake of a future and more universal advantage. Whilst that philosophy which, burying itself in the obscure part of our nature, regards the truth and falsehood of dogmas relating to the cause of the universe, and the nature and manner of man's relation with it, was thus stripping Power of its darkest mask, Political Philosophy, or that which considers the relations of man as a social being, was assuming a precise form. That philosophy indeed sprang from and maintained a connexion with that other as its parent. What would Swift and Bolingbroke and Sidney and Locke and Montesquieu, or even Rousseau, not to speak of political philosophers of our own age, Godwin, and Bentham, have been but for Lord Bacon, Montaigne and Spinoza, and the other great luminaries of the preceding epoch? Something excellent and eminent, no doubt, the least of these would have been, but something different from and inferior to what they are. A series of these writers illustrated with more or less success the principles of human nature as applied to man in political society. A thirst for accommodating the existing forms according to which mankind are found divided to those rules of freedom and equality which have been discovered as being the elementary principles according to which the happiness resulting from the social union ought to be produced and distributed, was kindled by these enquiries. Contemporary with this condition of the intellect all the powers of mankind, though in most cases under forms highly inauspicious *began* to develop themselves with uncommon energy. The mechanical sciences attained to a degree of perfection which, though obscurely foreseen by Lord Bacon, it had been accounted madness to have prophesied in a preceding age. Commerce was pursued with a perpetually increasing vigour, and the same area of the Earth was perpetually compelled to furnish more and more subsistence. The means and sources of knowledge were thus increased together with knowledge itself, and the instruments of knowledge. The benefit of this increase of the powers of man became, in consequence of the inartificial [8] forms into which mankind was distributed, an instrument of his additional evil. The capabilities of happiness were increased, and applied to the augmentation of misery. Modern society is thus an engine assumed to be for useful purposes, whose force is by a system of subtle mechanism augmented to the highest pitch, but which, instead of grinding corn or raising water acts against itself and is perpetually wearing away or breaking to pieces the wheels of which it is composed. [9] The result of the labours of the political philosophers has been the establishment of the principle of Utility as the substance, and liberty and equality as the forms according to which the concerns of human life ought to be administered. By this test the various institutions regulating political society have been tried, and as the undigested growth of the private passions, errors, and interests of barbarians and oppressors have been condemned. And many new theories, more or less perfect, but all superior to the mass of evil which they would supplant, have been given to the world.

Founding of the United States

The system of government in the United States of America was the first practical illustration of the new philosophy. Sufficiently remote, it will be confessed, from the accuracy of ideal excellence is that representative system which will soon cover the extent of that vast Continent. But it is scarcely less remote from the insolent and contaminating tyrannies under which, with some limitation of the terms as regards England, Europe groaned at the period of the successful rebellion of America. America holds forth the victorious example of an immensely populous, and as far as the external arts of life are concerned, a highly civilized community administered according to republican forms. It has no king, that is, it has no officer to whom wealth and from whom corruption flow. It has no hereditary oligarchy, that is it acknowledges no order of men privileged to cheat and insult the rest of the members of the State, and who inherit the right of legislating and judging which the principles of human nature compel them to exercise to their own profit and to the detriment of those not included within their peculiar class. It has no established Church, that is no system of opinions respecting the abstrusest questions which can be the topics of human thought, founded in an age of error and fanaticism, and opposed by law to all other opinions, defended by prosecutions, and sanctioned by enormous grants given to idle priests and forced from the unwilling hands of those who have an interest in the cultivation and improvement of the soil. It has no false representation, whose consequences are captivity, confiscation, infamy and ruin, but a true representation. The will of the many is represented in the assemblies and by the officers entrusted with the administration of the executive power almost as directly as the will of one person can be represented by the will of another. (This is not the place for dilating upon the inexpressible advantages [if such advantages require any manifestation] of a self-governing Society, or one which approaches it in the degree of the Republic of the United States.) Lastly, it has an institution by which it is honourably distinguished from all other governments which ever existed. It constitutionally acknowledges the progress of human improvement, and is framed under the limitation of the probability of more simple views of political science being rendered applicable to human life. There is a law by which the constitution is reserved for revision every ten years. Every other set of men who have assumed the office of legislation, and framing institutions for future ages, with far less right to such an assumption than the founders of the American Republic, regarded their work as the wisest and the best that could possibly have been produced: these illustrious men looked upon the past history of their species and saw that it was the history of his mistakes, and his sufferings arising from his mistakes; they observed the superiority of their own work to all the works which had preceded it, and they judged it possible that other political institutions would be discovered having the same relation to those which they had established which they bear to those which have preceded them. They provided therefore for the application of these contingent discoveries to the social state without the violence and misery attendant upon such change in less modest and more imperfect governments. The United States, as we would have expected from theoretical deduction, affords an example, compared with the old governments of Europe and Asia, of a free, happy, and strong people. [10] Nor let it be said that they owe their superiority rather to the situation than to their government. Give them a king, and let that king waste in luxury, riot and bribery the same sum which now serves for the entire expenses of their government. Give them an aristocracy, and let that aristocracy legislate for the people. Give them a priesthood, and let them bribe with a tenth of the produce of the soil a certain set of men to say a certain set of words. Pledge the larger portion of them by financial subterfuges to pay the half of their property or earnings to another portion, and let the proportion of those who enjoy the fruits of the toil of others without toiling themselves be three instead of one. Give them a Court of Chancery and let the property, the liberty and the interest in the dearest concerns, the exercise of the sacred rights of a social being depend upon the will of one of the most servile creations of that kingly and oligarchial and priestly power to which every man, in proportion as he is of an enquiring and philosophic mind and of a sincere and honourable disposition is a natural and necessary enemy. Give them, as you must if you give them these things, a great standing army to cut down the people if they murmur. If any American should see these words, his blood would run cold at the imagination of such a change. He well knows that the prosperity and happiness of the United States if subjected to such institutions would be no more.

The French Revolution

The just and successful Revolt of America corresponded with a state of public opinion in Europe of which it was the first result. The French Revolution was the second. The oppressors of mankind had enjoyed (O that we could say suffered) a long and undisturbed reign in France, and to the pining famine, the shelterless destitution of the inhabitants of that country had been added and heaped up insult harder to bear than misery. For the feudal system (the immediate causes and conditions of its institution having become obliterated) had degenerated into an instrument not only of oppression but of contumely, and both were unsparingly inflicted. Blind in the possession of strength, drunken as with the intoxication of ancestral greatness, the rulers perceived not that increase of knowledge in the subject which made its exercise insecure. They called soldiers to hew down the people when their power was already past. The tyrants were, as usual, the aggressors. The oppressed, having been rendered brutal, ignorant, servile and bloody by slavery, having had the intellectual thirst, excited in them by the progress of civilization, satiated from fountains of literature poisoned by the spirit and the form of monarchy, arose to take a dreadful revenge on their oppressors. Their desire to wreak revenge, to this extent, in itself a mistake, a crime, a calamity, arose from the same source as their other miseries and errors, and affords an additional proof of the necessity of that long-delayed change which it accompanied and disgraced. If a just and necessary revolution could have been accomplished with as little expense of happiness and order in a country governed by despotic as in one governed by free laws, equal liberty and justice would lose their chief recommendations and tyranny be divested of its most revolting attributes. Tyranny entrenches itself within the existing interests of the best and most refined citizens of a nation and says 'If you dare trample upon these, be free'. Though these terrible conditions shall not be evaded, the world is no longer in a temper to decline the challenge.

The French were what their literature is (excepting Montaigne and Rousseau, and some few of the . . .) [11] weak, superficial, vain, with little imagination, and with passions as well as judgements cleaving to the external forms of things. Not that they are organically different from the inhabitants of the nations who have become . . . or rather not that their organical differences, whatever they may amount to, incapacitate them from arriving at the exercise of the highest powers to be attained by man. Their institutions made them what they were. Slavery and superstition, contumely and the tame endurance of contumely, and the habits engendered from generation to generation out of this transmitted inheritance of wrong, created the thing which has extinguished what has been called the likeness of God in man. The Revolution in France overthrew the hierarchy, the aristocracy and the monarchy, and the whole of that peculiarly insolent and oppressive system on which they were based. But as it only partially extinguished those passions which are the spirit of these forms a reaction took place which has restored in a certain limited degree the old system. In a degree, indeed, exceedingly limited, and stript of all its antient terrors, the hope of the Monarchy of France, with his teeth drawn and his claws pared, may succeed in maintaining the formal witness of most imperfect and insecure dominion. The usurpation of Bonaparte and then the Restoration of the Bourbons were the shapes in which this reaction clothed itself, and the heart of every lover of liberty was struck as with palsy on the succession of these events. But reversing the proverbial expression of Shakespeare, it may be the good which the Revolutionists did lives after them, their ills are interred with their bones. But the military project of government of the great tyrant having failed, and there being even no attempt—and, if there were any attempt, there being not the remotest possibility of re-establishing the enormous system of tyranny abolished by the Revolution, France is, as it were, regenerated. Its legislative assemblies are in a certain limited degree representations of the popular will, and the executive power is hemmed in by jealous laws. France occupies in this respect the same situation as was occupied by England at the restoration of Charles II. It has undergone a revolution (unlike in the violence and calamities which attended it, because unlike in the abuses which it was excited to put down) which may be paralleled with that in our own country which ended in the death of Charles I. The authors of both Revolutions proposed a greater and more glorious object than the degraded passions of their countrymen permitted them to attain. But in both cases abuses were abolished which never since have dared to show their face. There remains in the natural order of human things that the tyranny and perfidy of the reigns of Charles II and James II (for these were less the result of the disposition of particular men than the vices which would have been engendered in any but an extra-ordinary man by the natural necessities of their situation) perhaps under a milder form and within a shorter period should produce the institution of a Government in France which may bear the same relation to the state of political knowledge existing at the present day, as the Revolution under William III bore to the state of political knowledge existing at that period.

The rise of the new Germany

Germany, which is, among the great nations of Europe, one of the latest civilized, with the exception of Russia, is rising with the fervour of a vigorous youth to the assertion of those rights for which it has that desire arising from knowledge, the surest pledge of victory. The deep passion and the bold and Aeschylean vigour of the imagery of their poetry, the enthusiasm, however distorted, the purity, truth and comprehensiveness of their religious sentiments, their language which is the many-sided mirror of every changing thought, their sincere, bold and liberal spirit of criticism, their subtle and deep philosophy mingling fervid intuitions into truth with obscure error (for the period of just distinction is yet to come) and their taste and power in the plastic arts, prove that they are a great People. And every great nation either has been or is or will be free. The panic-stricken tyrants of that country promised to their subjects that their governments should be administered according to republican forms, they retaining merely the right of hereditary chief magistracy in their families. This promise, made in danger, the oppressors dream that they can break in security. And everything in consequence wears in Germany the aspect of rapidly maturing revolution. [12]

Signs of regeneration in Spain

In Spain and in the dependencies of Spain good and evil in the forms of Despair and Tyranny are struggling face to face. That great people have been delivered bound hand and foot to be trampled upon and insulted by a traitorous and sanguinary tyrant, a monster who makes credible all that might have been doubted in the history of Nero, Christiern, Muley Ismael or Ezzelin—the persons who have thus delivered them were that hypocritical knot of conspiring tyrants, [13] who proceeded upon the credit they gained by putting down the only tyrant among them who was not a hypocrite, to undertake the administration of those arrondissements of consecrated injustice and violence which they deliver to those who the nearest resemble them under the name of the 'kingdoms of the earth'. This action signed a sentence of death, confiscation, exile or captivity against every philosopher and patriot in Spain. The tyrant Ferdinand, he whose name is held a proverb of execration, found natural allies in all the priests and military chiefs and a few of the most dishonourable of that devoted country. And the consequences of military despotism and the black, stagnant, venomous hatred which priests in common with eunuchs seek every opportunity to wreak upon the portion of mankind exempt from their own unmanly disqualifications [14] is slavery. And what is slavery—in its mildest form hideous, and, so long as one amiable or great attribute survives in its victims, rankling and intolerable, but in its darkest shape as it now exhibits itself in Spain it is the essence of all and more than all the evil for the sake of an exemption from which mankind submit to the mighty calamity of government. [15] It is a system of insecurity of property, and of person, of prostration of conscience and understanding, it is famine heaped upon the greater number and contumely heaped upon all, defended by unspeakable tortures employed not merely as punishments but as precautions, by want, death and captivity, and the application to political purposes of the execrated and enormous instruments of religious cruelty. Those men of understanding, integrity, and courage who rescued their country from one tyrant are exiled from it by his successor and his enemy and their legitimate king. Tyrants, however they may squabble among themselves, have common friends and foes. The taxes are levied at the point of the sword. Armed insurgents occupy all the defensible mountains of the country. The dungeons are peopled thickly, and persons of every sex and age have the fibres of their frame torn by subtle torments. Boiling water (such is an article in the last news from Spain) is poured upon the legs of a noble Spanish lady newly delivered, slowly and cautiously, that she may confess what she knows of a conspiracy against the tyrant, and she dies, as constant as the slave Epicharis, imprecating curses upon her torturers and passionately calling upon her children. These events, in the present condition of the understanding and sentiment of mankind, are the rapidly passing shadows, which forerun successful insurrection, the ominous comets of our republican poet perplexing great monarchs with fear of change.—Spain, having passed through an ordeal severe in proportion to the wrongs and errors which it is kindled to erase must of necessity be renovated. Spain produced Calderon and Cervantes, what else did it but breathe, thro' the tumult of the despotism and superstition which invested them, the prophecy of a glorious consummation? [16]

South America The independents of South America are as it were already free. Great Republics are about to consolidate themselves in a portion of the globe sufficiently vast and fertile to nourish more human beings than at present occupy, with the exception perhaps of China, the remainder of the inhabited earth. Some indefinite arrears of misery and blood remain to be paid to the Moloch of oppression. These, to the last drop and groan it will inflict by its ministers. But not the less are they inevitably enfranchised. The Great Monarchies of Asia cannot, let us confidently hope, remain unshaken by the earthquake which is shaking to dust the 'mountainous strongholds' of the tyrants of the Western world.

India Revolutions in the political and religious state of the Indian peninsula seem to be accomplishing, and it cannot be doubted but the zeal of the missionaries of what is called the Christian faith will produce beneficial innovation there, even by the application of dogmas and forms of what is here an outworn incumbrance. The Indians have been enslaved and cramped in the most severe and paralysing forms which were ever devised by man; some of this new enthusiasm ought to be kindled among them to consume it and leave them free, and even if the doctrines of Jesus do not penetrate through the darkness of that which those who profess to be his followers call Christianity, there will yet be a number of social forms modelled upon those European feelings from which it has taken its colour substituted to [17] those according to which they are at present cramped, and from which, when the time for complete emancipation shall arrive, their disengagement may be less difficult, and under which their progress to it may be the less imperceptibly slow. Many native Indians have acquired, it is said, a competent knowledge in the arts and philosophy of Europe, and Locke and Hume and Rousseau are familiarly talked of in Brahminical society. But the thing to be sought is that they should, as they would if they were free, attain to a system of arts and literature of their own.—Of Persia we know little, but that it has been the theatre of sanguinary contests for power, and that it is now at peace. The Persians appear to be from organization a beautiful refined and impassioned people and would probably soon be infected by the contagion of good.

Turkey

The Turkish Empire is in its last stage of ruin, and it cannot be doubted but that the time is approaching when the deserts of Asia Minor and of Greece will be colonized by the overflowing population of countries less enslaved and debased, and that the climate and the scenery which was the birthplace of all that is wise and beautiful will not remain for ever the spoil of wild beasts and unlettered Tartars.—In Syria and Arabia the spirit of human intellect has roused a sect of people called Wahabees, who maintain the Unity of God, and the equality of man, and their enthusiasm must go on 'conquering and to conquer' even if it must be repressed in its present shape. —Egypt having but a nominal dependence upon Constantinople is under the government of Ottoman Bey, a person of enlightened views who is introducing European literature and art, and is thus beginning that change which Time, the great innovator, will accomplish in that degraded country; and by the same means its sublime and enduring monuments may excite lofty emotions in the hearts of the posterity of those who now contemplate them without admiration.—The Jews, that wonderful people which has preserved so long the symbols of their union may reassume their ancestral seats and. . . . [18]

The West Indies

Lastly, in the West Indian islands, first from the disinterested yet necessarily cautious measures of the English Nation, and then from the infection of the spirit of Liberty in France, the deepest stain upon civilized man is fading away. Two nations of free negroes are already established; one, in pernicious mockery of the usurpation over France, an empire, the other a republic; both animating yet terrific spectacles to those who inherit around them the degradation of slavery and the spirit of dominion. [19]

Such is a slight sketch of the general condition of the hopes and aspirations of the human race to which they have been conducted after the obliteration of the Greek republics by the successful tyranny of Rome,—its internal liberty having been first abolished,—and by those miseries and superstitions consequent upon them, which compelled the human race to begin anew its difficult and obscure career of producing, according to the forms of society, the greatest portion of good.

England at the crisis of its destiny

Meanwhile England, the particular object for the sake of which these general considerations have been stated on the present occasion, has arrived, like the nations which surround it, at a crisis in its destiny. The literature of England, an energetic development of which has ever followed or preceded a great and free development of the national will, has arisen, as it were, from a new birth. In spite of that low-thoughted envy which would underrate, thro' a fear of comparison with its own insignificance, the eminence of contemporary merit, it is felt by the British that this is in intellectual achievements a memorable age, and we live among such philosophers and poets as surpass beyond comparison any who have appeared in our nation since its last struggle for liberty. For the most unfailing herald, or companion, or follower, of an universal employment of the sentiments of a nation to the production of a beneficial change is poetry, meaning by poetry an intense and impassioned power of communicating intense and impassioned impressions respecting man and nature. The persons in whom this power takes its abode may often, as far as regards many portions of their nature, have little correspondence with the spirit of good of which it is the minister. But although they may deny and abjure, they are yet compelled to serve that which is seated on the throne of their own soul. And whatever systems they may have professed by [20] support, they actually advance the interests of Liberty. It is impossible to read the productions of our most celebrated writers, whatever may be their system relating to thought or expression, without being startled by the electric life which there is in their words. They measure the circumference or sound the depths of human nature with a comprehensive and all-penetrating spirit at which they are themselves perhaps most sincerely astonished, for it is less their own spirit than the spirit of their age. They are the priests of an unapprehended inspiration, the mirrors of gigantic shadows which futurity casts upon the present; the words which express what they conceive not; the trumpet which sings to battle and feel not what it inspires; the influence which is moved not but moves. Poets and philosophers are the unacknowledged legislators of the world. [21]

Poetic renaissance and rebirth of Liberty

But, omitting these more abstracted considerations, has there not been and is there not in England a desire of change arising from the profound sentiment of the exceeding inefficiency of the existing institutions to provide for the physical and intellectual happiness of the people? It is proposed in this work (1) to state and examine the present condition of this desire, (2) to elucidate its causes and its object, (3) to show the practicability and utility, nay the necessity of change, (4) to examine the state of parties as regards it, and (5) to state the probable, the possible, and the desirable mode in which it should be accomplished.

Chapter II

On the Sentiment of the Necessity of Change

Sharpening of alternatives: despotism—or anarchy?

Two circumstances arrest the attention of those who turn their regard to the present political condition of the English nation—first, that there is an almost universal sentiment of the approach of some change to be wrought in the institutions of the government, and secondly, the necessity and the desirableness of such a change. From the first of these propositions, it being matter of fact, no person addressing the public can dissent. The latter, from a general belief in which the former flows and on which it depends, is matter of opinion, but one which to the mind of all, excepting those interested in maintaining the contrary is a doctrine so clearly established that even they, admitting that great abuses exist, are compelled to impugn it by insisting upon the specious topic, that popular violence, by which they alone could be remedied, would be more injurious than the continuance of those abuses. But as those who argue thus derive for the most part great advantage and convenience from the continuance of these abuses, their estimation of the mischiefs of popular violence as compared with the mischiefs of tyrannical and fraudulent forms of government are likely, from the known principles of human nature, to be exaggerated. Such an estimate comes too with a worse grace from them, who if they would, in opposition to their own unjust advantage, take the lead in reform, might spare the nation from the inconveniences of the temporary dominion of the poor, who by means of that degraded condition which their insurrection would be designed to ameliorate, are sufficiently incapable of discerning their own glorious and permanent advantage, tho' surely less incapable than those whose interests consist in proposing to themselves an object perfectly opposite to and utterly incompatible with that advantage. These persons propose to us the dilemma of submitting to a despotism which is notoriously gathering like an avalanche year by year, or taking the risk of something which it must be confessed bears the aspect of revolution. To this alternative we are reduced by the selfishness of those who taunt us with it. And the history of the world teaches us not to hesitate an instant in the decision, if indeed the power of decision be not already past.

Defects of the representative system

The establishment of King William III on the throne of England has already been referred to as a compromise between liberty and despotism. The Parliament of which that event was the act had ceased to be in an emphatic sense a representation of the people. The long Parliament was the organ of the will of all classes of people in England since it effected the complete revolution in a tyranny consecrated by time. But since its meeting and since its dissolution a great change had taken place in England. Feudal manners and institutions having become obliterated, monopolies and patents having been abolished, property and personal liberty having been rendered secure, the nation advanced rapidly towards the acquirement of the elements of national prosperity. Population increased, a greater number of hands were employed in the labours of agriculture and commerce, towns arose where villages had been, and the proportion borne by those whose labour produced the materials of subsistence and enjoyment to those who claim for themselves a superfluity of these materials began to increase indefinitely. A fourth class therefore made its appearance in the nation, the unrepresented multitude. Nor was it so much that villages which sent no members to Parliament became great cities, and that towns which had been considerable enough to send members dwindled from local circumstances into villages. This cause no doubt contributed to the general effect of rendering the Commons' House a less complete representation of the people. Yet had this been all, though it had ceased to be a legal and actual it might still have been a virtual Representation of the People. [22] But universally the nation became multiplied into a denomination which had no constitutional presence in the State. This denomination had not existed before, or had existed only to a degree in which its interests were sensibly interwoven with that of those who enjoyed a constitutional presence. Thus the proportion borne by the Englishmen who possessed the faculty of suffrage to those who were excluded from that faculty at the several periods of 1641 and 1688 had changed by the operation of these causes from 1 to 8 to 1 to 20. The rapid and effectual progress by which it changed from 1 to 20 to one to many hundreds in the interval between 1688 and 1819 is a process, to those familiar with the history of the political economy of that period, which is rendered by these principles sufficiently intelligible. The number therefore of those who have influence on the government, even if numerically the same as at the former period, was relatively different. And a sufficiently just measure is afforded of the degree in which a country is enslaved or free, by the consideration of the relative number of individuals who are admitted to the exercise of political rights. Meanwhile another cause was operating of a deeper and more extensive nature. The class who compose the Lords must, by the advantages of their situation as the great landed proprietors, possess a considerable influence over nomination to the Commons. This influence, from an original imperfection in the equal distribution of suffrage, was always enormous, but it is only since it has been combined with the cause before stated that it has appeared to be fraught with consequences incompatible with public liberty. In 1641 this influence was almost wholly inoperative to pervert the counsels of the nation from its own advantage. But at that epoch the enormous tyranny of the agents of the royal power weighed equally upon all denominations of men, and united all counsels to extinguish it; add to which, the nation, as stated before, was in a very considerable degree fairly represented in Parliament. The common danger which was the bond of union between the aristocracy and the people having been destroyed, the former systematized their influence through the permanence of hereditary right, whilst the latter were losing power by the inflexibility of the institutions which forbade a just accommodation to their numerical increase. After the operations of these causes had commenced, the accession of William III placed a seal upon forty years of Revolution.

1688 and the Oligarchy of Property

The government of this country at the period of 1688 was regal, tempered by aristocracy, for what conditions of democracy attach to an assembly one portion of which was imperfectly nominated by less than a twentieth part of the people, and another perfectly nominated by the nobles? For the nobility, having by the assistance of the people imposed close limitations upon the royal power, finding that power to be its natural ally and the people (for the people from the increase of their numbers acquired greater and more important rights whilst the organ through which those rights might be asserted grew feebler in proportion to the increase of the cause of those rights and of their importance) its natural enemy, made the Crown the mask and pretence of their own authority. At this period began that despotism of the oligarchy of party, which under colour of administering the executive power lodged in the king, represented in truth the interest of the rich. When it is said by political reasoners, speaking of the interval between 1688 and the present time, that the royal power progressively increased, they use an expression which suggests a very imperfect and partial idea. The power which has increased is that entrusted with the administration of affairs, composed of men responsible to the aristocratical assemblies, or to the reigning party in those assemblies, which represents those orders of the nation which are privileged, and will retain power as long as it pleases them and must be divested of power as soon as it ceases to please them. The power which had increased therefore is the power of the rich. The name and office of king is merely the mask of this power, and is a kind of stalking-horse used to conceal these 'catchers of men', whilst they lay their nets. Monarchy is only the string which ties the robbers' bundle. Though less contumelious and abhorrent from the dignity of human nature than an absolute monarchy, an oligarchy of this nature exacts more of suffering from the people because it reigns both by the opinion generated by imposture, and the force which that opinion places within its grasp.

National Debt At the epoch adverted to, the device of public credit was first systematically applied as an instrument of government. It was employed at the accession of William III less as a resource for meeting the financial exigencies of the state than as a bond to connect those in the possession of property with those who had, by taking advantage of an accident of party, acceded to power. In the interval elapsed since that period it has accurately fulfilled the intention of its establishment, and has continued to add strength to the government even until the present crisis. Now this device is one of those execrable contrivances of misrule which overbalance the materials of common advantage produced by the progress of civilization and increase the number of those who are idle in proportion to those who work, whilst it increases, through the factitious wants of those indolent, privileged persons, the quantity of work to be done. The rich, no longer being able to rule by force, have invented this scheme that they may rule by fraud. The most despotic governments of antiquity were strangers to this invention, which is a compendious method of extorting from the people far more than praetorian guards, and arbitrary tribunals, and excise officers created judges in the last resort, would ever wring. Neither the Persian monarchy nor the Roman empire, where the will of one person was acknowledged as unappealable law, ever extorted a twentieth part the proportion now extorted from the property and labour of the inhabitants of Great Britain. The precious metals have been from the earliest records of civilization employed as the signs of labour and the titles to an unequal distribution of its produce. The Government of a country is necessarily entrusted with the affixing to certain portions of these metals a stamp, by which to mark their genuineness; no other is considered as current coin, nor can be a legal tender. The reason of this is that no alloyed coin should pass current, and thereby depreciate the genuine, and by augmenting the price of the articles which are the produce of labour defraud the holders of that which is genuine of the advantages legally belonging to them. If the Government itself abuses the trust reposed in it to debase the coin, in order that it may derive advantage from the unlimited multiplication of the mark entitling the holder to command the labour and property of others, the gradations by which it sinks, as labour rises, to the level of their comparative values, produces public confusion and misery. The foreign exchange meanwhile instructs the Government how temporary was its resource. This mode of making the distribution of the sign of labour a source of private aggrandisement at the expense of public confusion and loss was not wholly unknown to the nations of antiquity.

Paper-money

But the modern scheme of public credit is a far subtler and more complicated contrivance of misrule. All great transactions of personal property in England are managed by signs and that is by the authority of the possessor expressed upon paper, thus representing in a compendious form his right to so much gold, which represents his right to so much labour. A man may write on a piece of paper what he pleases; he may say he is worth a thousand when he is not worth a hundred pounds. If he can make others believe this, he has credit for the sum to which his name is attached. And so long as this credit lasts, he can enjoy all the advantages which would arise out of the actual possession of that sum he is believed to possess. He can lend two hundred to this man and three to that other, and his bills, among those who believe that he possesses this sum, pass like money. Of course in the same proportion of bills of this sort, beyond the actual goods or gold and silver possessed by the drawer, pass current, they defraud those who have gold and silver and goods of the advantages legally attached to the possession of them, and they defraud the labourer and artizan of the advantages attached to increasing the nominal price of labour, and such a participation in them as their industry might command, whilst they render wages fluctuating and add to the toil of the cultivator and manufacturer.

The existing government of England in substituting a currency of paper for one of gold has had no need to depreciate the currency by alloying the coin of the country; they have merely fabricated pieces of paper on which they promise to pay a certain sum. The holders of these papers came for payment in some representation of property universally exchangeable. They then declared that the persons who held the office for that payment could not be forced by law to pay. They declared subsequently that these pieces of paper were the current coin of the country. [23] Of this nature are all such transactions of companies and banks as consist in the circulation of promissory notes to a greater amount than the actual property possessed by those whose names they bear. They have the effect of augmenting the prices of provision, and of benefiting at the expense of the community the speculators in this traffic. One of the vaunted effects of this system is to increase the national industry, that is, to increase the labours of the poor and those luxuries of the rich which they supply. To make a manufacturer work 16 hours when he only worked 8. To turn children into lifeless and bloodless machines at an age when otherwise they would be at play before the cottage doors of their parents. To augment indefinitely the proportion of those who enjoy the profit of the labour of others, as compared with those who exercise this labour. To screw up. . . . [24]

Oligarchy of fund-lords

The consequences of this transaction have been the establishment of a new aristocracy, which has its basis in funds as the old one has its basis in force. The hereditary landowners in England derived their title from royal grants—they are fiefs bestowed by conquerors, or church-lands. Long usage has consecrated the abstraction of the word aristocracy from its primitive meaning to that ordinary sense which signifies that class of persons who possess a right to the produce of the labour of others, without dedicating to the common service any labour in return. This class of persons, whose existence is a prodigious anomaly in the social system, has ever constituted an inseparable portion of it, and there has never been an approach in practice towards any plan of political society modelled on equal justice, at least in the complicated mechanism of modern life. Mankind seem to acquiesce, as in a necessary condition of the imbecility of their own will and reason, in the existence of an aristocracy. With reference to this imbecility, it has doubtless been the instrument of great social advantage, although that advantage would have been greater which might have been produced according to the forms of a just distribution of the goods and evils of life. The object therefore of all enlightened legislation, and administration, is to enclose within the narrowest practicable limits this order of drones. The effect of the financial impostures of the modern rulers of England has been to increase the number of the drones. Instead of one aristocracy, the condition to which, in the present state of human affairs, the friends of virtue and liberty are willing to subscribe as to an inevitable evil, they have supplied us with two aristocracies. The one, consisting in great land proprietors, and wealthy merchants who receive and interchange the produce of this country with the produce of other countries: in this, because all other great communities have as yet acquiesced in it, we acquiesce. Connected with the members of it is a certain generosity and refinement of manners and opinion which, although neither philosophy nor virtue, has been that acknowledged substitute for them which at least is a religion which makes respected those venerable names. The other aristocracy is one of attornies and excisemen and directors and government pensioners, usurers, stockjobbers, country bankers, with their dependents and descendants. These are a set of pelting wretches in whose employment there is nothing to exercise even to their distortion the more majestic faculties of the soul. Though at the bottom it is all trick, there is something frank and magnificent in the chivalrous disdain of infamy connected with a gentleman. There is something to which—until you see through the base falsehood upon which all inequality is founded—it is difficult for the imagination to refuse its respect, in the faithful and direct dealings of the substantial merchant. But in the habits and lives of this new aristocracy created out of an increase in public calamities, and whose existence must be determined by their termination, there is nothing to qualify our disapprobation. They eat and drink and sleep, and in the intervals of these things performed with most vexatious ceremony and accompaniments they cringe and lie. They poison the literature of the age in which they live by requiring either the antitype of their own mediocrity in books, or such stupid and distorted and inharmonious idealisms as alone have the power to stir this torpid imaginations. Their hopes and fears are of the narrowest description. Their domestic affections are feeble, and they have no others. They think of any commerce with their species but as a means, never as an end, and as a means to the basest forms of personal advantage. [25]

Misery of the poor under this system

If this aristocracy had arisen from a false and depreciated currency to the exclusion of the other, its existence would have been a moral calamity and disgrace, but it would not have constituted an oppression. But the hereditary aristocracy who had the political administration of affairs took the measures which created this other for purposes peculiarly its own. Those measures were so contrived as in no manner to diminish the wealth and power of the contrivers. The lord does not spare himself one luxury, but the peasant and artizan are assured of many *necessary* things. To support the system of social order according to its supposed unavoidable constitution, those from whose labour all those external accommodations which distinguish a civilized being from a savage arise, worked, before the institution of this double aristocracy, light hours. And of these only the healthy were compelled to labour, the efforts of the old, the sick and the immature being dispensed with, and they maintained by the labour of the sane, [26] for such is the plain English of the poor-rates. That labour procured a competent share of the decencies of life, and society seemed to extend the benefits of its institution even to its most unvalued instrument. Although deprived of those resources of sentiment and knowledge which might have been their lot could the wisdom of the institutions and social forms have established a system of strict justice, yet they earned by their labour a competency in those external materials of life which, and not the loss of moral and intellectual excellence, is supposed to be the legitimate object of the desires and murmurs of the poor. Since the institution of this double aristocracy, however, they have often worked not ten but twenty hours a day. Not that the poor have rigidly worked twenty hours, but that the worth of the labour of twenty hours, now, in food and clothing, is equivalent to the worth of ten hours then. And because twenty hours cannot, from the nature of the human frame, be exacted from those who before performed ten, the aged and the sickly are compelled either to work or starve. Children who were exempted from labour are put in requisition, and the vigorous promise of the coming generation blighted by premature exertion. For fourteen hours' labour, which they do perforce, they receive—no matter in what nominal amount—the price of seven. They eat less bread, wear worse clothes, are more ignorant, immoral, miserable and desperate. This then is the condition of the lowest and largest class, from whose labour the whole materials of life are wrought, of which the others are only the receivers or the consumers. They are more superstitious, for misery on earth begets a diseased expectation and panic-stricken faith in miseries beyond the grave. 'God', they argue, 'rules this world as well as that; and assuredly since his nature is immutable, and his powerful will unchangeable, he rules them by the same laws.' The gleams of hope which speak of Paradise seem like the flames in Milton's hell only to make darkness visible, and all things take their colour from what surrounds them. They become revengeful—

But the condition of all classes of society, excepting those within the privileged pale, is singularly unprosperous, and even they experience the reaction of their own short-sighted tyranny in all those sufferings and deprivations which are not of a distinctly physical nature, in the loss of dignity, simplicity and energy, and in the possession of all those qualities which distinguish a slave-driver from a proprietor. Right government being an institution for the purpose of securing such a moderate degree of happiness to men as has been experimentally practicable, [27] the sure character of misgovernment is misery, and first discontent and, if that be despised, then insurrection, as the legitimate expression of that misery. The public right to demand happiness is a principle of nature; the labouring classes, when they cannot get food for their labour, are impelled to take it by force. Laws and assemblies and courts of justice and delegated

The ends of government: connection between misery and mis-government

powers placed in balance and in opposition are the means and the form, but public happiness is the substance and the end of political institutions. [28] Whenever this is attained in a nation, not from external force, but from the internal arrangement and divisions of the common burthens of defence and maintenance, then there is oppression. And then arises an alternative between Reform, or the institution of a military Despotism, or a Revolution in which parties, one striving after ill-digested systems of democracy, and the other clinging to the outworn abuses of power, leave the few who aspire to more than the former and who would overthrow the latter at whatever expense, to wait for that modified advantage which, with the temperance and the toleration which both regard as a crime, might have resulted from the occasion which they let pass in a far more signal manner.

The propositions which are the consequences or the corollaries of the preceding reasoning, and to which it seems to have conducted us are:—

—That the majority of the people of England are destitute and miserable, ill-clothed, ill-fed, ill-educated.

—That they know this, and that they are impatient to procure a reform of the cause of this abject and wretched state.

—That the cause of this misery is the unequal distribution which, under the form of the national debt, has been surreptitiously made of the products of their labour and the products of the labour of their ancestors; for all property is the produce of labour.

—That the cause of that cause is a defect in the government.

—That if they knew nothing of their condition, but believed that all they endured and all they were deprived of arose from the unavoidable conditions of human life, this belief being an error, and one the endurance of which enforces an injustice, every enlightened and honourable person, whatever may be the imagined interest of his peculiar class, ought to excite them to the discovery of the true state of the case, and to the temperate but irresistible vindication of their rights.

A Reform in England is most just and necessary. What ought to be that reform?

The abominable doctrine of Malthus

A writer of the present day (a priest of course, for his doctrines are those of a eunuch and of a tyrant) [29] has stated that the evils of the poor arise from an excess of population, and after they have been stript naked by the tax-gatherer and reduced to bread and tea and fourteen hours of hard labour by their masters, and after the frost has bitten their defenceless limbs, and the cramp has wrung like a disease within their bones, and hunger and the suppressed revenge of hunger has stamped the ferocity of want like the mark of Cain upon their countenance, that the last tie by which Nature holds them to the benignant earth whose plenty is garnered up in the strongholds of their tyrants, is to be divided; that the single alleviation of their sufferings and their scorns, the one thing which made it impossible to degrade them below the beasts, which amid all their crimes and miseries yet separated a cynical and unmanly contamination, an anti-social cruelty, from all the soothing, elevating and harmonious gentleness of the sexual intercourse and the humanizing charities of domestic life which are its appendages—that this is to be obliterated. They are required to abstain from marrying under penalty of starvation. And it is threatened to deprive them of that property which is as strictly their birthright as a gentleman's land is his birthright, without giving them any compensation but the insulting advice to conquer, with minds undisciplined in the habits of higher gratification, a propensity which persons of the most consummate wisdom have been unable to resist, and which it is difficult to admire a person for having resisted. The doctrine of this writer is that the principle of population, when under no dominion of moral restraint, *is* outstripping the sustenance produced by the labour of man, and that not in proportion to the number of inhabitants, but operating equally in a thinly peopled community as in one where the population is enormous, being not a prevention but a check. So far a man might have been conducted by a train of reasoning which, though it may be shown to be defective, would argue in the reasoner no selfish or slavish feelings. But he has the hardened insolence to propose as a remedy that the poor should be compelled (for what except compulsion is a threat of the confiscation of those funds which by the institutions of their country had been set apart for their sustenance in sickness or destitution?) to abstain from sexual intercourse, while the rich are to be permitted to add as many mouths to consume the products of the labours of the poor as they please. (The rights of all men are intrinsically and originally equal and they forgo the assertion of all of them only that they may the more securely enjoy a portion.) If any new disadvantages are found to attach to the condition of social existence, those disadvantages ought not to be borne exclusively by one class of men, nor especially by that class whose ignorance leads them to exaggerate the advantages of sensual enjoyment, whose callous habits render domestic endearments more important to dispose them to resist the suggestion to violence and cruelty by which their situation ever exposes them to be tempted, and all whose other enjoyments are limited and few, whilst their sufferings are various and many. In this sense I cannot imagine how the advocates of equality could so readily have conceded that the unlimited operation of the principle of population affects the truth of these theories. On the contrary, the more heavy and certain are the evils of life, the more injustice is there in casting the burden of them exclusively on one order in the community. They seem to have conceded it merely because their opponents have insolently assumed it. Surely it is enough that the rich should possess to the exclusion of the poor all other luxuries and comforts, and wisdom and refinement, the least envied but the most deserving of envy among all their privileges!

What is the Reform that we desire? Before we aspire after theoretical perfection in the amelioration of our political state, it is necessary that we possess those advantages which we have been cheated of, and of which the experience of modern times has proved that nations even under the present conditions are susceptible. We would regain these. We would establish some form of government which might secure us against such a series of events as have conducted us to a persuasion that the forms according to which it is now administered are inadequate to that purpose.

We would abolish the national debt.

We would disband the standing army.

We would, with every possible regard to the existing rights of the holders, abolish sinecures.

We would, with every possible regard to the existing interests of the holders, abolish tithes, and make all religions, all forms of opinion respecting the origin and government of the Universe equal in the eye of the law.

We would make justice cheap, certain and speedy, and extend the institution of juries to every possible occasion of jurisprudence.

The National Debt: how contracted and who pay for it: how to abolish it

The national debt was contracted chiefly in two liberticide wars, undertaken by the privileged classes of the country—the first for the ineffectual purpose of tyrannizing over one portion of their subjects, the second, in order to extinguish the resolute spirit of obtaining their rights in another. The labour which this money represents, and that which is represented by the money wrung for purposes of the same detestable character out of the people since the commencement of the American war would, if properly employed, have covered our land with monuments of architecture exceeding the sumptuousness and the beauty of Egypt and Athens; it might have made every peasant's cottage, surrounded with its garden, a little paradise of comfort, with every convenience desirable in civilized life; neat tables and chairs, good beds, and a collection of useful books; and our ships manned by sailors well-paid and well-clothed, might have kept watch round this glorious island against the less enlightened nations which assuredly would have envied, until they could have imitated, its prosperity. [30] But the labour which is expressed by these sums has been diverted from these purposes of human happiness to the promotion of slavery, and that attempt at dominion, and a great portion of the sum in question is debt and must be paid. Is it to remain unpaid for ever, an eternal rent-charge upon the land from which the inhabitants of these islands draw their subsistence? This were to pronounce the perpetual institution of two orders of aristocracy, and men are in a temper to endure one with some reluctance. Is it to be paid now? If so what are the funds, or when and how is it to be paid? The fact is that the national debt is a debt not contracted by the whole nation towards a portion of it, but a debt contracted by the whole mass of the privileged classes towards one particular portion of those classes. If the principal were paid, the whole property of those who possess property must be valued and the public creditor, whose property would have been included in this estimate, satisfied out of the proceeds. It has been said that all the land in the nation is mortgaged for the amount of the national debt. This is a partial statement. Not only all the land in the nation, but all the property of whatever denomination, all the houses and the furniture and the goods and every article of merchandise, and the property which is represented by the very money lent by the fund-holder, who is bound to pay a certain portion as debtor whilst he is entitled to receive another certain portion as creditor. The property of the rich is mortgaged: to use the language of the law, let the mortgagee foreclose.

If the principal of this debt were paid, [31] it would be the rich who alone could, and justly they ought to pay it. It would be a mere transfer among persons of property. Such a gentleman must lose a third of his estate, such a citizen a fourth of his money in the funds; the persons who borrowed would have paid, and the juggling and complicated system of paper finance be suddenly at an end. As it is, the interest is chiefly paid by those who had no hand in the borrowing, and who are sufferers in other respects from the consequences of those transactions in which the money was spent.

The payment of the principal of what is called the national debt, which it is pretended is so difficult a problem, is only difficult to those who do not see who is the debtor, and who the creditor, and who the wretched sufferers from whom they both wring the taxes which under the form of interest is given by the former and accepted by the latter. It is from the labour of those who have no property that all the persons who possess property think to extort the perpetual interest of a debt, the whole of which the latter know they could not persuade the former to pay, but by conspiring with them in an imposture which makes the third class pay what the first neither received by their sanction nor spent for their benefit and what the second never lent to them. They would both shift from themselves and their posterity to the labour of the present and of all succeeding generations the payment of the interest of their own debt, because the payment of the principal would be no more than a compromise and transfer of property between each other, by which the nation would be spared 44 millions a year, which now is paid to maintain in luxury and indolence the public debtors and to protect them from the demand of their creditors upon them, who, being part of the same body, and owing as debtors whilst they possess a claim as creditors, agree to abstain from demanding the principal which they must all unite to pay, for the sake of receiving an enormous interest which is principally wrung out of those who had no concern whatever in the transaction. One of the first acts of a reformed government would undoubtedly be an effectual scheme for compelling these to compromise their debt between themselves.

Property, legitimate and illegitimate

When I speak of persons of property I mean not every man who possesses any right of property; I mean the rich. Every man whose scope in society has a plebeian and intelligible utility, whose personal exertions are more valuable to him than his capital; every tradesman who is not a monopolist, all surgeons and physicians, and artists, and farmers, all those persons whose profits spring from honourably and honestly exerting their own skill and wisdom or strength in greater abundance than from the employment of money to take advantage of their fellow-citizens' starvation for their profit, are those who pay, as well as those more obviously understood by the labouring classes, the interest of the national debt. It is the interest of all these persons as well as that of the poor to insist upon the payment of the principal.

For this purpose the form ought to be as simple and succinct as possible. The operations deciding who was to pay, at what time, and how much, and to whom, divested of financial chicanery, are problems readily to be determined. The common tribunals may be invested with legal jurisdiction to award the proportion due upon the several claim of each.

Labour and skill and the immediate wages of labour and skill is a property of the most sacred and indisputable right, and the foundation of all other property. And the right of a man to property in the exertion of his own bodily and mental faculties, or on the produce and free reward from and for that exertion is the most inalienable of rights. If however he takes by violence and appropriates to himself through fraudulent cunning, or receives from another property so acquired, his claim to that property is of a far inferior force. We may acquiesce, if we evidently perceive an overbalance of public advantage in submission under this claim; but if any public emergency should arise, at which it might be necessary to satisfy, by a tax on capital, the claims of a part of the nation by a contribution from such national resources as may with the least injustice be appropriated to that purpose, assuredly it would not be on labour and skill, the foundation of all property, nor on the profits and savings of labour and skill, which are property itself, but on such possessions which can only be called property in a modified sense, as have from their magnitude and their nature an evident origin in violence or imposture.

Thus there are two descriptions of property which, without entering into the subtleties of a more refined moral theory as applicable to the existing forms of society, are entitled to two very different measures of forbearance and regard. And this forbearance and regard have by political institutions usually been accorded by an inverse reason from what is just and natural. Labour, industry, economy, skill, genius, or any similar powers honourably and innocently exerted are the foundations of one description of property, and all true political institutions ought to defend every man in the exercise of his discretion with respect to property so acquired. Of this kind is the principal part of the property enjoyed by those who are but one degree removed from the class which subsists by daily labour. (Yet there are instances of persons in this class who have procured their property by fraudulent and violent means, as there are instances in the other of persons who have acquired their property by innocent or honourable exertion. All political science abounds with limitations and exceptions.)—Property thus acquired men leave to their children. Absolute right becomes weakened by descent, just because it is only to avoid the greater evil of arbitrarily interfering with the discretion of every man in matters of property that the great evil of acknowledging any person to have an exclusive right to property who has not created it by his skill or labour is admitted, and secondly because the mode of its having been originally acquired is forgotten, and it is confounded with property acquired in a very different manner; and the principle upon which all property justly exists, after the great principle of the general advantage, becomes thus disregarded and misunderstood. Yet the privilege of disposing of property by will is one necessarily connected with the existing forms of domestic life; and exerted merely by those who having acquired property by industry or who preserve it by economy, would never produce any great and invidious inequality of fortune. A thousand accidents would perpetually tend to level the accidental elevation, and the signs of property would perpetually recur to those whose deserving skill might attract or whose labour might create it.

But there is another species of property which has its foundation in usurpation, or imposture, or violence, without which, by the nature of things, immense possessions of gold or land could never have been accumulated. Of this nature is the principal part of the property enjoyed by the aristocracy and by the great fundholders, the majority of whose ancestors never either deserved it by their skill and talents or acquired and created it by their personal labour. It could not be that they deserved it, for if the honourable exertion of the most glorious and imperial faculties of our nature had been the criterion of the possession of property the posterity of Shakespeare, of Milton, of Hampden, would be the wealthiest proprietors in England. It could not be that they acquired it by legitimate industry, for, besides that the real mode of acquisition is matter of history, no honourable profession or honest trade, nor the hereditary exercise of it, evei in such numerous instances accumulated so much as the masses of property enjoyed by the ruling orders in England. They were either grants from the feudal sovereigns whose right to what they granted was founded upon conquest or oppression, both a denial of all right; or they were lands of the antient Catholic clergy which according to the most acknowledged principles of public justice reverted to the nation at their suppression, or they were the products of patents and monopolies, an exercise of sovereignty which it is astonishing that political theorists have not branded as the most pernicious and odious to the interests of a commercial nation; or in later times such property has been accumulated by dishonourable cunning and the taking advantage of a fictitious paper currency to obtain an unfair power over labour and the fruits of labour.

Property thus accumulated, being transmitted from father to son, acquires, as property of the more legitimate kind loses, force and sanction, but in a very limited manner. For not only on an examination and recurrence to first principles is it seen to have been founded on a violation of all that to which the latter owes its sacredness, but it is felt in its existence and perpetuation as a public burthen, and known as a rallying point to the ministers of tyranny, having the property of a snowball, gathering as it rolls, and rolling until it bursts.

The national debt, as has been stated, is a debt contracted by a particular class in the nation towards a portion of that class. It is sufficiently clear that this debt was not contracted for the purpose of the public advantage. Besides there was no authority in the nation competent to a measure of this nature. The usual vindication of national debts is that they are in an overwhelming measure contracted for the purpose of defence against a common danger, for the vindication of the rights and liberties of posterity, and that it is just that posterity should bear the burthen of payment. This reasoning is most fallacious. The history of nations presents us with a succession of extraordinary emergencies, and thro' their present imperfect organization their existence is perpetually threatened by new and unexpected combinations and developments of foreign or internal force. Imagine a situation of equal emergency to occur to England as that which the ruling party assume to have occurred as their excuse for burthening the nation with the perpetual payment of £45,000,000 annually. Suppose France, Russia, and Germany were to enter into a league against Britain, the one to avenge its injuries, the second to satisfy its ambition, the third to soothe its jealousy. Could the nation bear £90,000,000 of yearly interest? must there be twice as many luxurious and idle persons? must the labourer receive for 28 hours' work what he now receives for 14, what he once received for seven? But this argument. . .. [32]

What is meant by a Reform of Parliament? If England were a Republic governed by one assembly; if there were no chamber of hereditary aristocracy which is at once an actual and a virtual representation of all who attain through rank or wealth superiority over their countrymen; if there were no king who is as the rallying point of those whose tendency is at once to gather and to confer that power which is consolidated at the expense of the nation, then. . . . [33]

The advocates of universal suffrage have reasoned correctly that no individual who is governed can be denied a direct share in the government of his country without supreme injustice. If one pursues the train of reasonings which have conducted to this conclusion, we discover that systems of social order still more incompatible than universal suffrage with any reasonable hope of instant accomplishment appear to be that which should result from a just combination of the elements of social life. I do not understand why those reasoners who propose at any price an immediate appeal to universal suffrage, because it is that which it is injustice to withhold, do not insist, on the same ground, on the immediate abolition, for instance, of monarchy and aristocracy, and the levelling of inordinate wealth, and an agrarian distribution, including the parks and chases of the rich, of the uncultivated districts of the country. No doubt the institution of universal suffrage would by necessary consequence immediately tend to the temporary abolition of these forms; because it is impossible that the people, having attained the power, should fail to see, what the demagogues now conceal from them, the legitimate consequence of the doctrines through which they had attained it. A Republic, however just in its principle and glorious in its object, would through the violence and sudden change which must attend it, incur a great risk of being as rapid in its decline as in its growth. It is better that they should be instructed in the whole truth; that they should see the clear grounds of their rights, the objects to which they ought to tend; and be impressed with the just persuasion that patience and reason and endurance are the means of a calm yet irresistible process. A civil war, which might be engendered by the passions attending on this mode of reform, would confirm in the mass of the nation those military habits which have been already introduced by our tyrants, and with which liberty is incompatible. From the moment that a man is a soldier, he becomes a slave. He is taught obedience; his will is no longer, which is the most sacred prerogative of men, guided by his own judgement. He is taught to despise human life and human suffering; this is the universal distinction of slaves. He is more degraded than a murderer; he is like the bloody knife which has stabbed and feels not: a murderer we may abhor and despise; a soldier, is by profession, beyond abhorrence and below contempt.

Premature universal suffrage or Republicanism undesirable

Chapter III

Probable Means

That the House of Commons should reform itself, uninfluenced by any fear that the people would, on their refusal, assume to itself that office, seems a contradiction. What need of Reform if it expresses the will and watches over the interests of the public? And if, as is sufficiently evident, it despises that will and neglects that interest, what motives would incite it to institute a reform which the aspect of the times renders indeed sufficiently perilous, but without which there will speedily be no longer anything in England to distinguish it from the basest and most abject community of slaves that ever existed.

One motive. . . . [34]

The great principle of Reform consists in every individual giving his consent to the institution and the continuous existence of the social system which is instituted for his advantage and for the advantage of others in his situation. [35] As in a great nation this is practically impossible, masses of individuals consent to qualify other individuals, whom they delegate to superintend their concerns. These delegates have constitutional authority to exercise the functions of sovereignty; they unite in the highest degree the legislative and executive functions. A government that is founded on any other basis is a government of fraud or force and ought on the first convenient occasion to be overthrown. The first principle of political reform is the natural equality of men, not with relation to their property but to their rights. That equality in possessions which Jesus Christ so passionately taught is a moral rather than a political truth and is such as social institutions cannot without mischief inflexibly secure. Morals and politics can only be considered as portions of the same science, with relation to a system of such absolute perfection as Plato and Rousseau and other reasoners have asserted, and as Godwin has with irresistible eloquence systematised and developed. Equality in possessions must be the last result of the utmost refinements of civilization; it is one of the conditions of that system of society towards which, with whatever hope of ultimate success, it is our duty to tend. We may and ought to advert to it as to the elementary principle, as to the goal, unattainable, perhaps, by us but which, as it were, we revive in our posterity to pursue. We derive tranquillity and courage and grandeur of soul from contemplating an object which is, because we will it, and may be, because we hope and desire it, and must be

Equality of men

if succeeding generations of the enlightened sincerely and earnestly seek it.

But our present business is with the difficult and unbending realities of actual life, and when we have drawn inspiration from the great object of our hopes it becomes us with patience and resolution to apply ourselves to accommodating our theories to immediate practice.

Parliamentary reform—of what kind

That Representative Assembly called the House of Commons ought questionless to be immediately nominated by the great mass of the people. The aristocracy and those who unite in their own persons the vast privileges conferred by the possession of inordinate wealth are sufficiently represented by the House of Peers and by the King. Those theorists who admire and would put into action the mechanism of what is called the British Constitution would acquiesce in this view of the question. For if the House of Peers be a permanent representation of the privileged classes, if the regal power be no more than another form, and a form still more advisedly to be so regarded, of the same representation, whilst the House of Commons is not chosen by the mass of the population, what becomes of that democratic element upon the presence of which it has been supposed that the waning superiority of England over the surrounding nations has depended?

Any sudden attempt at universal suffrage would produce an immature attempt at a Republic. It is better that an object so inexpressibly great and sacred should never have been attempted than that it should be attempted and fail. It is no prejudice to the ultimate establishment of the boldest political innovations that we temporize so that when they shall be accomplished they may be rendered permanent.

Considering the population of Great Britain and Ireland as twenty millions and the representative assembly as five hundred, each member ought to be the expression of the will of 40,000 persons; of these two-thirds would consist of women and children and persons under age; the actual number of voters therefore for each member would be 13,333. The whole extent of the empire might be divided into five hundred electoral departments of parishes, and the inhabitants assemble on a certain day to exercise their rights of suffrage.

Mr Bentham and other writers have urged the admission of females to the right of suffrage; this attempt seems somewhat immature. Should my opinion be the result of despondency, the writer of these pages would be the last to withhold his vote from any system which might tend to an equal and full development of the capacities of all living beings.

Objections of secret ballot

The system of voting by ballot which some reasoners have recommended is attended with obvious inconveniences. It withdraws the elector from the eye of his country, and his neighbours, and permits him to conceal the motives of his vote, which, if concealed, cannot but be dishonourable; when, if he had known that he had to render a public account of his conduct, he would never have permitted them to guide him. There is in this system of voting by ballot and of electing a member of the *Representative Assembly* as a churchwarden is elected something too mechanical. The elector and the elected ought to meet one another face to face, and interchange the meanings of actual presence and share some common impulses, and, in a degree, understand each other. There ought to be the common sympathy of the excitements of a popular assembly among the electors themselves. The imagination would thus be strongly excited and a mass of generous and enlarged and popular sentiments be awakened, which would give the vitality of. . . . [36]

That republican boldness of censuring and judging one another which has indeed existed in England under the title of 'public opinion', though perverted from its true uses into an instrument of prejudice and calumny, would then be applied to its genuine purpose. Year by year the people would become more susceptible of assuming forms of government more simple and beneficial.

It is in this publicity of the exercise of sovereignty that the difference between the republics of Greece and the monarchies of Asia consisted. [37]

If the existing government shall compel the nation to take

the task of reform into its own hands, one of the most obvious consequences of such a circumstance would be the abolition of monarchy and aristocracy. Why, it will then be argued, if the subsisting condition of social forms is to be thrown into confusion, should these things be endured? Is it because we think that an hereditary king is cheaper and wiser than an elected President, or a House of Lords and a Bench of Bishops an institution modelled by the wisdom of the most refined and civilized periods, beyond which the wit of mortal man can furnish nothing more perfect? In case the subsisting Government should compel the people to revolt to establish a representative assembly in defiance of them, and to assume in that assembly an attitude of resistance and defence, this question would probably be answered in a very summary manner. No friend of mankind and of his country can desire that such a crisis should suddenly arrive; but still less, once having arrived, can he hesitate under what banner to array his person and his power. At the peace, Europe would have been contented with strict economy and severe retrenchment, and some direct and intelligible plan for producing that equilibrium between the capitalists and the land-holders which is derisively styled the payment of the national debt: had this system been adopted, they probably would have refrained from exacting Parliamentary Reform, the only secure guarantee that it would have been pursued. Two years ago it might still have been possible to have commenced a system of gradual reform. The people were then insulted, tempted and betrayed, and the petitions of a million of men rejected with disdain. [38] Now they are more miserable, more hopeless, more impatient of their misery. Above all, they have become more universally aware of the true sources of their misery. It is possible that the period of conciliation is past, and that after having played with the confidence and cheated the expectations of the people, their passions will be too little under discipline to allow them to wait the slow, gradual and certain operation of such a Reform as we can imagine the constituted authorities to concede.

Gradual reform probably too late, now

Upon the issue of this question depends the species of reform which a philosophical mind should regard with approbation. If Reform shall be begun by this existing government, let us be contented with a limited *beginning*, with any whatsoever opening; let the rotten boroughs be disfranchised and their rights transferred to the unenfranchised cities and districts of the nation; it is no matter how slow, gradual and cautious be the change; we shall demand more and more with firmness and moderation, never anticipating but never deferring the moment of successful opposition, so that the people may become habituated to exercising the functions of sovereignty, in proportion as they acquire the possession of it. If this reform could begin from within the Houses of Parliament, as constituted at present, it appears to me that what is called moderate reform, that is a suffrage whose qualification should be the possession of a certain small property, and triennial parliaments, would be a system in which for the sake of obtaining without bloodshed or confusion ulterior improvements of a more important character, all reformers ought to acquiesce. Not that such are first principles, or that they would produce a system of perfect social institutions or one approaching to such. But nothing is more idle than to reject a limited benefit because we cannot without great sacrifices obtain an unlimited one. We might thus reject a Representative Republic, if it were obtainable, on the plea that the imagination of man can conceive of something more absolutely perfect. Towards whatever we regard as perfect, undoubtedly it is no less our duty than it is our nature to press forward; this is the generous enthusiasm which accomplishes not indeed the consummation after which it aspires, but one which approaches it in a degree far nearer than if the whole powers had not been developed by a delusion.—It is in politics rather than in religion that faith is meritorious.

If the Houses of Parliament obstinately and perpetually refuse to concede any reform to the people, my vote is for universal suffrage and equal representation. But, it is asked, how shall this be accomplished in defiance of and in opposition to the constituted authorities of the nation, they who possess whether with or without its consent the command of a standing army and of a legion of spies and police officers, and hold the strings of that complicated mechanism with which the hopes and fears of men are moved like puppets? They would disperse any assembly really chosen by the people, they would shoot and hew down any multitude, without regard to sex or age, as the Jews did the Canaanites, which might be collected in its defence, they would calumniate, imprison, starve, ruin and expatriate every person who wrote or acted or thought or might be suspected to think against them; misery and extermination would fill the country from one end to another.

This question I would answer by another.

Will you endure to pay the half of your earnings to maintain in luxury and idleness the confederation of your tyrants as the reward of a successful conspiracy to defraud and oppress you? Will you make your tame cowardice and the branding record of it the everlasting inheritance of your posterity? Not only this, but will you render by your torpid endurance this condition of things as permanent as the system of caste in India, by which the same horrible injustice is perpetrated under another form?

Assuredly no Englishmen by whom these propositions are understood will answer in the affirmative; and the opposite side of the alternative remains.

When the majority in any nation arrive at a conviction that it is their duty and their interest to divest the minority of a power employed to their disadvantage, and the minority are sufficiently mistaken as to believe that their superiority is tenable, a struggle must ensue.

If the majority are enlightened, united, impelled by a uniform enthusiasm and animated by a distinct and powerful appreciation of their object, and feel confidence in their undoubted power—the struggle is merely nominal. The minority perceive the approaches of the development of an irresistible force, by the influence of the public opinion of their weakness, on those political forms of which no government but an absolute despotism is devoid. They divest themselves of their usurped distinctions; the public tranquillity is not disturbed by the revolution.

But these conditions may only be imperfectly fulfilled by the state of a people grossly oppressed and impotent to cast off the load. Their enthusiasm may have been subdued by the killing weight of toil and suffering; they may be panic-stricken and disunited by their oppressors, and the demagogues, the influence of fraud may have been sufficient to weaken the union of classes which compose them by suggesting jealousies, and the position of the conspirators, although it is to be forced by repeated assaults, may be tenable until the siege can be vigorously urged. The true patriot will endeavour to enlighten and to unite the nation and animate it with enthusiasm and confidence. For this purpose he will be indefatigable in promulgating political truth. He will endeavour to rally round one standard the divided friends of liberty, and make them forget the subordinate objects with regard to which they differ by appealing to that respecting which they are all agreed. He will promote such open confederation among men of principle and spirit as may tend to make their intentions and their efforts converge to a common centre. He will discourage all secret associations, which have a tendency, by making the nation's will develop itself in a partial and premature manner, to cause tumult and confusion. He will urge the necessity of exciting the people frequently to exercise their right of assembling, in such limited numbers as that all present may be actual parties to the proceedings of the day. [39] Lastly, if circumstances had collected a considerable number as at Manchester on the memorable 16th of August, if the tyrants command the troops to fire upon them or cut them down unless they disperse, he will exhort them peaceably to defy the danger, and to expect without resistance the onset of the cavalry, and wait with folded arms the event of the fire of the artillery and receive with unshrinking bosoms the bayonets of the charging battalions. [40] Men are every day persuaded to incur greater perils for a less manifest advantage. And this, not because active resistance is not justifiable when all other means shall have failed, but because in this

The conduct of true patriots

instance temperance and courage would produce greater advantages than the most decisive victory. In the first place, the soldiers are men and Englishmen, and it is not to be believed that they would massacre an unresisting multitude of their countrymen drawn up in unarmed array before them, and bearing in their looks the calm, deliberate resolution to perish rather than abandon the assertion of their rights. In the confusion of flight the ideas of the soldier become confused, and he massacres those who fly from him by the instinct of his trade. In the struggles of conflict and resistance he is irritated by a sense of his own danger, he is flattered by an apprehension of his own magnanimity in incurring it, he considers the blood of his countrymen at once the price of his valour, the pledge of his security. He applauds himself by reflecting that these base and dishonourable motives will gain him credit among his comrades and his officers who are animated by the same. But if he should observe neither resistance nor flight he would be reduced to confusion and indecision. Thus far, his ideas were governed by the same law as those of a dog who chases a flock of sheep to the corner of a field, and keeps aloof when they make a parade of resistance. But the soldier is a man and an Englishman. This unexpected reception would probably throw him back upon a recollection of the true nature of the measures of which he was made the instrument, and the enemy might be converted into the ally.

The patriot will be foremost to publish the boldest truths in the most fearless manner, yet without the slightest tincture of personal malignity. He would encourage all others to the same efforts and assist them to the utmost of his power with the resources both of his intellect and fortune. He would call upon them to despise imprisonment and persecution and lose no opportunity of bringing public opinion and the power of the tyrants into circumstances of perpetual contest and opposition.

All might however be ineffectual to produce so uniform an impulse of the national will as to preclude a further struggle. The strongest argument, perhaps, for the necessity of Reform, is the inoperative and unconscious abjectness to which the purposes of a considerable mass of the people are reduced. They neither know nor care—They are sinking into a resemblance with the Hindoos and the Chinese, who were once men as they are. Unless the cause which renders them passive subjects instead of active citizens be removed, they will sink with accelerated gradations into that barbaric and unnatural civilization which destroys all the differences among men. It is in vain to exhort us to wait until all men shall desire Freedom whose real interest will consist in its establishment. It is in vain to hope to enlighten them whilst their tyrants employ the utmost artifices of all their complicated engine to perpetuate the infection of every species of fanaticism and error from generation to generation. The advocates of Reform ought indeed to leave no effort unexerted, and they ought to be indefatigable in exciting all men to examine.

But if they wait until those neutral politicians whose opinions represent the actions of this class are persuaded that some effectual reform is necessary, the occasion will have passed or will never arrive, and the people will have exhausted their strength in ineffectual expectation and will have sunk into incurable supineness. It was principally the effect of a similar quietism that the populous and extensive nations of Asia have fallen into their existing decrepitude; and that anarchy, insecurity, ignorance and barbarism, the symptoms of the confirmed disease of monarchy, have reduced nations of the most delicate physical and intellectual organization and under the most fortunate climates of the globe to a blank in the history of man.

The reasoners who incline to the opinion that it is not sufficient that the innovators should produce a majority in the nation, but that we ought to expect such an unanimity as would preclude anything amounting to a serious dispute, are prompted to this view of the question by the dread of anarchy and massacre. Infinite and inestimable calamities belong to oppression, but the most fatal of them all is that mine of unexploded mischief which it has practiced beneath the foundations of society, and with which, 'pernicious to one touch' it threatens to involve the ruin of the entire building together with its own. But delay merely renders this mischief more tremendous, not the less inevitable. For the utmost may now be the crisis of the social disease which is rendered thus periodical, chronic and incurable.

The savage brutality of the populace is proportioned to the arbitrary character of their government, and tumults and insurrections soon, as in Constantinople, become consistent with the permanence of the causing evil, of which they might have been the critical determination.

Organization of opinion for reform

The public opinion in England ought first to be excited to action, and the durability of those forms within which the oppressors entrench themselves brought perpetually to the test of its operation. No law or institution can last if this opinion be decisively pronounced against it. For this purpose government ought to be defied, in cases of questionable result, to prosecute for political libel. All questions relating to the jurisdiction of magistrates and courts of law respecting which any doubt could be raised ought to be agitated with indefatigable pertinacity. Some two or three of the popular leaders have shown the best spirit in this respect; they only want system and co-operation. The taxgatherer ought to be compelled in every practicable instance to distrain, whilst the right to impose taxes, as was the case in the beginning of the resistance to the tyranny of Charles I is formally contested by an overwhelming multitude of defendants before the courts of common law. Confound the subtlety of lawyers with the subtlety of the law. The nation would thus be excited to develop itself, and to declare whether it acquiesced in the existing forms of government. The manner in which all questions of this nature might be decided would develop the occasions, and afford a prognostic as to the success, of more decisive measures. Simultaneously with this active and vigilant system of opposition, means ought to be taken of solemnly conveying the sense of large bodies and various denominations of the people in a manner the most explicit to the existing depositaries of power. Petitions, couched in the actual language of the petitioners, and emanating from distinct assemblies, ought to load the tables of the House of Commons. The poets, philosophers and artists ought to remonstrate, and the memorials entitled their petitions might shew the universal conviction they entertain of the inevitable connection between national prosperity and freedom, and the cultivation of the imagination and the cultivation of scientific truth, and the profound development of moral and metaphysical enquiry. [41] Suppose the memorials to be severally written by Godwin, Hazlitt and Bentham and Hunt, they would be worthy of the age and of the cause; radiant and irresistible like the meridian sun they would strike all but the eagles who dared gaze upon its beams with blindness and confusion. [42] These appeals of solemn and emphatic argument from those who have already a predestined existence among posterity, would appal the enemies of mankind by their echoes from every corner of the world in which the majestic literature of England is cultivated; it would be like a voice from beyond the dead of those who will live in the memories of men, when they must be forgotten; it would be Eternity warning Time.

Petitions of poets, philosophers and artists

Let us hope that at this stage of the progress of Reform, the oppressors would feel their impotence and reluctantly and imperfectly concede some limited portion of the rights of the people, and disgorge some morsels of their undigested prey. In this case, the people ought to be exhorted by everything ultimately dear to them to pause until by the exercise of those rights which they have regained they become fitted to demand more. It is better that we gain what we demand by a process of negociation which should occupy twenty years than that by communicating a sudden shock to the interests of those who are the depositaries and dependents of power we should incur the calamity which their revenge might inflict upon us by giving the signal of civil war. If, after all, they consider the chance of personal ruin, and the infamy of figuring on the page of history as the promoters of civil war preferable to resigning any portion how small soever of their usurped authority, we are to recollect that we possess a right beyond remonstrance. It has been acknowledged by the most approved writers on the English constitution, which has in this instance been merely a declaration of the superior decisions of eternal justice, that we possess a right of resistance. The claim of the reigning family is founded upon a memorable exertion of this solemnly recorded right. [43]

The last resort of resistance

The last resort of resistance is undoubtedly insurrection. The right of insurrection is derived from the employment of armed force to counteract the will of the nation. Let the government disband the standing army, and the purpose of resistance would be sufficiently fulfilled by the incessant agitation of the points of dispute before the courts of common law, and by an unwarlike display of the irresistible number and union of the people.

The calamity of civil war

Before we enter into a consideration of the measures which might terminate in civil war, let us for a moment consider the nature and the consequences of war. This is the alternative which the unprincipled cunning of the tyrants has presented to us, and which we must not shun. There is secret sympathy between Destruction and Power, between Monarchy and War; and the long experience of all the history of all recorded time teaches us with what success they have played into each other's hands. War is a kind of superstition; the pageantry of arms and badges corrupts the imagination of men. How far more appropriate would be the symbols of an inconsolable grief—muffled drums, and melancholy music, and arms reversed, and the livery of sorrow rather than of blood. When men mourn at funerals for what do they mourn in comparison with the calamities which they hasten with every circumstance of festivity to suffer and to inflict! Visit in imagination the scene of a field of battle or a city taken by assault, collect into one group the groans and the distortions of the innumerable dying, the inconsolable grief and horror of their surviving friends, the hellish exultation and unnatural drunkenness of destruction of the conquerors, the burning of the harvests and the obliteration of the traces of cultivation—to this, in a civil war, is to be added the sudden disruption of the bonds of social life, and 'father against son'.

If there had never been war, there could never have been

tyranny in the world; tyrants take advantage of the mechanical organization of armies to establish and defend their encroachments. It is thus that the mighty advantages of the French Revolution have been almost compensated by a succession of tyrants (for demagogues, oligarchies, usurpers and legitimate kings are merely varieties of the same class) from Robespierre to Louis XVIII. War, waged from whatever motive, extinguishes the sentiment of reason and justice in the mind. The motive is forgotten, or only adverted to in a mechanical and habitual manner. A sentiment of confidence in brute force and in a contempt of death and danger is considered the highest virtue, when in truth, and however indispensable, they are merely the means and the instrument, highly capable of being perverted to destroy the cause they were assumed to promote. It is a foppery the most intolerable to an amiable and philosophical mind. It is like what some reasoners have observed of religious faith; no fallacious and indirect motive to action can subsist in the mind without weakening the effect of those which are genuine and true. The person who thinks it virtuous to believe, will think a less degree of virtue attaches to good actions than if he had considered it as indifferent. The person who has been accustomed to subdue men by force will be less inclined to the trouble of convincing or persuading them.

These brief considerations suffice to show that the true friend of mankind and of his country would hesitate before he recommended measures which tend to bring down so heavy a calamity as war.

I imagine however that before the English Nation shall arrive at that point of moral and political degradation now occupied by the Chinese, it will be necessary to appeal to an exertion of physical strength. If the madness of parties admits no other mode of determining the question at issue, . . . [44]

When the people shall have obtained, by whatever means, the victory over their oppressors and when persons appointed by them shall have taken their seats in the Representative Assembly of the nation, and assumed the control of public affairs according to constitutional rules, there will remain the great task of accommodating all that can be preserved of antient forms with the improvements of the knowledge of a more enlightened age, in legislation, jurisprudence, government and religious and academical institutions. The settlement of the national debt is on the principles before elucidated merely an arrangement of form, and however necessary and important is an affair of mere arithmetical proportions readily determined; nor can I see how those who, being deprived of their unjust advantages, will probably inwardly murmur, can oppose one word of open expostulation to a measure of such irrefragable justice.

There is one thing which certain vulgar agitators endeavour to flatter the most uneducated part of the people by assiduously proposing, which they ought not to do nor to require; and that is Retribution. Men having been injured, desire to injure in return. This is falsely called an universal law of human nature; it is a law from which many are exempt, and all in proportion to their virtue and cultivation. The savage is more revengeful than the civilized man, the ignorant and uneducated than the person of a refined and cultivated intellect; the generous and . . . [45]

END OF MS

NOTES

The Statesman's Manual

1 (p. 7). *A reading public.* Coleridge refers to the phenomenon which had appeared towards the latter end of the eighteenth century, of an uncultivated and untrained 'public' which indulged in 'desultory' reading, chiefly of the 'circulating library' variety: a habit which he bracketed alone with swinging on a gate and spitting over bridges as means of filling up intellectual vacuity. See the first footnote to chapter III of his *Biographia Literaria.* His letters after 1815 are studded with references to this ominous phenomenon: see especially *Unpublished Letters* (ed. E. Leslie Griggs), vol. II, pp. 193-5, where he prophecies a return to esotericism. The point is important because it forms part of Coleridge's indictment of the general mental debilitation of his age and of his plea for the guardianship of standards by a responsible 'clerisy' and the re-education of the 'educated' (note 7). The general question can be studied in Q. D. Leavis, *Fiction and the Reading Public*, and a good deal of useful information can be found in Amy Cruse, *The Englishman and his Books.*

2 (p. 7). *Patrick Colquhoun* (1745-1820), manufacturer, Metropolitan Police Magistrate, inventor of the soup-kitchen, and collector of statistics. His *Treatise on the Wealth, Power and Resources of the British Empire in every Quarter of the World* was published in 1814.

3 (p. 8). I.e. the surviving fragments of a 'clerisy'—see Coleridge's extended conception of this 'learned order' in the *Church and State*, chapters V and VI.

4 (p. 9). *The discipline adopted. . . .* Joseph Lancaster, (1778-1838) founder of the 'Lancastrian Schools'—the first at Borough Road, Southwark in 1798—was a pioneer of 'modern' methods of school discipline, replacing the traditional flogging methods by appeals to the children's love of emulation, hatred of ridicule, etc. See his *Improvements in Education.* Coleridge refers in a footnote to Robert Southey's account of Lancaster's disciplinary inventions in his tract on *The New, or Madras System, of Education* and gives his own opinion that 'the true perfection of discipline in a school is—the maximum of watchfulness with the minimum of punishment'.

5 (p. 9). *The 'liberal idea'*. . . . Lancaster found his chief supporters among Nonconformists, especially the Quakers, and the religious instruction given in the Lancastrian schools was 'undenominational'. Coleridge's objection to this, couched as it is in the language of contemporary Anglican intolerance, was really far more philosophically based and intellectually respectable than that of Sarah Trimmer and the rest of the critics of Lancaster. It is part and parcel of the extremely impressive criticism of 'plain and simple Christianity' which he develops in the Second Lay Sermon (see pp. 86-9).

6 (p. 9). *Dr Bell's original and unsophisticated plan*. . . . The Rev. Dr Andrew Bell (1753-1832) published a pamphlet in 1797 called *An Experiment in Education* describing his use of the notorious 'Monitorial' method of instruction in a school at Madras, where he had been chaplain and superintendent. His 'original and unsophisticated plan', by which, it was claimed, a 'School or Family may teach itself', however large it might grow, by the mere multiplication of Monitors under *one* Master, appealed enormously to an age that worshipped cheapness and mass-production. Coleridge himself could call it 'this vast moral steam-engine'. His preference for Bell over Lancaster is here based on the fact that in Bell's schools (those of the 'National Society', founded in 1811) the religious instruction was according to the doctrines of the Established Church.

7 (p. 10). Re-education of the governing class. Amidst all the clamour of the 'Education-mad', at this time, for popular education, Coleridge steadily insisted that the proper preliminary to the efficient education of the labouring classes was the re-education of the upper classes—or of the teachers. To 'spur-arm the toes of society' or to 'enlighten the higher ranks *per ascensum ab imis*', would result in the plebification, not the popularization, of science. See the final paragraph of chapter VII of *The Constitution of the Church and State*.

8 (p. 10). This sentence is Coleridge's philosophical rendering of the idea expressed in Shelley's famous statement that 'poets are the unacknowledged legislators of the world'. From a manuscript note, it is evident that he was prepared to regard 'Ideas' in the world of mind as equivalent to 'Gentlemen' in the social scale. From the reference to Plato's Republic (p. 32), and the discussion of the symbolic 'tri-unity' of the human mind (pp. 32-4), it is possible to work out both the extent, and the limitations, of Coleridge's acceptance of the Platonic parallelism.

9 (p. 10). It is this reading of experience in the light of philosophy that makes Coleridge's criticism radical, and preserves him from Burke's tendency towards a certain superstition about tradition, 'our ancestors', 'the old ways', etc.

10 (p. 10). See Appendix B.

11 (p. 12). This passage requires to be studied along with Coleridge's discussion of 'Symbol' (p. 25). It is fully treated in the Introduction, pp. x-xi.

12 (p. 12). Cf. *Unpublished Letters*, vol. II, p. 327.

13 (p. 14) Opening paragraph of chapter III of *Church and State*, and *Table Talk*, 13 July 1832: 'I have read all the famous histories . . . but I never did so for the story itself as a story. The only interesting thing to me was the principles to be evolved from, and illustrated by, the facts. . . .' N.B. Coleridge's professed indifference for 'things contingent and transitory' as obscuring 'things of now, for ever, and which were always' (*Anima Poetae*, chapter III, Thursday, 19 April 1804). The latter passage is an early example of Coleridge's treatment of historical events as symbols of the Ideas in history and of that plea for the philosophical reading of history in order that it shall 'teach the science of the future in its perpetual elements' (i.e. become prophetic) which it was the purpose of these passages on Scriptural History to convey. See Introduction, pp. xiii-xvi.

14 (p. 15). Machiavelli.

15 (p. 16). Coleridge's 'recluse genius', and the mode of his operation under society, should be compared with Shelley's 'Poet as legislator' (pp. 201-2, following).

16 (p. 16). N.B. Coincidence, not causation. Coleridge insists that civil, social and domestic habits etc. *coincide* with the prevalent metaphysical system. He is always careful to insist on coincidence, correspondence, inter-action, never upon the priority of one to the other. See the letter to Lord Liverpool, written at about this time (1817): all history and experience attest that 'the taste and character, the whole tone of manners and feeling, and above all the religious (at least the theological) and the political tendencies of the public mind have ever borne such a close correspondence, so distinct and evident an analogy to the predominant system of speculative philosophy . . . a reaction and interdependence on both sides, but a powerful, most often indirect, of the last on all the former'. (*Political Thought of S. T. Coleridge*, ed. R. J. White, p. 211.) The view is interestingly illustrated from art and architecture in this letter.

17 (p. 16). Cf. Wordsworth on 'Ideas and popular movements', p. 170 following.

18 (p. 17). See note 18 to Wordsworth's *Convention of Cintra.*

19 (p. 18). See note 45 to Wordsworth's *Convention of Cintra.*

20 (p. 18). Cf. *Biographia Literaria*, chapter XII, thesis X.

21 (p. 19). See Appendix A, p. 31.

22 (p. 19). Cf. Shelley on the promotors of everyday utility: 'They follow the footsteps of poets, and copy the sketches of their creations into the book of common life.' pp. 203-4, following.

23 (p. 19). *Knowledge a spring and principle of action.* This observation gives us the core of Coleridge's theory of knowledge: that the only true knowledge is that which we have so made a part of ourselves that it modifies our actions, in the sense that we *become* what we *know*. It is expressed over and over again throughout his work, and all through his life.

24 (p. 20). *David Hume*, b. Edinburgh, 1711, d. 1776. Published his *History of England* between 1754 and 1761.

25 (p. 21). Cf. Wordsworth, p. 179, following, and note 31 to the *Convention of Cintra.*

26 (p. 21). See Appendix A, p. 34.

27 (p. 21). Cf. Wordsworth, p. 143, following, and note 11 to the *Convention of Cintra.*

28 (p. 22). Coleridge was liable to claim all and every one of his intellectual heroes of the past as 'Platonists'. In an entry under 1805 (chapter III) of *Anima Poetae*, the list includes Philip Sidney, Shakespeare, Milton, Bacon, Harrington, Swift and Wordsworth. The insistence with which he included the great master of induction in this galley is perhaps rather more impressive than the evidence he produced. He is generally content merely to mention him in the same breath as Plato: e.g. in the opening chapter of *Church and State*, we have: 'Plato often names ideas laws; and Lord Bacon, the British Plato, describes the Laws of the material universe as the Ideas in nature.' More extended is the statement of the case in *A Treatise on Method*, ed. A. D. Snyder, pp. 40-7. (See also Note 61, below.) The important point here, however, is that Coleridge attributes to Bacon the 'sublime' thought that an Idea 'containeth an endless power of semination' and cites his great aphorism 'Scientia et potentia in idem coincidunt'. He had taken the motto: KNOWLEDGE IS POWER for his paper, THE WATCHMAN, as a young man in the 1790's. By the time he came to write the *Lay Sermons* he was

perfectly in possession of the Platonic connotation of this apparently trite statement, and it is significant that he quotes a seventeenth-century *English* philosopher as his authority. It is perhaps the clearest example of his master-intention throughout these works,—to return to the tradition of English Platonism where it had last flowered before its eclipse by 'sensational' or 'mechanical' philosophy during the later part of the seventeenth century (see his account of this process in Appendix A, pp. 37-9, following). To grasp this is to grasp not only the philosophical, but also the political, essence and intention of the *Lay Sermons*.

29 (p. 22). Cf. note 11 to *The Convention of Cintra*.

30 (p. 22). *Rights of property as the spheres and necessary conditions of free agency*. This, the moral basis of property-rights, is here merely mentioned by way of example, and Coleridge nowhere developed it fully. Its political bearings are discussed, however, in chapter x of *Church and State*, and there is an interesting note which embodies the idea in *Notes, Theological, Political, and Miscellaneous*, ed. Derwent Coleridge, 1853, p. 211.

31 (p. 22). The intuitive knowledge of 'the poorest amongst us' of the idea of free-will is illustrated in chapter I of *Church and State*. Coleridge was fond of stressing that while 'it is the privilege of the few to possess an idea—of the generality of men it might be more truly affirmed that they are possessed by it.' Hence the 'ventriloquial' nature of Truth: it may speak from any 'dirty corner or straw moppet'—e.g. from Cobbett! (See *Table Talk*, 13 December 1819).

32 (p. 23). It seems, from the context, that Coleridge's meaning would be clearer if he had said 'wholly from outside of yourselves', since he is declaiming against the fruitfulness of knowledge *ab extra* as contrasted with the creative and modifying power of knowledge in his own sense as 'self-production'.

33 (p. 24). See the extension of this passage in *The Friend*, Introductory Essays 16, and 'First Landing-Place', Essay 4.

34 (p. 25). See passage on 'Symbol', p. 25, and discussion of Coleridge on historical events as symbolic of Ideas, Introduction, pp. xiii-xvi. It is in passages like this that one sees how greatly J. S. Mill was astray in relating Coleridge to 'that series of great writers and thinkers, from Herder to Michelet, by whom history . . . has been made a science of causes and effects'. (Essay on Coleridge in *Dissertations and Discussions*, 1840.) See also note following.

35 (p. 26). Elsewhere Coleridge expressed the same thought thus: 'The directing Idea of History is to weave a Chain of Necessity the particular Links in which are free acts—or—to present that which is necessary, as a Whole, consistently with the moral freedom of each particular act—or—to exhibit the moral necessity of the Whole in the freedom of the Components—the resulting chain as necessary, each particular Link remaining free.' ('Autograph Notebook', in *Coleridge on Logic and Learning*, by A. D. Snyder.) This idea of History should be compared with Coleridge's idea of Poetry: 'The common end of all *narrative*, nay, of *all*, Poems is to convert a *series* into a *whole*: to make those events which, in real or imagined History move on in a *strait* Line, assume to our understandings a *circular* motion—the snake with its Tail in its mouth.' (*Unpublished Letters*, vol. II, p. 128.) See Introduction, pp. xiii-xiv.

36 (p. 27). Cf. *Biographia Literaria*, chapter XII, thesis III, *et seq.*

37 (p. 28). See Appendix B.

38 (p. 29). *The axioms of the unthinking.* The 'unthinking' are possessed *by* ideas, and their utterances may therefore be 'ventriloquial' of Truth (see note 31, above).

39 (p. 29). *The ethereal intuition of our own Newton.* When, in 1801, Coleridge was working out his creative philosophy of mind, he had boldly termed Newton 'a mere materialist,' adding that 'the souls of five hundred Sir Isaac Newtons would go to the making up of a Shakespeare or a Milton'. (*Letters*, p. 352.) He was to blush for the presumptuousness of these opinions, later. By the time he wrote the *Lay Sermons* he was ready to affirm that Newton, and every great scientist, apprehended truth with the self-same direct and intuitive reason which produced great works of art. 'Hypothesis, be it observed', he wrote in 1818, in his *Treatise on Method*, 'can never form the groundwork of a true scientific method, unless when the hypothesis is either a true *Idea* proposed in an hypothetical form, or at least the symbol of an Idea as yet unknown, of a Law as yet undiscovered. . . .' (*Coleridge's Treatise on Method*, ed. A. D. Snyder, pp. 17-25.) An interesting discussion of the place of 'sudden illumination' in scientific and mathematical discovery is to be found in Henri Poincaré, *Science et Méthode* (chapter on 'L'invention mathématique'). For the whole question of Coleridge's thought on the methods of Science, see A. D. Snyder, *Coleridge on Logic and Learning* (pp. 16-32).

40 (p. 32). For assistance in reading, it should be noted that Coleridge

now proceeds to elaborate what he has laid down in the previous paragraphs.

41 (p. 33). *Jacobinism.* Coleridge claimed that he was the first to analyse the true nature of Jacobinism, and the short statement that follows should be expanded by reference to his *Essays on His Own Times*, ed. by His Daughter, 1850, vol. III, pp. 687-8, and 692-4. The most important of these passages are printed in *The Political Thought of S. T. Coleridge*, ed. R. J. White, pp. 118-20. There is an interesting example of his early definition of Jacobinism in *Essays*, vol. II, pp. 542-452 (quoted also in *Political Thought*, pp. 55-6). See also note 40 to *The Convention of Cintra.*

42 (p. 33). Cf. the passages on Rights and Duties in Coleridge's *Two Addresses on Sir Robert Peel's Bill* (1818), from which the relevant passages are quoted in *Political Thought* (pp. 216-21).

43 (p. 35). See note 26 to *The Convention of Cintra.* Coleridge appears to have thought himself the Roland to Napoleon's Oliver, and that the great tyrant knew it. See his references to Napoleon's efforts to get the philosophic journalist into his clutches during his stay in Italy in 1806 (*Biographia Literaria*, chapter x).

44 (p. 36). It is noteworthy that Coleridge does not attribute the 'Modern dilemma'—fashionably known as 'the dissociation of sensibility'—or the divorce of the Reason and the Understanding —to the rise of capitalism, or any such easy origin. Indeed, he would probably have considered this to be putting the cart before the horse. He allows no alibi for 'our own act and deed'.

45 (p. 36). It is this impregnation by the Imagination of the materials collected by the Understanding that produces great poetry. It was the phenomenon which struck Coleridge so mightily when he first heard Wordsworth read his *Guilt and Sorrow* in 1797: 'the original gift of spreading the tone, the atmosphere, and with it the depth and height of the ideal world, around forms, incidents, and situations. . . .' (*Biographia Literaria*, chapter IV). He no sooner felt this, than he sought to understand it; and it was from this, probably the most profound experience of his life, that the complete re-orientation of his mind in the direction of a philosophy of Ideas took its origin. It should be noticed, however, that he does not equate Imagination with Reason, although he often seems to come very near to doing so. The process of Imaginative impregnation of the Understanding as the poetic process is examined in fascinating detail in *The Road to Xanadu*, by J. Livingston Lowes

(see especially chapter III). See also note 1 to Shelley's *Defence of Poetry*.

46 (p. 37). *Science itself put on a sensual and selfish character. . . .* It is important to notice that Coleridge's lament over the 'usurpations of the insulated Understanding' is not in any sense a lament over the advances of science; and that he rather deplores the effect of these usurpations upon the methods and objectives of science itself. He would say that the absence of the ideal method had tended to subject true science (*Scientia*) to mere technology. See, for example, his plea for the ideal method in science in his *Treatise on Method* (ed. A. D. Snyder), pp. 16-25, and the section on 'The Potential Scientist' in A. D. Snyder's *Coleridge on Logic and Learning*.

47 (p. 38). *Debtor and creditor accounts on the ledgers of self-love. . . .* A fairly literal description of Bentham's *Felicific Calculus*, by which pains and pleasures were to be measured in a 'hay-balance' (as Carlyle called it), and legislation made into an exact science.

48 (p. 38). *A French nature. . . .* 'A little effusion of old English *Gall contra Gallos*', Coleridge called this kind of remark. He knew himself to indulge in it frequently. France was the land of the Understanding *par excellence*; he claimed to have overthrown French metaphysics, but was proud to know nothing of French manners—and to care less.

49 (p. 40). N.B. the direct appeal to the scientist to employ the ideal method. Cf. note 46 above.

50 (p. 41). See *The Friend*, The First Landing-Place, Essay 6.

51 (p. 43). Cf. the passage on 'the axioms of the unthinking', p. 29 above.

52 (p. 45). The two final paragraphs are intimately connected with the lengthy discussion of 'Plain and simple Christianity' in the second sermon, pp. 86-9.

53 (p. 46). The light of Reason, Coleridge has already insisted, is not a personal possession (p. 37 above), but the Understanding is a *peculiam* which differs in extent and value from man to man, and according as a man possesses more or less of it we say that he is a 'man of talent'. How much of it he will possess must depend to a great extent on fortuitous circumstances—birth, education, opportunity, etc., and it is for this reason, as well as for the reason that Talent is the expression of the Understanding, that Coleridge so strongly objects to government by 'Men of Talent'. Reference should be made, here, to the warning against entrusting power to

merely 'talented' or 'clever' men—the Sons of the Understanding —which occurs in chapter X of *Church and State.* What Coleridge had to say on this point of government by 'An Aristocracy of Talent' in *Church and State*, it may be added, he had already said in an article in *The Courier* in 1809 (See *Essays*, vol. II, pp. 652-6), i.e. nearly twenty years earlier. 'The aristocracy of Talent', he had concluded, '. . . exists . . . wherever the understanding, or calculating faculty, which is properly the executive branch of self-government, has usurped that supreme legislative power which belongs *jure divino* to our *moral* being.' The passage is reprinted in *Political Thought*, p. 127.

54 (p. 47). Coleridge liked quoting himself, and this passage occurs several times in his works. See, for example, the passage in the second Sermon, p. 84 following, and under 'C' in chapter VII of *Church and State.*

55 (p. 47). *Holofernes and Costard.* Schoolmaster and Clown in Shakespeare's *Love's Labour Lost.*

56 (p. 47). *Condillac*, Etienne Bonnot de (1715-80), *Philosophe* of the circle of Diderot, author of *Traité des Sensations* (1754) and *Cours d'études* (13 vols, 1767-73). Established systematically the principles of John Locke in France: more especially that all mental contents are sensations. Coleridge's special *bête noir* as the extreme exponent of the Sensational Psychology.

57 (p. 48). *The Schoolmen.* Coleridge was one of the first thinkers of modern times, in England, at least, to re-examine the 'exploded nonsense' of the Schoolmen. He came to suspect quite early that there was a good deal of what he called 'omne meus oculos' about modern notions of the 'darkness' of the 'Dark Ages', and in 1801 he spent some weeks reading in the Library of the Dean and Chapter of Durham Cathedral, whence he wrote to Southey that he was reading Duns Scotus: 'I mean to set the poor old Gemman on his feet again; and in order to wake him out of his present lethargy, I am burning Locke, Hume and Hobbes under his nose.' (*Letters*, p. 358.) This course of study, as well as his reading of the Platonists and the Germans, helped him along the path to his matured philosophical position. 'God bless the old Schoolmen!' he exclaims, in 1803, 'they have been my best comforts, and most instructive companions, for the last two years. Could you believe', he adds, 'that I could have come to this?' (*Unpublished Letters*, vol. I, p. 298.) The Schoolmen, he asserts, 'had *wells*: we are flooded ankle-high'.

(*Letters*, p. 424.) For his more considered opinions on the Schoolmen, see the passage from his 'Logic' cited in A. D. Snyder's *Coleridge on Logic and Learning*, p. 114.

58 (p. 48). *Edward Stillingfleet* (1635-99), Bishop of Worcester 1689-99 liberal divine, author of *Vindication of the Doctrine of the Trinity* (1696) in criticism of Locke's *Reasonableness of Christianity* (1695).

59 (p. 51). *Table Talk of John Selden* (1584-1654): 'Without School divinity a Divine knows nothing Logically, nor will be able to satisfy a rational Man out of the Pulpit.' See heading: 'Minister Divine' (p. 126, Pickering Edition, 1847).

60 (p. 52). 'Whatever you may think about this my work at a first glance, wait and see whether there may not be method in what appears to you to be madness.' The passage is by Giordano Bruno (c. 1548-1600), disciple of Nicolas of Cusa and Copernicus, who died at the hands of the Inquisition.

61 (p. 53). Cf. *Unpublished Letters*, vol. II, pp. 264-6, where the final statement is repeated, with the important addition: 'He for whom Ideas are constitutive, will in effect be a Platonist—and in those, for whom they are regulative only, Platonism is but a hollow affectation.' He goes on to include among the Platonists, Shakespeare, Milton, Dante, Michael Angelo and Rafael, and adds 'Lord Bacon, who never read Plato's Works, taught pure Platonism in his *great* work, the *Novum Organum*, and abuses his divine predecessor for fantastic nonsense, which he had been the first to explode'. On which side of the fence Coleridge himself stood is abundantly clear from the whole tenor of the first Lay Sermon. He was fond of asserting that every man is born either an Aristotelian or a Platonist, and it was no doubt with considerable pleasure that he affirmed that the opposition between the two perennial schools of philosophy would only be resolved at the Greek Kalends, 'or when two Fridays meet'. (See *Coleridge on Logic and Learning*, ed. A. D. Snyder, p. 125.)

A Lay Sermon on the Existing Distresses and Discontents

1 (p. 60). Coleridge claimed to have taught his age to reason and to judge concerning art, character, and public policy, with reference to *principles*. See his remarkable letter, asserting this claim, to Daniel Stuart, 12 Sept. 1814 (*Letters*, pp. 627-34). It was the

characteristic which made Burke a 'scientific statesman; and therefore a seer' because 'every principle contains in itself the germs of a prophecy. . . .' (*Biographia Literaria*, chapter X). It is here that Coleridge consciously assumes the mantle of Burke. (For the prophetic and seminal power of principles, or ideas, see note 28 to *The Statesman's Manual.*)

2 (p. 61). Cf. Wordsworth, p. 213, and note 30 to *The Convention of Cintra.*

3 (p. 63). How literally Coleridge intended this reference to principles to be, may be seen from his writing a long metaphysical letter to the Prime Minister, Lord Liverpool, at the crisis of post-war disorder in 1817, urging the 'rescue of speculative philosophy from false principles of reasoning'—'at least' Lord Liverpool endorsed this strange missive, 'I believe this is Mr Coleridge's meaning, but I cannot well understand him.' (See Yonge's *Life of Lord Liverpool*, vol. II, pp. 300-7: and *Political Thought*, pp. 209-16.) In 1815, when we were at war with the United States, he wrote to an American that 'even now it would not be too late'—for a peaceful settlement —'if the Spirit of Philosophy could be called down on Ministers and Governments'. (*Unpublished Letters*, vol. II, p. 153.)

4 (p. 67). Twenty years earlier, as the youthful Editor of *The Watchman*, Coleridge had urged upon his fellow Patriots: 'We should certainly never attempt to make proselytes by appeals to the selfish feelings—and consequently should plead *for* the oppressed, not *to* them.' (*Essays on His Own Times*, vol. I, pp. 29-30; and *Political Thought*, p. 41.) This is but one example of his remarkable consistency.

5 (p. 69). *Liberty of the Press.* Cf. *Unpublished Letters*, vol. II, pp. 194-5, where he chastises the Cobbetts and the Hunts as demagogues and liberticides. 'Hateful under all names, these wretches are most hateful to me as Liberticides.' He fears that their activities 'must end in the Suspension of Freedom of all kind'. This letter was written in the same year that he published the second *Lay Sermon.*

6 (p. 73). Cf. *Table Talk*, 11 May 1830. 'In my judgment, no man can rightly apprehend an abuse till he has first mastered the idea of the use of an institution.'

7 (p. 76). *The War-taxes.* The Liverpool Government abandoned the Property Tax (Income Tax) in 1816, in fulfilment of the pledge given by Pitt when the tax was introduced in 1798 that it should

be 'for and during the continuance of the war and no longer'. They abandoned it under the pressure of popular clamour, led by the City of London, to the detriment of any prospect of reducing indirect taxation—which reduction might have eased the discontents of the time.

8 (p. 77). Many writers of the time deplored the decay of manners among the farmers and yeomen, notably Cobbett. See *Rural Rides* (Cole), vol. 1, pp. 265-8.

9 (p. 78). Although Coleridge attributes many of our ills to the War, he adds in a footnote his tribute to 'its golden side'. The War had galvanized us into thought; it had compelled the people at large to realize 'that national honesty and individual safety, private morals and public security, mutually grounded each other, that they were twined at the very root'; it had produced 'manly sobriety' and academic strenuosity at the Universities, and a widespread realization that an illiterate populace was 'a magazine of combustibles left roofless while madmen and incendiaries were letting off their new invented blue-lights and fire-rockets in every direction'.

10 (p. 81). In a footnote Coleridge entreats the reader's attention to the word '*over*-balance'. He does not wish to be thought hostile to the spirit of commerce, to which he attributes 'the largest proportion of our actual freedom . . . and at least as large a share of our virtues as our vices'. Nor does he wish to inculpate individuals or classes. 'It is not in the power of a minister or of a cabinet to say to the current of national tendency, "Stay here!" or "Flow there".' He concludes that the excess of commercial spirit can only be remedied 'by the slow progress of intellect, the influence of religion, and irresistible events guided by Providence'.

11 (p. 82). *A learned and philosophic public*. Not, it should be observed, a 'populace'.—'From a popular philosophy and a philosophic populace, Good sense deliver us!'—Coleridge is pleading for a 'Clerisy'. In the penultimate paragraph of chapter VII of *Church and State* he declares: 'a truth which I hold it the disgrace and calamity of a professed statesman not to know and acknowledge—that a permanent, nationalized, learned order, a national clerisy or church, is an essential element of a rightly constituted nation, without which it wants the best security alike for its permanence and its progression'. His views on the *institution* of the Clerisy, learned order, or church, should be consulted at large in chapters V to VIII of the same work.

12 (p. 83). *A work on the point of publication.* Possibly a reference to the *Biographia Literaria*, which appeared this year (1817), but the point is uncertain in view of Coleridge's frequent references to works from his pen that are either 'in the press' or 'on the point of publication', but which never appeared.

13 (p. 83). See note on the application of the 'Ideal' method to Science: *Statesman's Manual*, note 46.

14 (p. 84). An elaboration of the point made on p. 61, that men are now better than their principles. See Wordsworth, *Convention of Cintra*, p. 179 below, and note 30.

15 (p. 85). *A civilized community.* In *Church and State*, concluding paragraph of chapter VI, Coleridge states his distinction between cultivation and civilization: 'this most valuable of the lessons taught by history . . . that a nation can never be a too cultivated, but may easily become an over-civilized race.' It is the distinction that he had made in *The Friend*, between the 'expensively be-school-mastered, be-tutored, be-lectured' young man, and 'educated' young men; between 'varnished' and 'polished'; between the 'perilously over-civilized' or 'pitiably uncultivated'—and the truly cultivated'. (Section 2, Essay 10.)

16 (p. 86). *Plain and simple Christianity.* The following paragraphs are Coleridge's contribution to the assault upon the tendency to reduce Christianity to a simple scheme of Utilitarian ethics, which might be said to have begun with John Locke's *Reasonableness of Christianity* (1695) and to have culminated in William Paley's *Principles of Moral and Political Philosophy* (1785). Reference should be made, here, to Appendix B of the *Statesman's Manual*, pp. 48-52, above. It is hardly necessary to point out that these passages also represent Coleridge's most important contribution to the study of Protestantism in its relation to the rise of Capitalism.

17 (p. 95). This brief philosophic schematic division of 'modern' history into two periods: 1460-1688 (Platonic) and 1688 onwards (Mechanic), should be set against the larger philosophical schematization to be found in *The Friend*, Section 2, Essay 10 (Essay 9 in the 1818 edition), and in *A Treatise on Method* (ed. A. D. Snyder), pp. 47-51. The wider reference enables one to see that the two periods since 1640 are but the latest pair of opposites in the dialectic of history. According to the operation of 'the moral law of polarity' (*Table Talk*, 5 April 1832), it was to be expected that the swing of the pendulum towards another era of Platonic, vital, or spiritual

philosophy would be noticeable in Coleridge's own life-time. Indeed, he professes to see signs of this: see pp. 46 and 48.

18 (p. 97). This passage should be compared with Shelley's quasi-religious conception of the function of poetry (pp. 202-3, below). Here it may be noted that Coleridge thinks of religion as 'contracting universal truths into individual duties' (p. 33 above), and more generally as doing the duty of philosophy for the generality of mankind. 'It is folly to think of making all, or the many, philosophers. . . . But the existence of a true philosophy . . . is indispensable to a sound state of religion in all classes.' *Church and State*, chapter VII, final paragraph.

19 (p. 100). *Coalition system in Christianity.* See the passages on 'Undenominational religious instruction' in the *Statesman's Manual*, p. 9, and notes 5 and 6.

20 (p. 101). *Periodical revolutions of credit.* J. S. Mill gave it as his opinion, rather rashly, that in political economy Coleridge wrote 'like an arrant driveller' and that 'it would have been well for his reputation had he never meddled with the subject'. (Essay on Coleridge in *Dissertations and Discussions*, 1840.) Coleridge, in his turn, thought the Political Economy of the Smith-Ricardo-Malthus-Mill school 'solemn humbug . . . a multitude of sophisms, but not a single just and important result which might not be far more convincingly deduced from the simplest principles of morality and commonsense'. (*Unpublished Letters*, vol. II, p. 349.) That a writer of primarily religious and philosophical intentions should include in his survey of the contemporary discontents a vivid description of what we now call 'the trade-cycle' is, however, rather remarkable. Statistics were still in an elementary stage of development, and the *Economist* did not appear until 1843. Tooke, Macpherson and Colquhoun, together with published parliamentary papers, had already some useful data, but anything like a scientific study of the phenomenon was still a long way in the future. See W. W. Rostrow, *British Economy of the Nineteenth Century*, 1948, chapters II and V.

21 (p. 104). Coleridge made his tour of Scotland, in company for part of the time with the Wordsworths, in August 1803. (See *Letters*, pp. 431-41, and *Unpublished Letters*, vol. I, pp. 272-8.) Perhaps it is some indication of the earnestness of the itinerant philosopher's enquiries among the peasantry that he was 'taken for a spy and clapped into Fort Augustus'. (*Letters*, p. 435.) But he appears to

have been irresistible to spy-catchers: witness the famous episode of 'Spy-Nozy' in chapter x of *Biographia Literaria.*

22 (p. 108). The peculiar character of landed property. Coleridge adds here a footnote to the effect that 'the very idea of individual or private property . . . was originally confined to moveable things'—precious stones, precious metals, coin, merchandise, and—in some cases—livestock. The class of citizens and burgesses, who dealt in and privately owned such property, was able to grow up under the protection of the Bishops and Abbots, in the vicinity of whose churches markets could be peaceably conducted. 'To the feudal system we owe the forms, to the Church the substance of our liberty . . . the origin of towns and cities . . . the holy war waged against slavery and villenage. . . .' (Cf. paragraph 2 of chapter VIII of *Church and State.*) Landed property, however, was always viewed as a *trust*,—fiduciary—and held in return for the performance of duties (final paragraph of chapter IV, *Church and State*). Coleridge was concerned that we should return to this conception. 'When shall we return to a sound conception of the right to property—namely, as being official, implying and demanding the performance of commensurate duties! Nothing but the most horrible perversion of humanity and moral justice, under the specious name of political economy, could have blinded men to this truth as to the possession of land—the law of God having connected indissolubly the cultivation of every rood of earth with the maintenance and watchful labour of man. But money, stock, riches by credit, transferable and convertible at will, are under no such obligations; and, unhappily, it is from the selfish, autocratic possession of *such* property that our landowners have learnt their present theory of trading with that which was never meant to be an object of commerce.' (*Table Talk*, 31 March 1833.) J. S. Mill thought that the revival of the idea of a trust inherent in landed property was 'the greatest service which Coleridge has rendered to politics in his capacity of a Conservative philosopher'. (Essay on Coleridge in *Dissertations and Discussions*, 1840.)

23 (p. 109). This somewhat negative attitude to state interference is perhaps rendered more positive by the last sentence of the paragraph. In the year after these sentences were written, Coleridge took an active part in securing support for Sir Robert Peel's Factory Bill of 1818, to limit the hours of work of children in cotton-mills. His *Two Addresses on Sir Robert Peel's Bill* were privately printed

in 1913 by Sir Edmund Gosse. (See also *Political Thought*, pp. 216-21.) Here he insists that 'there is no species of property which the legislature does not possess and exercise the right of controlling and limiting, as soon as the right of the individuals is shown to be disproportionately injurious to the community'.

24 (p. 110). *Agricultural State of the Kingdom, in February, March and April* 1816, being the substance of the replies to a circular letter sent by the Board of Agriculture to every part of the Kingdom.

25 (p. 112). The notorious 'Speenhamland System', introduced in 1795, by which the wages of agricultural labourers were supplemented out of the rates, tended to reduce the independent labourer to the status of a pauper. (See *The Village Labourer*, by J. L. and B. Hammond, chapters VI and VII.)

26 (p. 114). *The Spenceans.* The followers of Thomas Spence, (1750-1814), a Newcastle schoolmaster who delivered a lecture before the Philosophical Society of that town in 1775 expounding a plan for a communist commonwealth in which the land would be administered as a national joint-stock. 'Spence's Plan', which he propaganded for the rest of his life in its original simplicity, became a mild jest among the more sophisticated 'philosophical' Radicals, like Place and Joseph Hume; but the fact that a 'Spencean Society' was founded after its author's death, and that it attracted into its body certain firebrands like the Watsons, Thistlewood, and others, gave rise to a good deal of alarm in the breast of Lord Sidmouth, the Home Secretary during the dangerous years 1812-22. Secret Committees of both Houses of Parliament reported that the 'Spenceans' were planning a general, armed insurrection for the overthrow of private property and all established institutions. 'Poor visionaries' the original followers of Spence may have been, as Coleridge called them; but at this time 'Spencean' meant to the general public what 'Bolshy' meant in the 1920's. Spence's original lecture is included in *The Pioneers of Land Reform*, Bohn's Popular Library (No. 81), and there is a useful short account of his ideas in *A History of British Socialism*, by M. Beer, vol. I, part II, chapter 2, section ii.

27 (p. 115). *State Lotteries.* The British Government ran annual lotteries (generally at £10 a ticket and for annuities as prizes) between 1709 and 1824, when the practice was abolished. Between 1793 and 1824, an annual profit of £346,765 was made by the Government in this way. Spencer Perceval, whose Act of 1806 somewhat restricted the

practice, was Coleridge's 'Idea of a great and good, and most simple, great man'. (*Unpublished Letters*, vol. II, p. 82.)

28 (p. 116) *Personally and in detail.* The necessity for personal and individual effort, for *detailed* application of general principles of conduct, was a constant theme with Coleridge throughout his political career. The true duty of the Patriot, he told his fellow Radicals of the 1790's, was to be '*personally* among the poor'. The generalized benevolence of the professional philanthropist always repelled him. (*Essays on His Own Times*, vol. I, pp. 21-4: compare with *Table Talk*, 14 August 1833—'I have never known a trader in philanthropy who was not wrong in heart somewhere or other.') In his famous 'Character of Mr Pitt' (*Morning Post*, 1800. Printed in *Essays*, vol. II, pp. 320-9, and in *Political Thought*, pp. 68-74) he attacks the great statesman for his 'GENERAL PHRASES, unenforced by one *single image*, one *single fact* of real national amelioration. . . .' In his *Addresses* in support of Peel's Factory Bill of 1818, he begs the reader to 'individualize the sufferings which it is the object of this Bill to remedy, follow up the detail in some one case with a human sympathy. . . .' (*Addresses*, ed. Gosse, and *Political Thought*, p. 220.) In the year before his death, 1833, he writes: '. . . from the very outset I hoped in no advancement of humanity but from individual minds and morals working onward from Individual to Individual. . . . This in my first work, the *Conciones ad Populum*, I declared, in my 23rd year: and to this I adhere in my present 63rd.' (*Unpublished Letters*, vol. II, p. 452.)

THE CONVENTION OF CINTRA

1 (p. 126). The British forces which landed in Portugal in the summer of 1808 were, in fact, diverted from other theatres of war. The 10,000 which landed under Sir Arthur Wellesley at Mondega Bay, and pushed forward to defeat Junot at Vimiero on 21 August, had been intended for South America. Sir John Moore's force of 10,000 which followed, was diverted to Portugal from the Baltic.

2 (p. 127). Wordsworth here refers to that considerable section of English opinion which regarded the war with the French Revolution as an attempt to thwart the French people in their choice of their own form of Government. It was the French invasion of Switzerland, the classic land of Liberty, that marked the turning-

point in the struggle between native patriotism and ideological attachment to France which afflicted Wordsworth, Coleridge, Southey, and many other generous young minds in these years. Its effect on them was somewhat similar to the effect of the Russian invasion of Finland upon the minds of honest English admirers of the Soviet Union in 1939. It did not diminish their faith in the original principles of the Revolution, but it convinced them that the French had forfeited their claim to represent and champion them. Coleridge's *Ode to France* (1798) is the great poetic document of this phase of Romantic re-orientation.

3 (p. 130). The victory of Vimiero was won on 21 August, within a week or two of the landing. The Convention was signed on 30 August.

4 (p. 132). The revolt of the Spanish people against the French first received some kind of organization in Asturias—appropriately, since it was from Asturias that Spain had been reconquered from the Moors. It was the Council of Asturias which, from Oviedo, declared for the people against the authorities and formally declared war on the French on 25 May 1808. Seville, however, was to challenge Oviedo as the capital of resistance. A rich city on the Guadalquivir, within practical range of such centres as Cadiz, Granada, Cordoba, Malaga, San Roque and Jaen, Seville elected a revolutionary Council, or Junta, which was soon calling itself 'The Supreme Council of Spain and the Indies'. Documents like the one entitled *Precautions*, which Wordsworth quotes, represent the shrewd directive influence of the Junta of Seville in the cause of national resistance.

5 (p. 133). The enthusiasm of the Romantic poets for the Spanish Rising was quite untinged by enthusiasm for Legitimacy, or the Bourbons. 'A detestable race' Southey called them, at the height of his Toryism. Wordsworth here refers to Spanish loyalty to their Bourbon rulers as a 'failing of excess' and elsewhere is unsparing of his references to the 'decrepitude' of the old Monarchy. When Napoleon advanced upon Spain, the old King, Carlos IV, abdicated in favour of his son, Fernando VII. The latter might have had the whole nation at his back had he possessed either the courage or the intelligence to lead them. Napoleon lured both father and son into France, secured their abdication of their claims to the throne, and set up his brother, Joseph Bonaparte, in their place. It is not clear whether Wordsworth refers to Carlos IV or to Fernando VII as

the 'Sovereign' to whom the Spaniards failed in 'excessive loyalty'. Anyhow, they were equally worthless.

6 (p. 137). The Romantics, unlike the Utilitarians of Bentham's generation, evinced a moral scepticism about the claims of the new republic of the United States to represent the best hopes of liberty and enlightenment. Wordsworth's reference should be compared with (1) Coleridge's reference in his letter to Lord Liverpool in 1817 (*Political Thought*, p. 214): 'like a horde of Americans, a people without a history. . .' and his scepticism about the possibility of a national fusion of North and South (*Table Talk*, 15 May 1833); and (2) Shelley's view that, while the Constitution of the United States was perfectly adjusted to representing the will of the people 'as it is', it made no provision for securing that that will should be 'wise and just'. See note 10, *Philosophical View of Reform*.

7 (p. 138). National calamity as a form of Divine Chastisement, and a disguised blessing, was a favourite theme of the Romantics. Compare Wordsworth's passage with Coleridge, *Fears in Solitude* (lines 29-174), of 1798, and *Unpublished Letters*, vol. I, pp. 282-3. Coleridge saw a French invasion of his country in 1798, and again in 1803, as a moral judgment upon his country's wickedness (the over-filled 'commercial gourd', etc.), just as Wordsworth saw the French invasion of Spain in 1808. Shelley saw greater reason for hope of moral revival in a renaissance of poetry (pp. 205-6, below).

8 (p. 141). *Sir Hew Dalrymple* (1750-1830), Lieutenant-General in command of the Gibraltar Garrison, 1806; command of the Army in Portugal, 1808; chiefiy responsible for negotiating the Convention; General, 1812. His principal fault appears to have been his ignorance of many points in the situation in Portugal, a situation into which he had been intruded very recently. (See Napier's *Peninsular War*, Book II, chapter V.)

9 (p. 142). Napier's view is (*op. cit.* conclusion of chapter VI), that the Convention 'although some of its provisions were objectionable in point of form, and others imprudently worded, yet taken as a whole, it was a transaction fraught with wisdom and prudence'—and this upon both political and military grounds.

10 (p. 143). The distinction between Genius and Talent is fundamental not only to the Romantic conception of Poetry, but to Romantic ideas on Government and Politics. See note 53 to *The Statesman's Manual*.

11 (p. 143). It follows from the Romantics' theory of knowledge, and

of the constitution of the human mind, that a people—like an individual—can only be awakened to and sustained in great action and endeavour by the call of 'Principles' or, as Coleridge preferred to call them, 'Ideas'. This passage recalls Coleridge's statements in *The Statesman's Manual* (pp. 16, 17, 21 and 22, and Introduction, p. xxx).

12 (p. 144). Of the three Generals responsible for the Suspension of Arms and the Convention,—Sir Hew Dalrymple, Sir Harry Burrard, and Sir Arthur Wellesley,—only Wellesley was employed again.

13 (p. 147). This passage is of paramount importance for understanding the Romantic doctrine of nationality, and of nationality as the only secure basis for internationalism. It should be compared with the passages on the Law of Nations in Coleridge's *The Friend* (1809-10), Section 1 (Principles of Political Knowledge), Essays 13 and 14.

14 (p. 147). The following passage from a letter written to Major-General Sir Charles W. Pasley, K.C.B., on his 'Military Policy and Institutions of the British Empire' in 1811, further explicates Wordsworth's theory of nationality as the basis of internationalism, in a healthy balance of power: 'I wish to see Spain, Italy, France and Germany, formed into independent nations; nor have I any desire to reduce the power of France further than may be necessary for that end. Woe be to that country whose military power is irresistible! I deprecate such an event for Great Britain scarcely less than for any other land. . . . If a nation have nothing to oppose or to fear without, it cannot escape decay and concussion within. Universal triumph and absolute security soon betray a State into abandonment of that discipline, civil and military, by which its victories were secured. If the time should ever come when this island shall have no more formidable enemies by land than it has at this moment by sea, the extinction of all that it previously contained of good and great would soon follow. Indefinite progress undoubtedly there ought to be somewhere; but let that be in knowledge, in science, in civilization, in the increase of the numbers of the people, and in the augmentation of their virtue and happiness. But progress in conquest cannot be indefinite; and for that very reason, if for no other, it cannot be a fit object for the exertions of a people, I mean beyond certain limits, which of course, will vary with circumstances. My prayer, as a patriot, is, that we may always have, somewhere or other, enemies capable of resisting us, and keeping us at arm's

length.' (*Memoirs* of W. Wordsworth, vol. I, pp. 406-20; and *Prose Works of W. Wordsworth*, ed. A. B. Grosart, vol. I, p. 204.)

15 (p. 149). This was, in fact, the political objective of the British Government: to clear the French out of Portugal as quickly as possible in order to use the country safely as a base for further military operations in the Peninsula. Napier defends the *Convention* on these grounds (See *History of the War in the Peninsula*, Book II, chapter v), where Wellesley's view is quoted, with approval, as in favour of a Convention by which a strong French force might be removed economically from Portugal and 'an actual gain made both of men and time, for the further prosecution of the war in Spain'.

16 (pp. 153, 157). That the Generals exceeded their powers in negotiating the Convention is untrue; in the enquiry which followed they were declared to have acted according to their best judgment and with proper promptitude. Wordsworth's appeal against the Convention to universal moral law, or the principles of reason and justice which inhere in the nature of things, was a legitimate exercise of moral indignation, but needless to say it would possess no validity at international law.

17 (p. 159). The right to petition, safeguarded by the Bill of Rights, could not be in question; but the terms of the City Petition undoubtedly laid its framers open to the charge of pre-judging the issue.

18 (p. 161). How the philosophic statesman is to judge whether *Vox Populi* be *Vox Dei*, or whether it be *Vox Diaboli* is more philosophically explained by Coleridge in *Table Talk*, 29 April 1832: 'I can only know by trying the thing called for by the prescript of reason and God's will.' The reference of Wordsworth to the loud voice of the people as 'possessed either by the Godhead or the Demon' is a paraphrase of a passage from Sir Philip Sydney, and is quoted and commented upon by Coleridge in his *Church and State* (1830), chapter I. The whole question of *Vox Populi* in the writings of Wordsworth and Coleridge is discussed in the Introduction, pp. xxxiv-xxxv.

19 (p. 163). See note 11 above.

20 (p. 164). Cf. Coleridge writing in *The Courier* on the Spanish rising: 'That there is an invisible spirit that breathes through a whole people, is participated in by all, though not by all alike; a spirit which gives a colour and character to their virtues and vices, so that the same actions . . . are yet not the same in a Spaniard as they

would be in a Frenchman, I hold for an undeniable truth, without the admission of which all history would be riddle. . . .' (1810. See *Essays on His Own Times*, ed. by Sarah Coleridge, 1850, vol. II, pp. 668-9: also, *Political Thought of S. T. Coleridge*, ed. R. J. White, p. 142.) The same analogy occurs in Coleridge's letter to Lord Liverpool, 1817: '. . . in all political revolutions, whether for the weal or chastisement of a nation, the people are but the sprigs and boughs in a forest, tossed against each other, or moved all in the same direction, by an agency in which their own will has the least share.' (*Political Thought*, p. 216.) He employed the metaphor in refuting the Hartleian theory of the Association of Ideas as early as 1803: 'I almost think that ideas *never* recall ideas, as far as they are ideas, any more than the leaves in a forest create each others' motion. The breeze it is that runs through them—it is the soul, the state of feeling.' (*Letters of S. T. Coleridge*, ed. E. H. Coleridge, p. 428: also, *Political Thought*, p. 50.)

21 (p. 165). 'There is (I cannot refrain from observing) in the Catholic religion, and in the character of its priesthood especially, a source of animation and fortitude in desperate struggles. . . .' Wordsworth wrote, in a passage which has been omitted from his text. He cites the example of Padre St Iago Sass of Zaragoza, who played alternately the part of priest and soldier with great bravery, and became both Captain in the army and Chaplain to the Commander-in-chief. Not all the priests, however, were like Padre St Iago Sass. The Jesuit Father Calvo of Valencia was hanged by the Council of Valencia for hounding on the patriots to the most fearful atrocities.

22 (p. 169). Cf. Coleridge, who addresses his second *Lay Sermon* to Higher Classes, and opens it with an adjuration to them to 'walk in the light of your own knowledge'. Their habits of reflection, he tells them, should at least be equal to their opportunities of leisure. (See above, p. 59.)

23 (p. 169). Cf. Coleridge's 'Character of Mr Pitt' which appeared in the *Morning Post*, in 1800 (*Essays on His Own Times*, 1850, vol. II, pp. 320-9; also in *Political Thought*, pp. 68-74). Coleridge's animadversions upon Pitt's education afford a perfect example of Wordsworth's point.

24 (p. 170). Burke on 'the routine statesman': 'Men too much conservant in office are rarely minds of remarkable enlargement. Their habits of office are apt to give them a turn to think the

substance of business not to be much more important than the forms in which it is conducted. These forms are adapted to ordinary occasions; and therefore persons who are nurtured in office do admirably well as long as things go on in their common order; but when the high roads are broken up, and the waters out, when a new and troubled scene is opened, and the file affords no precedent, then it is that a greater knowledge of mankind and far more extensive comprehension of things is requisite, than ever office gave, or than office can ever give.' (*Speech on American Taxation*, 1774.)

25 (p. 171). Walter Bagehot's view, that the best type of constitutional statesman is a man of first-rate ability and second-rate ideas. (*Biographical Studies*, 'The Character of Sir Robert Peel'.)

26 (p. 176). Cf. Coleridge's frequently repeated characterization of Bonaparte as one of the 'Molochs of human nature' in whom the Will, unbalanced by Reason and Religion, has become 'Satanic pride and rebellious self-idolatry in the relations of the spirit to itself, and remorseless despotism relatively to others . . . the fearful resolve to find in itself alone the one absolute motive of action'. These 'Molochs', Coleridge insists, 'are indebted for the larger portion of their meteoric success to their total want of principle' and to their 'daring to say with their whole heart, "Evil, be thou my good". . .!' (*The Statesman's Manual*, pp. 34-5 above). He had shown, writing in *The Courier* in 1809, that once a man has dared to say this, 'the means of accomplishing a given end are multiplied incalculably, because all means are considered as lawful. He who has once said with his whole heart, Evil, be thou my good! has removed a world of obstacles the very decision that he will have no obstacles but those of force and brute matter.' (*Essays on His Own Times*, vol. II, pp. 657-8; also, *Political Thought*, p. 76.) The identity of Coleridge's and Wordsworth's views on Napoleon—that they expressed their views in the same year (1809) in almost identical terms—need raise no issue of plagiarism. It sprang from personal intercourse, and a shared moral philosophy.

27 (p. 176). This view of Bonaparte as an example of moral regression is shared by Coleridge. 'None but the Vulgar felt about Napoleon as they do about Alexander' he wrote, c. 1820. 'Napoleon was an APE. . . . War at present ought to be spoken of by all men of genius as contemptible, vulgar, the dotage of second childhood, the lechery of barrenness.' (See *Political Thought*, pp. 149-50.)

28 (p. 178). Moved in the House of Commons by Lord Henry Petty, 21 February 1809: defeated by 50 votes, (203:153). Hansard, *Parliamentary Debates*, XII, 1809, 897-975. The Motion was, in fact, two-fold: the second part attributed the causes and circumstances of the Convention 'in a great measure' to the misconduct and neglect of His Majesty's Ministers.

29 (p. 178). *The non-existence of a wide-ranging intellect* was regarded by Coleridge, too, as the principal defect of the age. *Vide* numerous passages in the *Lay Sermons* (pp. 46-7 and 97-9), and in his letters, e.g. 'No real information can be given, no important errors overthrown in Politics, Morals, or Literature without requiring some effort of Thought . . . consequently, I am like a Physician who prescibes exercise with the dumb bells to a Patient paralytic in both arms.' (*Unpublished Letters*, vol. II, p. 22.)

30 (p. 179). The 'enlightened Friend' was, of course, Coleridge, and the observation quoted is to be found in the second *Lay Sermon*, p. 61 above. See also Coleridge's reference to 'the Castlereagh gang' for his literal use of the word 'unprincipled', in *Unpublished Letters*, vol. II, pp. 223-4.

31 (p. 179). Cf. Coleridge: 'Woe to that man who, on circumstances which vitally affect the weal and woe of the whole human race, in time and for eternity, can reason in as cold-blooded a tone as if he were demonstrating a problem in geometry.' (See *Political Thought*, pp. 57-8.)

32 (p. 181). Wordsworth cites the Legislative Union of England, Scotland and Ireland, and the amalgamation of the large and numerous fiefs of France, as examples of beneficial loss of independence.

33 (p. 181). See note 14 above.

34 (p. 183). The whole of this paragraph, and its predecessor, should be carefully collated with its parallel passages in Coleridge's *The Statesman's Manual* (pp. 37-9 above) and in Shelley's *Defence of Poetry* (pp. 205-6 below). The significance of such collation is discussed in the Introduction, pp. xxi-xxiii.

35 (p. 183). This *union of peace with innocent and laudable animation* might almost be the germ of Coleridge's later theory of the polarity of the forces of 'Permanence' and 'Progression' in the Body Politic. (See *Church and State* (1830), chapter II.)

36 (p. 185). 'Has not the hereditary possession of a landed estate been proved by experience to generate dispositions equally favourable to loyalty and established freedom?' Coleridge asked, in the *Morning*

Post, in 1800 (*Essays on His Own Times*, vol. II, p. 273). He was not necessarily referring to great proprietors. The point is worked out in the *Second Lay Sermon*: 'As the specific ends of agriculture are the maintenance, strength and security of the State, so (I repeat) must its ultimate ends be the same as those of the State. . . .' (p. 109 above).

37 (p. 185). Wordsworth's romantic faith in the natural virtues of the poor, or of the peasant, was not shared by Coleridge. Having addressed the higher and the middle classes in his First and Second Lay Sermons, he intended (he tells us) to address a third to the working-classes. (See *Unpublished Letters*, vol. II, p. 179.) The fact that this was never written was due more to his procrastination than his belief that it was unnecessary.

38 (p. 186). It should never be forgotten that Wordsworth maintained his faith in the original goodness of the Revolution, despite its deplorable course. In a passage omitted here, he insisted that Napoleonic France, the scourge of Europe, 'with all the terrible features which it has gradually assumed, is a child of noble parents —Liberty and Philanthropic Love. Perverted as the creature in which it has grown up to (rather, into which it has passed),— from no inferior stock could it have issued. It is the Fallen Spirit, triumphant in misdeeds, which was formerly a blessed Angel.'

39 (p. 187). The whole ground of difference between subject and serf, between a commonwealth and a slave-plantation,—the whole meaning of constitutional government,—Coleridge held, evolved out of the Idea of the distinction between Persons and Things, 'all social law and justice being grounded on the principle that a person can never, but by his own fault, become a thing, or, without grievous wrong, be treated as such. . . .' (*Church and State*, chapter I.) This doctrine lies behind Wordsworth's distinction here.

40 (p. 187). *Jacobinism.* What Wordsworth means by Jacobinism is to be understood in the light of the analysis of the phenomenon in its moral and philosophical bearings given in Coleridge's first *Lay Sermon* (pp. 32-3), and note 41 to that work.

41 (p. 187). *Condillac.* See note 56 to Coleridge's first *Lay Sermon.*

42 (p. 191). The *Memoirs* of Sir Philip Warwick, edited and reprinted by Sir Walter Scott, 1802. First published from original MS, London, 1701.

43 (p. 191). See note 21 above.

44 (p. 193). Wordsworth frequently paraphrases Burke's famous description of 'Community'—the partnership between the dead, the living, and the yet unborn. It is noteworthy that here, however, at the conclusion of a castigatory essay, he shows a certain Augustinian, even Calvinistic, selectiveness: it is the timeless community of the good, the brave and the wise to which he would summon us.

45 (p. 193). Cf. Coleridge, *The Friend* (1809-10), Introductory Essays 16: 'There is a wisdom higher than prudence, to which prudence stands in the same relation as the mason and carpenter to the genial and scientific architect. . . . The widest maxims of prudence are like arms without hearts, disjointed from those feelings which flow forth from principles as from a fountain.' (Quoted also in *Political Thought*, p. 95.)

A Defence of Poetry

1 (p. 199). *Reason and Imagination.* It is evident from the nature of Shelley's distinction that he is using *Reason* in the sense of *ratione*, —the analysing, classifying, calculating, experiential faculty, which Coleridge preferred to denominate *Understanding*: the faculty which deals with particulars rather than with universals. He accepts, that is to say, what we now know as 'the eighteenth-century' connotation of the word. Coleridge tended to equate the word with *intellectus*, to restore it—he would have said—to its highest dignity as the faculty of intuitive knowledge of ultimate truth. As a philosopher-poet, he was aware that the *insight* afforded to man by his Reason was akin to, if not identical with, *Imagination*. Briefly, Shelley and Coleridge agree upon the sovereign insight afforded by the Imagination, but whereas Coleridge will call this faculty Reason when he is talking in terms of philosophy, Shelley reserves the term Reason for what Coleridge calls the 'Subaltern faculty—the Understanding.' (See pp. 31, 35 and 36 above, and Introduction, p. xxii.)

2 (p. 199). Here, by his acceptation of 'a principle within the human being' which *adjusts* and *accommodates* what is given from without, Shelley departs from (if he had ever accepted) the mechanistic, or sensational, philosophy of mind which, in its extreme form (e.g. in La Mettrie and Condillac) made man 'the victim of his senses'; which denied all intuitive knowledge; and which, involved the

tabula rasa theory of mind. (Cf. Coleridge on sensationalism, or the mechanistic theory, p. 38 above.)

3 (p. 200). It is implied that Shelley accepts the fact of the existence of an 'indestructible order' in the nature of things: an order which is apprehended *in* them by the poetic imagination, not an order which is imposed *upon* them by the classifying philosopher.

4 (p. 200). Philosophically rendered, this faculty of the poet of beholding the future in the present, emerges in Coleridge as the apprehension of the Ideas, or Principles, of which historic events, persons, etc. are the transitory forms or modes. Thus the statement, of which Coleridge is so fond: 'Every principle contains in itself the germs of a prophecy.' This is the link between Shelley's 'poet as legislator' and Coleridge's 'philosophic statesman'. (See Introduction, pp. xxxviii and xxxix.)

5 (p. 201). *Images which participate in the life of truth.* Cf. Coleridge's definition of a symbol: 'A symbol always partakes of the reality which it renders intelligible.' (See p. 25 above.)

6 (p. 201). Philosophers as Poets, and Poets as Philosophers. This equation is fundamental to the political thought of the Romantic poets. Shelley's paragraph can be paralleled by many almost identical passages in Coleridge. See final section of chapter XV of *Biographia Literaria*: 'No man was ever yet a great poet, without being at the same time a profound philosopher' (re. Shakespeare); Lectures on Shakespeare, *passim* (e.g. 'Shakespeare the morning star, the guide and the pioneer, of true philosophy'—'he should be styled a philosophical aristocrat' etc.); *Treatise on Method* (ed. A. D. Snyder), pp. 25-36. Coleridge's works are likewise strewn with references to poetic-philosophic-Platonism of Milton, Bacon, etc. As for Wordsworth, he once wrote to his 'dearest William'—'you were a great poet by inspirations, and in the moments of revelation . . . a thinking feeling philosopher habitually . . . your Poetry was your Philosophy under the actions of strong winds of feeling . . .' *Unpublished Letters*, vol. I, p. 266.

7 (p. 203). Mrs Barbauld's criticism of the *Ancient Mariner*, that it 'had no moral', was countered by Coleridge with the remark that it had too much, and that its chief fault 'was the obtrusion of the moral sentiment so openly on the reader as a principle or cause of action in a work of such pure imagination'. (*Table Talk*, 31 May 1830.)

8 (p. 203). This notion of poetry as a 'luxury', 'an agreeable diversion', something 'extra' to the 'real' business of life, set in during the

latter part of the seventeenth century. It was bound up with the advancing cult of 'Utility' as the measure of all things by a commercial culture; the popularity of John Locke as its spokesman; the advance of technology, and the spread of the (properly) plain, naked, sober use of words by the scientists into other spheres of experience; in fact, the phenomenon which Mr Eliot has called 'the dissociation of sensibility'. (See Michael Roberts, *The Modern Mind* and R. C. Knights, *Explorations*—essay on Bacon.) It was against this usurpation of all spheres of life and experience by the instrument of 'the Understanding', and the reduction of poetry and its powers of Reason, Imagination and Insight, that Shelley is protesting—as Coleridge protests in his passages on the usurpation of the Understanding in the first *Lay Sermon* (See p. 37 above). The poets were upholding the claims of a higher utility than that of the 'Utilitarians'.

9 (p. 204). If Shelley had given instances here, no doubt he would have cited the *bêtes noirs* of Coleridge and Wordsworth: Condillac, La Mettrie, etc. . . . (See note 56 of *The Statesman's Manual.*)

10 (p. 204). *First principles which belong to the imagination.* . . . See notes 2 and 3 above.

11 (p. 204). It is at this point that Shelley makes the transition from his account of philosophical error to his account of social evils. The eclipse of that insight which a wide-spread cultivation of the poetic imagination gives to a society has led to the misuse of the technical discoveries of modern times, greatly to the advantage of the economically strong and sorely to the disadvantage of the economically weak. The whole of this passage, and the two following paragraphs, give Shelley's version of what Coleridge was saying about the decay of vital philosophy in the *Lay Sermons* (especially pp. 45-7), and what Wordsworth has to say on pp. 182-3 of the *Convention of Cintra*. (See note 34 of the latter, and Introduction pp. xxiii-xxiv.)

12 (p. 205). N.B. Similarity of this phrase to that of Wordsworth on p. 183.

13 (p. 205). *The creative faculty, which is the basis of all knowledge.* The clearest statement of Shelley's acceptance of a non-sensational theory of knowledge. (See note 2 above.)

14 (p. 206). See Keats' Sonnet to Haydon (1817): 'Great spirits now on earth are sojourning. . . .'

A Philosophical View of Reform

1 (p. 211). The adjuration is of the pure milk of Godwin. See *Political Justice*, *passim*, and in particular the conclusion of chapter II of Book I: 'perfectibility is one of the most unequivocal characteristics of the human species, so that the political, as well as the intellectual state of man, may be presumed to be in a course of progressive improvement.'

2 (p. 211). Shelley here embarks on an examination of the history of Europe since the fall of the Roman Empire in the light of the twin Godwinian texts: (i) that government is 'nothing more than a scheme for enforcing by brute violence the sense of one man or set of men upon another,' (*Political Justice*, Book IV, chapter I); and (ii) that (in consequence) 'the history of mankind is little else than the history of crimes', (*Political Justice*, Book I, chapter II). Comparison with Book I, chapter II of Godwin's work, however, reveals the vast superiority of Shelley in both historical sense and breadth of vision. Compare, again, his survey of the intellectual history of Europe in *Defence of Poetry*.

3 (p. 213). Shelley's regret for the temporary eclipse of Dutch republicanism was based on a very tenuous experience of that form of government by the people of Holland. Holland was 'liberated' by the armies of the French Revolution and enjoyed a short existence as 'The Batavian Republic' (founded 1795) until Napoleon set up his brother Joseph as King of Holland. At the Peace Settlement of 1815, Holland and Belgium were united under a Dutch monarch in the Kingdom of the Netherlands, largely for strategic purposes. Belgium gained its independence from Holland in 1839.

4 (p. 214). The makers of the Revolution of 1688 'acknowledged and declared' no principles, this or any other. The Bill of Rights was a wholly practical list of grievances suffered under James II, and the new monarchs were required to promise to abstain from giving such causes for complaint in future. The Revolution Settlement contained no theorizing whatever upon the nature or the sources of sovereign authority. The principle advanced by Shelley, here, was largely the product of the successful maintenance of the settlement over the next century and a half, together with the wide acceptance of traditional Whig doctrine adumbrated in John Locke's second *Treatise on Civil Government* (1690).

5 (p. 215). The abstract right of the people to cashier an unsatisfactory government was nowhere advanced as a principle in 1688, although a resolution that James II had broken 'the original contract between King and People' was passed by both Houses of Parliament. The principle itself was crystallized by Locke and the Whig apologists, so that it emerged clearly, and even crudely, in the political theorizing of radical reformers at the time of the American and the French Revolutions. It was its advocacy by Dr Price, the Unitarian spokesman of the Society for Commemorating the Revolution in Great Britain in his famous Old Jewry sermon of 1789, that evoked Burke's immortal counter-attack in 'Reflections on the Revolution in France' (1790). Shelley, in this passage ranges himself with the thorough-going Radical interpreters of the English Revolution.

6 (p. 215). Here, in a footnote, occurs an unfinished sentence which Shelley may have intended to work into the above passage: 'Regular and graduated systems of alternate slavery and tyranny, by which all except the lowest and largest class were to be gainers in the materials of subsistence and ostentation at the expense of that class, the means being fraud and force, were established in the shape of feudal monarchies upon the ruins of the. . . .'

7 (p. 215). For Shelley's views on the comparative importance, for human well-being, of the Lockeian school of philosophy and the poets, see p. 204 above.

8 (p. 217). *Inartificial*, is given in the MS. It seems that Shelley is here referring to such 'forms' as nations and classes, and one might have assumed that to a Godwinian philosopher such forms would be rather 'artificial'. Possibly there was a slip of the pen.

9 (p. 217). Compare the parallel passage in *Defence of Poetry*, p. 204 above, and Wordsworth's passage on modern man's enslavement to mechanism, p. 183 above.

10 (p. 219). Footnote by Shelley: 'Its error consists not in the not representing the will of the people as it is, but in not providing for the full development and the most salutary condition of that will. For two conditions are necessary to a theoretically perfect government, and one of them alone is adequately fulfilled by the most perfect of practical government, the Republic of the United States: to represent the will of the people as it is. To provide that that will should be as wise and just as possible. In a certain extent the mere representation of public will produces in itself a wholesome

condition of it, and in this extent America fulfills imperfectly and indirectly the last and most important condition of perfect government.'

11 (p. 220). Incomplete sentence in MS.

12 (p. 222). This passage seriously misrepresents what actually took place at the Congress of Vienna in the matter of constitutional government for the German states. For 'panic-stricken tyrants' should be read 'the German Committee of the Vienna Congress'. This Committee, constituted by the Great Powers on 14 October 1814, confronted by the menace of Napoleon's return from Elba, reached agreement on 9 June 1815, after much wrangling, on the terms of a 'Federal Act' for Germany. Under Article XIII of this Act, each sovereign was obliged to grant a representative constitution to his subjects within a year. The promise was, however, subsequently emasculated by revision in the Diet. The time-limit was removed, and the obligation upon the Princes was weakened by substituting the word 'will' for 'shall'. Apart from the Duke of Saxe-Weimar who granted his dominions a constitution in May 1816—before the Diet opened—the Princes generally avoided or evaded their obligations. The Diet, under Metternich's leadership, took the line that it was an internal matter for each state to settle within itself. Thus Article XIII of the Federal Act became no more than a guarantee to the German people of 'an unlimited right of expectation'. When Shelley refers to Germany wearing 'the aspect of rapidly maturing revolution', he is evidently making the most of such manifestations of liberal and patriotic fervour as the 'rag' staged by the students of the University of Jena at the Wartburg Festival in 1817 and the murder of the revolutionary journalist, Kotzebue, by a Jena student in 1819: events which led to the imposition of the notorious Carlsbad Decrees by the Federal Diet.

13 (p. 223). *That hypocritical knot of conspiring tyrants*. The Quadruple Alliance (Britain, Austria, Russia and Prussia) which had overthrown Napoleon—distinguished by Shelley from his conquerors in the phrase 'the only tyrant among them who was not a hypocrite'.

14 (p. 223). The celibacy of the clergy was something of an obsession with Shelley. Compare his offensive reference to Malthus—who by the way, had a wife and family—on page 239.

15 (p. 223). *The mighty calamity of government*. While Shelley calls government a calamity, it is plain that he accepts it as a lesser evil.

Its right function is that of 'securing such a moderate degree of happiness to men as has been experimentally practicable', and, indeed, 'public happiness is the substance and the end of political institutions' (pp. 237-8). This represents a departure from the strict doctrine of Godwin and the anarchists, for whom 'institution' is the worst of evils.

16 (p. 224). Even while Shelley was writing, events in Spain were moving towards the insurrection of 1820, when Ferdinand VII was compelled to grant the 'Constitution of 1812'. In April 1823, however, 95,000 French troops entered Spain and re-established the absolutism of Ferdinand.

17 (p. 225). For 'to' read 'for'. MS error.

18 (p. 226). Sentence uncompleted in MS.

19 (p. 226). The Slave Trade was abolished throughout the British Empire by the Ministry of All-the-Talents, mainly as a result of the insistence of Charles James Fox and his friends, in 1807. Slavery itself was abolished in 1833. These measures were rather the results of the animated social conscience produced by Evangelical religion than 'the infection of the spirit of Liberty in France'. The two nations of free negroes to which Shelley refers were 'The Black Republic' of Haiti, or San Domingo, where a bloody slave-revolt was stimulated by agents of the French Republic in 1791; and where the negro Dessalines had proclaimed himself Emperor in 1804; and the Republic of Liberia, founded by manumitted American slaves in 1820.

20 (p. 227). For 'by' read 'to'. MS error.

21 (p. 227). Compare the final sentence of *Defence of Poetry* (p. 206 above) where 'philosophers' are omitted.

22 (p. 229). *Virtual representation.* The theory of Virtual Representation, which was frequently used in defence of the unreformed House of Commons, rested upon the assumption that the mass of the people were included (occupationally) in the main 'interests' that were actually represented, and that they did not require direct and separate representation as a class. It was, indeed, the emergence of a distinct working-class, whose members could scarcely be said to find representation in the divers 'national interests' represented in Parliament, or—as Shelley puts it—whose interests could no longer be supposed to be 'interwoven with that of those who enjoyed a constitutional presence',—it was this change which made direct representation of 'the people' necessary. The substitution of repre-

sentation of persons for representation of interests, which Coleridge saw to be the significance of the Bill of 1832, and deplored as a departure from 'the Idea' of the Constitution, was necessitated by changes in the social structure which Shelley was acute enough to understand and accept. This passage reveals his powers as a social observer at their best.

23 (p. 234). The Bank of England suspended Cash Payments in 1797, and the suspension was continued throughout the War. In 1816 Parliament sanctioned suspension for a further two years. In 1819 it was provided that the Bank should resume Cash Payments at a date no further distant than 1821. Actually, the Bank resumed them at once. Shelley's complaint that paper-money, issued in large quantities, and therefore depreciating in value (depreciation at the peak-period of 1814 was about 25%), was a prime cause of the high price of provisions, was widely held at the time; as was his view that the government's currency policy had raised up a vulgar aristocracy of Fund-lords. Cobbett, who claimed to have put the question in its true light in his tract *Paper against Gold, and Glory against Prosperity* (1810-11 and 1815), railed against the social consequence of this policy year in, year out.

24 (p. 234). Omission in MS.

25 (p. 236). For further observations on the new aristocracy, see Shelley's pamphlet *On the Death of Princess Charlotte* (1817).

26 (p. 236). *Sane*, i.e. 'healthy'.

27 (p. 237). See note 15 above.

28 (p. 238). See note 15 above.

29 (p. 239). See note 14 above.

30 (p. 241). Footnote to MS: 'This sum could not have amounted to less than two thousand millions. It would be a curious problem in political economy to calculate the precise degree of comfort and of ornament *represented by it*.'

31 (p. 242). Footnote to MS: 'After due reductions had been made so as to make an equal value, taking corn for the standard, be given as was received.'

32 (p. 247). Sentence incomplete in MS.

33 (p. 247). Sentence incomplete in MS.

34 (p. 249). Sentence incomplete in MS.

35 (p. 249). Footnote by Shelley: 'This is impossible in great nations and the most enlightened theorists have therefore proposed dividing them into a great multiplicity of federated republics.' This probably

refers to little more than the fifteenth chapter of the third book of Rousseau's Social Contract.

36 (p. 251). Sentence incomplete in MS.

37 (p. 251). Shelley's opposition to the secret ballot should be compared with the somewhat similar views of John Stuart Mill as expressed in *Representative Government* (1861), chapter X.

38 (p. 252). Shelley here refers to the culmination of a period of Radical petitioning which had, properly speaking, opened in 1812 with the founding of the Hampden Clubs by Major John Cartwright. In the autumn of 1816, Sir Francis Burdett and Lord Cochrane inaugurated a nation-wide petitioning movement at a public meeting in Westminster. The petitions gathered from the country districts were carried to London by delegates in the first days of 1817. The leaders of the movement disagreed, at the last moment, on the terms to be demanded: whether universal, or merely ratepayer, suffrage. A striking account of this rift is given in chapter III of Samuel Bamford's *Passages in the Life of a Radical.* In the end, Burdett declined to present a petition demanding universal suffrage, and the task fell upon the hare-brained Lord Cochrane. That the petitions were 'rejected with disdain' by the House of Commons is substantially true. But not even the optimistic Cartwright ever claimed that the number of signatures obtained exceeded several thousand. 'The petitions of a million of men' is a wild exaggeration. (See E. Halevy, *History of the English People, 1815-30*, Part I, chapter I, section 2.)

39 (p. 255). Shelley's advocacy of assembly in 'limited numbers' probably reflects his awareness of both the tragedy and the futility of what happened on the occasion of the 'Manchester Massacre', popularly referred to as 'Peterloo', on 16 August 1819: the event which stirred him to compose *A Philosophical View of Reform.* There may have been as many as 50,000 or 60,000 people assembled, in an orderly fashion, on that occasion, and it is obvious that the great majority of them could have had little idea of what was going on, and far less have been 'actual parties to the proceedings of the day'. Instead, they served, for all their orderly behaviour, to bring about the tragedy as soon as force was used against the more active participants: most of the injuries suffered were caused by the pressure of the multitude itself. The authorities, however, imagined that the organizers of the meeting were pursuing a policy of 'collecting them [i.e. the masses] in numerous and tumultuous meetings where they

might be taught to estimate their own numerical force'. (See Memorandum to Lord Liverpool, by Lord Grenville, 12 November 1819, in C. D. Yonge's *Life of Lord Liverpool*, vol. II, p. 420.) Moreover, Shelley himself, in his poem, *The Masque of Anarchy*, which was composed in memory of Peterloo, is somewhat more enthusiastic for the impact of *numbers* than he is in his pamphlet. He bids his countrymen—

> Rise, like Lions after slumber
> In unvanquishable number. . .
> Ye are many—they are few.

40 (p. 255). Cf. the admonition in *The Masque of Anarchy*:

> And if then the tyrants dare
> Let them ride among you there,
> Slash, and stab, and maim, and hew,—
> What they like, that let them do.
> With folded arms, and steady eyes,
> And little fear, and less surprise,
> Look upon them as they slay
> Till their rage has died away.

Shelley's resolute faith in the moral power of non-resistance, and indeed the whole treatment of the relation of means to ends in the latter pages of the pamphlet, is the most notable example of his Godwinian heritage.

41 (p. 259). One such petition, at least, went to Lord Liverpool, the Prime Minister, in the shape of a long, philosophical letter from Coleridge, shewing almost precisely the connections between national prosperity and freedom, and between the cultivation of the philosophic imagination and the furtherance of scientific truth, which Shelley desired. It is printed in C. D. Yonge's *Life of Lord Liverpool*, vol. II, pp. 300-7. (See Introduction, p. ix.) Shelley does not mention Coleridge as a possible writer of 'memorials' of this kind. He was, like Hazlitt, under the mistaken impression that Coleridge had turned to 'the unclean side.' Coleridge, on the other hand, recognized the potential ally in Shelley: he believed that, had he met Shelley, he could have helped him.

42 (p. 259). The eagles and the meridian sun. An evident echo of the celebrated passage in Milton's *Areopagitica*: 'an eagle mewing her mighty youth, and kindling her undazzled eyes at the full midday beam. . . .'

43 (p. 260). This 'solemly recorded right'—of resistance—refers to the clause in the Declaration of Rights of 1689: 'That the Subjects which are Protestants may have Arms for their Defence suitable to their Conditions and as allowed by Law.' Blackstone in his *Commentaries on the Laws of England* (1765-9) described the right of the subject to bear arms in self-defence as 'a public allowance, under due restrictions, of the natural right of resistance and self-preservation when the sanctions of society and laws are found insufficient to restrain the violence of oppression' (vol. I, 143-4). The right of resistance was frequently appealed to in the age of the French Revolution. It is discussed in Halevy's *History of the English People in 1815*, Part I, chapter 2, section 8.

44 (p. 261). Sentence incomplete in MS.

45 (p. 262). MS concludes with uncompleted sentence.

INDEX

Note. *The tables of contents which precede each of the texts afford a fairly comprehensive subject-index. The following is an index of proper names, and of the introduction, together with some headings for cross-reference. Large and important subjects are given in capitals.*